STREETWISE

ELIJAH ANDERSON

Race,

Class,

and Change

STREETWISE

in an

Urban

Community

THE UNIVERSITY OF CHICAGO PRESS

Chicago and London

The University of Chicago Press, Chicago 60637
The University of Chicago Press, Ltd., London
© 1990 by The University of Chicago
All rights reserved. Published 1990
Paperback edition 1992
Printed in the United States of America
16 15 14 13 12 11 10 09 08 07   10 11 12 13 14

ISBN-13: 978-0-226-01816-4 (paper)
ISBN-10: 0-226-01816-4 (paper)

Library of Congress Cataloging-in-Publication Data
Anderson, Elijah.
    Streetwise : race, class, and change in an urban community /
Elijah Anderson.
        p.   cm.
    Includes bibliographical references.
    1. Inner cities—Pennsylvania—Philadelphia.   2. Gentrification—
Pennsylvania—Philadelphia.   3. Neighborhood—Pennsylvania—
Philadelphia.   I. Title.
HN80.P5A53   1990
307.3'362'0974811—dc20   90-34048
                                                                 CIP

⊚ The paper used in this publication meets the minimum requirements of
the American National Standard for Information Sciences—Permanence of
Paper for Printed Library Materials, ANSI Z39.48-1992.

To Caitlin, Luke, and Nancy

Contents

Preface

*F*rom summer 1975 through summer 1989, I did fieldwork in the general area I call the Village-Northton, which encompasses two communities—one black and low income to very poor (with an extremely high infant mortality rate), the other racially mixed but becoming increasingly middle to upper income and white. When my wife Nancy and I moved to the Village in 1975, I had not planned to study the area; but this changed as I encountered the local community and discovered what seemed an ideal urban laboratory. I found the Village one of the most culturally and ethnically diverse areas of the city, where wealthy people and poor people, gays, hippies, students, Jews, WASPs, Italian-Americans, Irish-Americans, newly arrived Southeast Asians, Ethiopians, Zambians, Pakistanis, Iranians, and others lived together in relative comity. First I came to know the setting informally, simply experiencing its everyday life, making contacts almost by accident, and learning cultural rules from these experiences as any newcomer might. I became so intrigued by the neighborhood that I decided to study it formally. After acquiring research funding from the National Institute of Justice, I began to interview residents more formally and to write field notes.

Over the course of fourteen years, various issues emerged and subsided. I came to focus on the nature of street life and public culture—how this diverse group of people "got it on" or related to one another in public. What was the nature of local street life? What were the prescriptions and proscriptions of public behavior? For me these issues persisted, a logical outgrowth of my previous book *A Place on the Corner* (Anderson 1978). To gain an effective point of view, I spent many hours on the streets, talking and listening to the people of the neighborhood. To obtain further understanding I photographed the setting, videotaped street corner scenes, recorded interviews, and got to know all kinds of people, from small-time drug dealers to policemen, middle-class whites, and outspoken black community activists. I hung out with various residents and interviewed many of them extensively. I frequented neighborhood bars, laundromats, and carryouts and attended brunches, parties, and community gatherings. From 1985 through 1987 I was an active board member of the Village-Northton Educational Fund, a racially mixed group of community activists concerned with improving the quality of local public-school education. As my research focus became more refined, it also expanded to include issues important to those I was coming to know, for whom I would serve as a communication link to an outside audience.

Particularly during the 1980s, the problems of United States cities grew more and more insistent, if not intractable to many. With rising unemployment, brought on in part by increasing "deindustrialization" and the exodus of major corporations, the local black community suffered. The employment lives of its members are further complicated by continuing racial prejudice and discrimination, which often frustrate efforts to make effective adjustments to these changes and the emerging reality. Many who have difficulty finding work in the regular economy become ever poorer and may join the criminal underground, which promises them huge financial rewards, a certain degree of "coolness," and happiness—that seems never to fully materialize. Yet in hot pursuit, many alienated young people commit themselves to this way of life, adopting its morality and norms and serving as role models for other youths. In this way the drug economy has become elaborated, and drug use has grown widespread among the local poor. As the black community of Northton has undergone social deterioration, the adjacent Village has experienced "spillover" crime and public incivility.

These developments had profound consequences for the more general area I was studying, requiring further refinement of my research plans from a limited ethnographic representation of the gentrifying neighborhood of the Village to a more inclusive study of the relationship between it and the adjacent black ghetto of Northton. I found that I could not truly understand the Village independent of Northton, and vice versa, particularly where the two communities met, and that realization posed insistent sociological and ethnographic questions. How do these diverse peoples get it on? How are their everyday public lives shaped and affected by the workings of local social institutions? What is the culture of the local public spaces? What is the public social order? Is there one? How are the social changes in the two communities affecting the residents of both?

From the mid-1970s through the 1980s, moving to the city and refurbishing inner-city areas seemed to young professionals like a brilliant idea, and a good investment to boot. They could afford an inner-city home that they could treat as a starter house, and the antique bargains held a special allure. Many were alienated from the life-styles of their suburban parents and sour on what the suburbs represented to them—social and cultural homogeneity—and they saw the city as a place where they might define their own lives in a different manner, close to their work and play. This group contributed to the process we know today as gentrification. Yet commitment to such projects had its costs and brought some uncertainty. Crime in the street and wariness about strangers have always been recognized as costs of living in the city, but today many feel such realities have become worse. With looming municipal budget deficits, higher local taxes, a decline in city services, and growing inner-city poverty, drug use, and crime, many gentrifiers have come to see their own fortunes as inextricably linked to those of the nearby ghetto. They realize that changes in the neighboring black community directly and indirectly affect not only their sense of well-being but also their property values. This acknowledgment has slowed down—but not yet reversed—the process of gentrification.

I mean my descriptions and analyses to convey my understanding of the way social relations are shaped by these changes—how individuals come to interpret and negotiate the public spaces in the community I have been studying. Much of what I learned came through informal interviews and direct ethnographic observation over an extended period, and it draws on my experiences in the Village-Northton and in nearby communities that share some of the area's more prominent features. In a sense, over time I became my own informant. What emerges, then, is to a certain extent conceptual and abstract, but it reflects my sense of what is true.

I like to think of this study as a beginning. I intend to continue working from the data base collected here, producing occasional ethnographic essays. I hope others will follow me in trying to disentangle the various questions uncovered by this study. If that provocation is initiated, this book will have achieved its goal.

My work was supported by the United States Bureau of the Census, contract 50YABC-J-66015, by grant 80-NI-AX-0003 from the National Institute of Justice, and by a grant from the United States Department of Health and Human Services, Office of Minority Health. The views, opinions, and findings contained in this book are my own and should not be construed as an official Bureau of the

Census position, policy, or decision unless so designated by other official documentation.

Earlier versions of some of the material in this book have been published in *Social Class and Democratic Leadership*, ed. Harold J. Bershady (Philadelphia: University of Pennsylvania Press, 1989), *The New Urban Reality*, ed. Paul Peterson (Washington, D.C.: Brookings Institution, 1985), *Annals of the American Academy of Political and Social Science* 501 (January 1989): 59–78, and *Society* 21, 1 (December 1983) (© 1983 by Transaction Publishers; published by permission).

Over so many years of ethnographic research and writing, I have incurred numerous debts. Though I cannot acknowledge every one, I would like to thank the following friends and colleagues who have commented on portions of this work and helped me in all sorts of ways: Victor Lidz, Harold Bershady, Charles Bosk, Fred Block, Samuel Z. Klausner, Philip Rieff, Philip Morgan, Samuel Preston, William Labov, Carol Stillman, Alison Anderson, James Kurth, Aaron Porter, Luke Harris, Herman Wrice, Karen Kauffman-Knibbe, Gerald Jaynes, Janie Freeman, Lois Bye, Christine Szczepanowski, George Funderberg, Frank Furstenberg, Jr., Demie Kurz, Jack Katz, Rachel Bedard, Leonard Braitman, Kirk Wattles, Karen Keyes, Gerard Bye, Gerald D. Suttles, David Kairys, Roosevelt Dicks, Karen Faulkner, Ted Hershberg, Elizabeth Martin, Lee Rainwater, Renée Fox, the Reverend Fletcher J. Bryant, Arthur Paris, Robert Washington, Howard Arnold, Dell Hymes, Ira Harkavy, Martin Kilson, the late Erving Goffman, William J. Wilson, Michael B. Katz, Cara Crosby, Antonio McDaniels, Tom Gavin, Ralph Smith, Harold Haskins, and Howard S. Becker. Kirk Wattles compiled the tables in the Appendix. I owe enormous gratitude to the many people of the community who allowed me to enter their social world and shared their local knowledge with me, but who must remain anonymous. My wife Nancy and I, particularly at the beginning, did the fieldwork for this project jointly, and without her collaboration and constant support, this book would not have been written.

Introduction

A round the nation, urban residents feel intimidated by their streets, parks, and other public places, particularly after dark or when too many strangers are present. The national problem of safe streets has become especially acute in the city, particularly in underclass ghetto communities and adjacent areas undergoing transitions in race, class, and culture. The margins of the ghetto can be scenes of tension as they become gentrified and are slowly absorbed by a wider community made up primarily of middle- and upper-income people who for the most part are white.

Housing in these marginal areas is inexpensive but promises a high return on investment. Local prices ebb and flow somewhat arbitrarily, strongly influenced by an area's "hot" or "trendy" reputation. The housing itself is generally old, even vintage, which for many is an important part of its attraction; and some people genuinely value the novelty and social diversity of such neighborhoods.

In cities in some parts of the country, a fluctuating movement advances house by house and block by block as sometimes unwitting middle- to upper-income newcomers struggle to "reclaim" neighborhoods from the poorer residents who have come to be identified with the inner city. Finding it practical to live close to work and play, many pay higher and higher rents for apartments, while others fashionably renovate spacious old houses built by the gentry of an earlier period. Some buy property to sell it again to the highest bidder; they are in effect speculating.

Such prime but often undiscovered city neighborhoods increase in financial value, particularly when the old dwellings are restored to something approaching their original elegance and are inhabited by well-to-do people. In time these newcomers, because of their professional status and (usually but not always) their white skin, are able to alter the earlier perception of the area as a marginal neighborhood. Making visible use of the neighborhood, they imbue it with a certain social distinction. They are then joined by others of their own social class and, through their individual purchases and collective residence, form a subculture of well-off urban people who for the

1

time being may feel under siege by local crime and public incivility, but who eventually threaten to overwhelm their predecessors.

In establishing their presence, the newcomers make social, cultural, economic, and territorial claims that sometimes confuse and upset their neighbors. Some move in next door to relatively poor people; they may even actively "seek a deal" by canvassing door to door and offering a price below market value, attempting to buy residents out.

As real estate deals are consummated property values usually rise, and taxes follow suit. Home improvement loans suddenly become available, houses get refurbished, long-vacant apartment buildings are renovated, and the neighborhood is physically improved. City services are revitalized and local schools become more attentive to their charges, though the newcomers approach these institutions cautiously, if at all. An area perceived as on the verge of becoming a slum slowly turns around and in time is redefined as quaint, historic, and desirable. As prices rise the poorer residents, who tend to be renters, find themselves compelled to move—sometimes, if they are black, into the adjacent ghetto.

Typically this ghetto has also undergone social change in recent years. Older black residents remember better days when life was more orderly and civilized, when crime and drugs were almost unknown, when young people respected their elders, and when the men worked in good jobs and took care of their families. But now many of the older, decent people are gone. After working to pay for a home, many have died and left their property to poverty-stricken relatives who lack the money or the priorities to keep it up; people's morale and the physical appearance of the area have declined, undermining the sense of community. The offspring of some have become upwardly mobile and have found the neighborhood incompatible with their developing status and sense of identity. As this group emerges socially and economically, its members tend to become steadily more distant from the ghetto community, eventually expressing this distance by literally moving away. Their departure has diminished an extremely important source of moral and social leadership within the black community. In pursuit of status and employment, and out of genuine concern for their own survival, the black middle class and those who aspire to it increasingly leave the ghetto behind.

In their wake, unemployment, crime, drug use, family disorganization, and antisocial behavior have become powerful social forces. With severely limited education and skills, younger and poorer blacks who are left behind have little chance to participate in the regular economy. The jobs that do exist for them are usually low paying or many miles away. Young blacks in particular are caught in an employment bind. To many young men, the underground economy of drugs and vice looks attractive.

The interpersonal trust and moral cohesion that once prevailed are undermined, and an atmosphere of distrust, alienation, and crime pervades the area, further disrupting its social organization. One of the community's most important institutions has become a casualty of these changes—the relationship between "old heads" and young boys. Traditionally, the "old head" was a man of stable means who believed in hard work, family life, and the church. He was an aggressive agent of the wider society whose acknowledged role was to teach, support, encourage, and in effect socialize young men to meet their responsibilities regarding work, family, the law, and common decency. The young boy, usually a single man in his late teens or early twenties, had confidence in the old head's ability to impart useful wisdom and practical advice about life. Often the old head acted as surrogate father to those who needed attention, care, and moral support.

But today, as meaningful employment has become increasingly scarce for young blacks and as crime and drugs have become a way of life for many, the old head is losing his prestige and authority. With the expansion of the drug culture and its opportunities for large sums of quick money, street-smart young boys are concluding that the old head's lessons about life and the work ethic are no longer relevant. Today, too, many of those who in earlier times might have become old heads have left the ghetto with the middle class exodus or have simply disengaged.

A new role model is emerging and competing with the traditional old head for the hearts and minds of young boys. He is young, often a product of the street gang, and at best indifferent to the law and traditional values. This "new" old head is in many respects the antithesis of the traditional one. If he works at the low-paying jobs available to him, he does so grudgingly. More likely he makes ends meet, part time or full time, in the drug trade or some other area of the underground economy.

This emerging role model derides family values and has a "string" of women. He may feel little obligation toward them and the chil-

3

dren he has fathered, but on "mother's day," when welfare checks come to these single mothers, he expects his share. On the local street corners, his self-aggrandizement consumes his whole being as he attempts to impress people through displays of material success like expensive clothes and fancy cars. Eagerly awaiting his message are the unemployed young black men, demoralized by what they see as a hopeless financial situation and inclined to emulate his style and values. For some who follow this model, great though often fleeting financial success may be in store. More often a trail of un-fulfilled dreams, broken lives, jail, and even death awaits.

Female old heads have suffered a fate similar to that of the men. As poverty and hopelessness become pervasive and drugs proliferate, the community "mother"—once an omnipresent figure on the neigh-borhood porches and in local beauty shops and corner groceries—has also undergone a serious decline in numbers, prestige, and authority. Serving as important exterior role models, these women repeatedly and insistently told attentive boys and girls "what was good for them," at times physically disciplining them. The few such women who remain active in the community are overwhelmed by a virtual proliferation of "street kids"—children almost totally without pa-rental supervision, left to their own devices—and they lament the decline of the local community. The families of these youngsters often are casualties of the rampant drug culture. As family care-takers and role models disappear or decline in influence, and as un-employment and poverty become more persistent, the community, particularly its children, becomes vulnerable to a variety of social ills, including crime, drugs, family disorganization, generalized de-moralization, and unemployment.

As the social life of the ghetto deteriorates, those living in middle-class areas nearby, newcomers and old-timers alike, feel the impact. Adjusting to the local neighborhood reality, many try to coexist and others flee. In addition to their interest in the status of the commu-nity and the rise in property values, most residents are very concerned about safety in public. As sometimes strange bedfellows (conservative and liberal, black and white, gays and straights), they join their di-verse counterparts in local struggles to fight crime and otherwise pre-serve an ideal character for the neighborhood, forming town watches and shoring up local municipal codes that might discourage un-desirables and encourage others more to their liking.

In their conversations with neighbors, both blacks and whites assume that the main offenders are young, black, and male. Some residents refer to them euphemistically as "kids," while really thinking of them as ruthless street criminals who recognize no bounds. At night, when crack addicts and others roam the streets, breaking into cars, scavenging and stealing items of little cash value such as house plants, garden hoses, doormats, garbage cans, and toys, or simply harassing people, the residents become even more set in their perceptions, and they often adopt a siege mentality.

In these circumstances, intolerance surfaces in the residents' relations with unknown blacks, particularly males. The teenagers who walk through the streets with their "boom boxes" seem even more obnoxious. Decent, well-intentioned white people wonder whether they are becoming racist as they catch themselves studying the anonymous black man, defensively seeing him first as a predator and seeking not to become his prey. Many worry about a figure lurking in the shadows, hiding in a doorway or behind a clump of bushes, ready to pounce on an unsuspecting victim. Law-abiding users of the streets, encountering a group of young black males, picture them as a "wolf pack"—out to "hit" (mug) anyone who looks vulnerable.

Accordingly, residents black and white, male and female, young and old become suspicious of unfamiliar black males they encounter, particularly as they venture warily into the streets at night, wondering if they will get home safely. In trying to be careful, some whites agonize about the way they keep anonymous black men at a safe physical and social distance. But growing numbers appear indifferent and comfortable about such distancing behavior, viewing it as simply one more urban survival tool. Still others, including newly arrived young Asian males, identify with the young blacks, adopting their clothing styles, speech, and public behavior, and thus lend fresh meaning to the term "assimilation." Whereas some residents simply give up and flee, apologizing to the neighbors and friends they leave behind and bewailing inadequate police protection and the high crime rate, others tough it out, learning and refining a peculiar etiquette for surviving in public places, and often developing a profound street wisdom in the process.

This street wisdom is largely a state of mind, but it is demonstrated through a person's comportment. It represents a perspective gained through public interaction, the give and take of street life. This perspective allows one to "see through" public situations, to anticipate what is about to happen based on cues and signals from those one encounters. In essence, a "streetwise" person is one who understands "how to behave" in uncertain public places.

One gains street wisdom through a long and sometimes arduous process that begins with a certain "uptightness" about the urban environment, with decisions based on stereotypes and simple rules of public etiquette. Given time and experience, the nervousness and fear give way to a recognition that street life involves situations that require selective and individualized responses—in this complicated environment, applying broad stereotypes simply will not do. After much practice, a person may operate with a certain aplomb, easily maneuvering through what were once viewed as "tricky" situations. The process is like learning to drive an automobile. The novice may hesitate and navigate uncertainly, but an experienced driver moves through complicated traffic patterns with little apparent thought. The same principles of driving are employed in both cases, but in the latter they are almost effortlessly applied.

Through public experience, a person becomes deeply familiar with elements of the neighborhood—drug dealers, policemen, the local grocer, poor people, homeless people, and middle class families and individuals making up the community's social fabric. But perhaps most important, one gains some working conception of how these elements fit together.

In these circumstances the person neither takes the streets for granted nor recoils from them but becomes alive to dangerous situations, drawing on a developing repertoire of ruses and schemes for traveling the streets safely. In a word, the person learns street sense, how to behave in a sensible manner. In becoming something more than a passive reactant to public situations, the individual becomes proactive and to some degree the author of public actions.

1

o

The

Village

Setting

*T*he Village-Northton area, a community within Eastern City, is a "case study" of an urban neighborhood facing the problems that accompany racial and class transition. Northton is predominantly black, residents range from low income to very poor. The Village is at present racially mixed, but it is becoming increasingly white and middle to upper income. The history of the general area is interwoven with the growth and expansion of Eastern City.[1]

The Village was first settled in the 1800s by well-to-do people who could afford to commute across the Tyler River to the center of Eastern City or to maintain summer homes along the river's west bank. The first landowners built large houses on their estates, but in time these holdings were cut up and additional homes were built there. Neighborhoods developed, with general stores, churches, and schools. During the 1850s, 1860s, and 1870s, many elaborate Victorian houses were built that remain to this day. Some inhabitants branched out farther west into an area that is still wealthy and suburban.

During the late 1800s and early 1900s, the land to the north and west of the Village was overtaken by industrial development. Small factories emerged, and homes were built nearby at a rapid pace. One

1. "The Village-Northton" is a convenient descriptive pseudonym, since the community has qualities of smallness, quaintness, and remoteness often associated with villages. There is no connection with Greenwich Village in New York, for instance, though that area may share some of the same problems and solutions worked out by the residents of the "Village" of this book. "Eastern City" and other place-names and personal names are also pseudonyms.

7

of the most prominent of these working-class neighborhoods was Northton, just north of the Village. In many respects Northton was like a company town, with its small, sooty, close-packed dwellings. The social history of the area is evident in its architecture, the scale of the houses, the size of the lots, and the craftsmanship of the facades. Walking through, one gains the impression that much of Northton was built for a class that worked for, not alongside, the inhabitants of what is now the Village.

One version of community lore says that Northton was settled by newly arrived Irish and German immigrants who were employed in local industries or as servants in the large homes across Bellwether Street and near the town square that once served as a dropping-off point for farmers' produce. In time Bellwether Street became a boundary that separated the working class from the wealthy. During the early twentieth century this boundary was often violated by middle-class Irish and German proprietors of local shops and businesses, who were eager to obtain Village property. The wealthy viewed the up-and-coming Northtonians as invaders, and with each inroad the social definition of the Village was altered.

The steam engine brought even greater change. Rails were laid along the bank of the Tyler River, not far from the Village. Trains left great billows of smoke and soot, and residents had trouble keeping their clothes and houses clean. This invasion of technology, along with the invading lower classes, encouraged the earlier inhabitants of the once pastoral setting to seek a new environment. They left the sooty Village to the middle-class Irish and Germans and to the remnants of their own group who would not move elsewhere.

The Irish and Germans were joined by blacks from the South, who were attracted to Northton during and after World War II when, in search of a better life, many migrated north and settled in similar white working-class areas, often despite strong physical resistance. The blacks eventually succeeded the Irish and Germans and claimed Northton; the whites fled to other parts of the western section of Eastern City and to working-class and middle-class suburbs.

In time the blacks threatened the border areas of the Village, where slumlords found they could make good money by renting them their subdivided mansions and townhouses. The whites of the Village, some of whom by now were refugees from Northton, offered waning resistance. They reluctantly accepted pockets of black settlement within the Village, often on the least desirable blocks. The immediate result was distinct white working-class and middle-class areas coexisting, not always peacefully, with growing enclaves of blacks who had recently migrated from the ghetto of Northton. Moreover, Bellwether Street increasingly became a geographic and social boundary separating races as well as classes; other informal boundaries developed on the edges of the white community. These boundaries were defended, sometimes violently, by white gangs. As one black resident of Northton who remembers the forties and fifties declared:

◉ *Yeah, I can remember the time when you had to have a pretty good pair of sneakers [for running] if you wanted to get through the Village. The white [Irish] boys would get you for crossing the line.* ◉

What had once separated the lace-curtain Irish from the Irish working class now separated blacks from whites, though the racial boundaries were less permeable than the class boundaries had been.

During this period, the Village was undergoing great changes in density and appearance. As financial depressions took their toll, houses were sold to be subdivided and rented out. The Village went from a neighborhood of upper-income homeowners to one inhabited primarily by working-class and middle-class renters. Landlords bent on earning quick profits from makeshift apartments "ruined" a good number of spacious homes. Ceilings were dropped, rooms were divided, and separate stairs and entrances were added. A living space that had once accommodated one family could now hold two or three, ensuring a nice profit for the landlord. But though the stone mansions and townhouses were gradually turned into multiple-family dwellings, lot sizes remained the same. The towering sycamores still spread a lush canopy over the brick walks. These factors preserved the area's potential to be restored to something approaching its former glory.

The Liberal Era

During the 1950s, when the Korean War was ending and civil rights was becoming a major political issue, a group of liberal and civic-minded Quakers established a cooperative in one of the grand old houses of the Village. They called themselves the Village Friends, and they passionately supported pacifism, racial integration, and economic egalitarianism. The Village Friends invited blacks and others to live in their communal dwellings. They condoned biracial and interethnic marriages among their members. The group even be-

gan buying dilapidated buildings, refurbishing them, and renting
them out to the "right kind of people," including university students
of color and others who had difficulty finding decent housing in the
Village or nearby. It was the time of the "Beat generation," and the
Village Friends developed their own version of Bohemian values,
modified to emphasize their commitment to racial equality and
other liberal goals. Because they were especially concerned with
brotherhood and equality between the races, their most immediate
mission was to develop an integrated and egalitarian community—
issues that deeply concern their successors to this day.

Some of their neighbors, particularly the conservative middle-
class Irish and German Villagers, looked on the Friends with suspicion, if not outrage, calling them communists and "nigger lovers."
One middle-aged white woman who was involved in this movement
and remembers the 1950s in the Village said:

◑ *The way I saw it happening was the Village Civic Association
was so racist and so strong that they talked people into cutting their
houses up into apartments rather than selling them because there
was no white market for houses at that point. The Irish population
was fleeing, and there was no incoming white population. Or things
would happen like they would sell the houses to their plumber or
carpenter, and he would cut them up. Most of the conversions were
just terrible. They were done by mechanics, not by architects. And
usually they were people who did work in the neighborhood. And
they rented those houses. Probably there was still a white market for
renting, and they were renting to whites until the buildings got so
run down that they couldn't rent to whites. Then they would rent
them to blacks, and of course the blacks were poor. And then came
the professional group that was mostly white. Oh, we [the Village
Development Association] tried so hard to get black professionals to
move into [the Village]. But they wouldn't be caught dead there,
ha-ha. It just was not a place where they wanted to live, not that
there were that many black professionals to begin with. It just didn't
work. Our group grew from Friends Cooperative Houses, and the
racist group was called the Village Civic Association, and VDA was
formed out of the need for Friendship Co-op to survive. It was a development company that was supported from investments by residents. The board said we needed a civic effort. And they really
inspired a new civic organization, Village Neighbors. At that time it
was decided not to infiltrate the Civic Association and to take it over*

but to start a new group, because the Civic Association had such a bad reputation in the black neighborhoods surrounding the area. Apparently, in the thirties they had sound trucks on the streets, admonishing people not to sell to Negroes and not to rent to Negroes. They were infamous in the black community. So we decided that to take over the Civic Association would be to take over an organization with such a negative image that it wouldn't be worth our while, that we'd better start a new organization. So we did, and the racist Village Civic Association just went down the drain. Our group, the Village Development Association, bought at least forty-three properties. We started out on a quota basis, renting and selling to all kinds of people. ◖

Despite the criticism of the conservative Irish and German residents, the Friends adhered to their stated goals: "To keep the Village from becoming a land speculator's paradise" and "to make the Village the kind of place where all different kinds of people can live." Meanwhile, the Bellwether Street boundary was showing signs of weakness. Numbers of poor blacks were concentrated on the periphery of the Village. Slumlords continued to buy run-down buildings, making a minimum of cosmetic repairs and renting them at exorbitant rates to the poorest class of blacks from Northton and other parts of the city. The middle-class Irish and Germans, as well as the Village Friends and some of the blacks themselves, could rally together against this trend, for none wanted the "wrong kind of blacks" for neighbors. As the Friends competed with other whites for control over Village resources, the hidden restrictions in their own conception of the kind of blacks who were to be tolerated became evident. They were most hospitable to educated, "decent" blacks who would contribute to neighborhood stability, thus creating an ambiance of racial integration and harmony.

The Village Development Association, a society of civic-minded and concerned Villagers that included many Friends, emerged. Individuals and families contributed to the association's fund for buying up properties, renovating them, and selling or renting them to desirable tenants, black or white. The association held integrated picnics, parties, and parades to celebrate progressive social attitudes and to attract support from liberal whites and "decent" blacks from around the city. A neighborhood movement of sorts developed as the members attempted to save the Village from the hands of "the racists." One informant explained that some of the Irish "saw what kind of

people we were bringing in, and they became tolerant, if not accepting." In time the social and political environment was altered as
some of the conservatives moved and others died. In the early 1960s
there was some friction with those who remained, but this eventually faded as new issues gained prominence in the neighborhood.

During the sixties, the Village Friends and their neighbors formed
coalitions based on their common interests. Through its transactions, which often had to be carried out quietly, the Village Development Association accumulated numerous properties from owners
who would not sell to blacks and other minorities. This association
constituted an ecological invasion force, helping to change the character of the neighborhood to what it was during the sixties and seventies—culturally diverse, racially mixed, and socially tolerant. As
one forty-year-old black artist who lived in the Village through the
1950s and 1960s said proudly, "You know how it was everywhere else
during the sixties? Well, it was like that in the Village in the fifties!"
Such is the pride with which some longtime Villagers describe the
good old days.

With the advent of the Vietnam War and the protests against it,
the Village became a magnet for adherents of the youthful counterculture, including some antiwar activists and draft resisters. The
Central Committee for Conscientious Objectors, with headquarters
in the Village, attracted young men in need of draft counseling—and
their sympathizers. The workers from an underground print shop
that specialized in producing phony identification for draft resisters
seeking admission to Canada lived and housed clients in the roomy
homes and apartments of the Village. An ethos of political radical-
ism developed, and the Federal Bureau of Investigation was reputed
to be infiltrating the neighborhood because an act of trespass and de-
struction on government property had been traced to the Village. A
variety of individuals of liberal or radical political persuasion united
to defend the Village from what they viewed as harassment by the
FBI. As one middle-aged white lawyer who brought a lawsuit against
the FBI in defense of the community recalls:

❍ *For reasons I never knew—or was never sure were good reasons—the FBI seemed convinced that people living in the Village
had done it [destroyed government property]. And they sent over a
hundred agents in, some undercover, some not. And they began
a whole range of activities. . . . They would be standing in little*

groups on corners, and you'd walk by and they'd hassle you. This is the FBI people.

This community [the Village] reacted to the FBI harassment politically. So lawyers—myself and other lawyers—talked about bringing a suit. We did bring a suit, which we eventually won. There was a series of committee meetings, and we decided there would be an early warning system, there would be a list of lawyers who would come any time there was an incident. There were horns, gas-driven horns, and they were put in these four collectives, in the four corners of the Village. And when the FBI was hassling anybody, everybody knew that you could go to any one of these four houses and one of these horns would go off, and everybody would surround the FBI and tell them to stop. Not physically. It was always nonviolent. No one had any intention of fighting with them, or anything like that.

They were knocking people off bicycles—anybody who was on parole or probation, they would be taking them in their cars, threatening to send them back to jail. But just the presence of two hundred people would make them stop pushing around that guy on the bike.

That was a very political conflict with the FBI, which then took on a very countercultural aspect at the street fair. The street fair consisted of a lot of political speeches and stuff . . . a series of booths, it was very creative. There was a booth where there was a big glowering picture of J. Edgar Hoover. And this woman would take a polaroid picture of you so you'd have yourself with J. Edgar Hoover. There were pictures of all the undercover FBI people we could get pictures of, and you could throw darts at their pictures. Lots of live rock music, lots of food, painting—body painting, you know—all sixties counterculture stuff. Well, this was a major thing. Nobody had ever that openly challenged the FBI. And we brought a lawsuit. It was all quite incredible. And the other incredible thing is that no one ever talked to them. When they asked questions, they got nowhere. They didn't even get close.

It [political activism] was all a very uplifting thing. It also showed the power of people who individually are real powerless compared to this huge federal agency, and the armed agents all around. But when they got it together and took a stand, it [the confrontation] made the FBI look foolish. ◐

Within the Village, following these developments, important distinctions were being made between conservatives and liberals and radicals, between those who owned their own homes and those who rented, between young and old, and between black and white. But perhaps even more important social and economic distinctions revolved around the issue of "squatting" rights in the crumbling buildings of the East Village, an area bordering the campus of Eastern Technical University. The owners of some of the largest, most dilapidated apartment buildings there were unwilling or unable to keep the premises in repair and rented, so nonpaying occupants squatted in them. Many of the buildings lay vacant while the University and the Eastern City Redevelopment Commission made long-term plans for the area, and when it finally acted and began to demolish the buildings, the squatters protested with direct action, including sit-ins and civil disobedience.

Though plumbing, wiring, and other amenities were ancient, the apartments were large and charming with their bay windows, fireplaces, oak floors, and sixteen-foot ceilings. The more conventional members of the community associated these dilapidated old buildings with drug dealers, "deserters from the armed services," runaway teenagers, and students; and such old dwellings, and the life-styles then associated with them, were in marked contrast to the white middle-class suburban homes where many of the squatters had been raised, though a number were from blue-collar neighborhoods of city. More conventional people often stereotyped the youthful counterculture as being centered on "getting high on dope or alcohol," loud music, "the politics of revolution," and sex. But the recollections of one involved activist of the period suggest a more complex reality:

⊙ *There were really two kinds of generally countercultural sorts of things going on: There was this large number of political activists that spanned the left side of the spectrum; liberal to various forms of radical. And most of them were most involved in anti–Vietnam War work. And there were several collective houses. Many of them formerly were from houses from the development association, including my own. I bought one of those houses in '71. I had the title, but we lived collectively, with six people, and shared all expenses.*

There were many such communes in the Village. Part of the culture was to be against the extreme forms of individualism that characterized laissez-faire capitalism. The youths tended to see this as a negative. There was a sense of community. People thus didn't live in their own apartment. So you don't live in a family. You live with men and women together, children were fine, and you shared housework, cooking. You had group meetings about anything that happened. Dialogue about anything. Endless dialogue. That was a very important norm. To live collectively, and to emphasize community. And everybody was involved in some aspect or another of political work. Some went on to go to ———. Two of the women went on to Ivy Medical School, doctors, but also even in their medical education and later, you know, did progressive sorts of medical stuff. And so. And they were very serious, long-term, committed people.

Then there was a group of just plain counterculture. Dope—not heroin, [Gut] marijuana, acid, when that was in—and lots of loud music. Politics of revolution, in a way the counterculture of that time to me had a way of talking like it was revolutionary, but it was more life-style. Some of them, or most all of them, would talk revolution. The more serious political people, you know, weren't so sure, "What do we mean revolution? You talking about taking over the state, in the United States?" you know. "What does that mean?" you know, and "How could that be accomplished?" Or "Is it a good thing?" So, there was, I think, a lot of merger and intermixing, particularly at parties, which there were lots of, and socially, and street fairs, and sometimes the countercultural side would predominate but more often the political would predominate. ◐

The disaffected young residents of the East Village saw their mission as bringing to fruition a true countercultural life-style. Food cooperatives were started. One still thrives in an old apothecary shop on the fringe of the neighborhood and draws members from all over the Village and, to a lesser extent, Northton. The building itself is old. The copper scrollwork around the doors and windows is corroded green but intact, and a symbolic staff with coiled snake adorns the archway as one passes into the bustling food store. The smell of nuts, grains, and fruit recalls the days of the general store, before supermarkets packaged, bottled, and froze their goods. The Co-op claimed to sell no foods that contained preservatives. Moreover, it sold many products (such as yogurt) in biodegradable containers. Even the bulk dog food was "all natural." The ethos of the Co-op was hard work, good nutrition, sharing, and equality. Its image in the seventies was of mainly white, and a few black, blue-jeans-clad men and women, of beards and long hair, old pickup trucks, and mixed-breed dogs tied to poles out front.

People with little money who wanted to find others like themselves sought out establishments like the Co-op and gravitated to the abandoned apartment buildings in East Village. Some of the sons and daughters of the original Village Friends chose to "drop out" and join what became known as the "hippies" and "squatters." The controversy over squatting showed up the differences between generations and in differences of economic interests that did not separate the older Irish and German inhabitants from their former rivals, the Village Friends. Both factions of the "old guard," after all, were primarily homeowners, an important distinction. Compared with the squatters and hippies, the Village Friends' generation looked patently conservative.

Among the youthful counterculture, there was sometimes a missionary zeal to create a "humane life-style" in contrast to the more conventional society. This ideal was to be free of racism, materialism, and "mindless conventionality." Such values were often hammered out in social gatherings, and discussions sprang up when people were ostensibly meeting for other purposes. For example, when such people gathered to discuss strategy for dealing with Eastern Technical University's plans for the neighborhood, many encountered one another closely for the first time. Until specific actions were organized, group meetings appeared to be no more than venting sessions, but actually, as in the FBI case, community building was occurring. In such meetings people were able to identify with one another, even with those very different from themselves. For instance, on an October evening in 1977:

⊙ *Wednesday evening . . . some thirty-five people sat around the table in the old casket company. Issue after issue was raised and dropped. It was a motley group, but there were only three blacks. Those present represented what seemed very much like the Village counterculture. There was blue-jeans-clad John Davis, a downtown lawyer, who offered his services to the group free of charge. There were Sylvia and Maureen, a biracial gay couple who lived down the street from the casket company. Tom, a long-haired "hippy-looking" Vietnam veteran, vowed he would never move from his house. "They'll have to carry me out," he roared. The others listened to him politely, and then one person after another entered the conversation with their own thoughts. David Wright, a struggling artist who spends his days as a short-order cook at a downtown restaurant, said, "Somebody's making out on these changes [in the community]." "They want the whole area [East Village]," someone else said.*

Khalem (formerly George Ferguson), a young Black Muslim bent on making his way as an actor or a singer, sat quietly by, checking out the meeting. Michael Berman, an architect who had just purchased a home in the Village, waved his hand for the floor. He suggested tactics for the group in its battle with the Redevelopment Commission. There was much camaraderie that night, as people sipped hot coffee and tea and munched on cookies. The meeting was like a large social gathering whose primary but unspoken purpose seemed to be to let off steam. Many felt their living spaces were threatened, and they were fired up. At 9:45 the meeting ended abruptly and people began filing out onto the dark streets of the Village, their concerns seemingly placed on hold until the next announcement of a meeting (found mysteriously on local utility poles and bulletin boards). ○

Although the counterculture youths felt at odds with middle-class white society and the Quakers at times seemed to be among "the enemy," they shared the Friends' goal of living in harmony with their black neighbors. In their minds such contacts, because of the persistence of racism, became a yardstick with which to measure one's decency and commitment to liberal social values. Indeed, many found inspiration, if not affirmation, in their relationships with blacks of the Village and the nearby ghetto. Many such young whites assumed that many older and conventional whites were intolerant of blacks, if not out and out racist; thus by embracing blacks they were in effect distinguishing themselves from such "grown-ups." They would struggle to get to know black people, perhaps making close friends with some. The youths had a tendency to look upon the blacks as "authentic" victims, and some would venerate "black" lifestyles, self-consciously demonstrating their own lack of prejudice. Through the music they chose to listen to, they celebrated the subculture of blacks as they understood it. On visits to their homes it was not uncommon to hear the sounds of Miles Davis, Billie Holiday, Bessie Smith, B. B. King, and other influential black blues and jazz musicians. In claiming an affinity if not solidarity with blacks, some would go so far as to adopt the fashions of the nearby ghetto. On the streets of the Village in the 1970s, middle-class white youths could be seen wearing dashikis (African shirts), work clothes, and wide-brimmed bordello hats. In conversations with blacks, often insensitive to class and social background differences among blacks, they would spike their language with "man," "cool," and "right on," imi-

17

tating the lower-income blacks with whom they shared the neighbor-hood streets and sometimes their beds. Such shows of familiarity with the black subculture were displays of "hipness" that distanced them from the wider white society and, some believed, drew them spiritually and politically closer to blacks, though some blacks were offended by their actions. For many of the white youths this demonstrative closeness was a sign of racial salvation, placing them firmly on the morally correct side of the continuing struggle for racial equality.

With such complicated activities being worked out in the public places of the Village, and with the prevalence of the liberal value of tolerance that corresponded to them, many saw the community even more clearly as a haven for political refugees. At the same time, the Village claimed strong loyalties from its inhabitants. What some current Villagers refer to as the good old days still come to life as one walks the streets with a former resident and learns, "This was the 3500 Co-op" or "That's the old headquarters for the VCCO [Village Committee for Conscientious Objectors]." Consequently many residents praised the Village as the most liberal or radical part of the city and did not want to live anywhere else. Tied to its countercultural values, many remained there for a long time, leaving only when the neighborhood "changed" or when skyrocketing housing prices forced them out. As one former countercultural man who now lives in the suburbs stated:

◑ *One of the reasons I left was that I thought it was over. This feeling of community. And it was interracial, and that was a big part. The different communities were acting together to make things better. And really working, not perfectly, you know. There were problems, there would be fights at street fairs once in a while, but generally they were acting together to make things better, and succeeding. And I guess the point in time was the ACT thing. That was the conversion time for me.* ◑

Over time, though, some of the former squatters have become renters, perhaps settling on the same block or in an apartment building owned by a member of their group they once viewed as "straight." There was a mad rush whenever one of the few affordable rental units became available. With each successive move, the former squatters seemed less committed to their old attitudes that downplayed accumulating property and "respectability." Others of the youthful counterculture lived in various houses where rents were relatively cheap, sometimes finding themselves between the "straight" and the "hip" worlds. It was not unusual to see young people who worked straight jobs during the day and at night or on the weekends lived the life of the hippie. For instance:

○ *Mary Harmon, a twenty-five-year-old (white) nurse at Memorial Hospital, lived alone in a one-bedroom apartment on Topaz Street. Each day she left for work at approximately 2:30 P.M. and returned home about midnight. Mary seemed to be a something of a contradiction in that she held a responsible position, yet her lifestyle belied her ability to be responsible. When leaving for work or coming home, she was neat in her crisp nurse's uniform. But right up till the time she had to leave for work, and on weekends, she would live as a "stone hippy," dressed in ragged jeans, walking around the neighborhood barefoot, and getting high on large amounts of marijuana with her friends.* ○

And again:

○ *Thirty-year-old (white) Jason Greene worked in a downtown brokerage house. He usually left for work in his suit and tie "work clothes," but in the evening he could be seen on the streets in his hippie outfit, blending in with his friends of the counterculture. In this context, he did not project the usual image of a person employed by a brokerage company.* ○

Many such people became politically and socially more conservative, or "straight," as they aged and took on family responsibilities. A few have become homeowners and even landlords and have resolved some of their political and social dilemmas by taking an active role in local civic affairs. Some continue to thrive in the area as they have grown socially and politically committed to it. Over the years, they have contributed greatly to its peculiar atmosphere of social tolerance, encouraging the conception of a "Village type of person." As one white informant said during the early 1980s, "There's something about the Village and the Village person. This is the greatest place to live. I wouldn't live anywhere else. You couldn't pay me to live out there among the squares in the 'burbs."

And as another (white female) informant said of the early 1970s:

○ *I guess one of the things that comes to my mind the most that I never found anywhere else, and that I think really was starting to happen in the Village when I left [1979]. . . . The thing that seemed to happen every day in all kinds of situations was that you got a lot of different kinds of people, talking to each other, being out on the street, at community meetings, at the playground. . . . People just talked to each other all the time. There was a strong community feeling. You had all kinds of interactions about issues with all kinds of people. Groups don't always talk to each other like that, across groups in informal settings, across racial lines. But not just across racial lines. There was a student population in the Village. And I'm not talking about just the Tech fraternities. I'm talking about the [graduate] students from Ivy University and Tech and other schools in the city, who lived in the apartment buildings and houses in the area. So you got a lot of talk across age lines, which I think is real rare in a community. There wasn't always family connection there. It was just because you lived in this community. You had students talking to adults. They were young adults themselves.*

And across racial lines, too. In the early days of the 1970s, you had a lot more cross-economic talking going on. I never got the sense in the Village that the real gentrification was going on until around 1976 and 1977, just about the time we were leaving. It [the community] suddenly became more polarized. But before then you had people with a middle-class orientation, who saw the Village as a good investment but also chose to live there for other reasons, like the diversity of the area. The thing about living in the Village was that people actively chose the community, and it was for so many similar reasons. There just was an understanding there, of who you were in a way. There was the Village person, who preferred to live in the Village. The Village person was somebody who wanted to be ac-cepted very much for themselves—in other words, this is who I am. I only want the trappings of such a person. I've kind of left behind some other things. And also, he or she was a person who had an openness. "I may not agree with what you say, but don't keep it to yourself because I want to hear it. So let me know about it." People were unpretentious. They would dress in a laid-back way and act down to earth. Such a person could be spotted on the streets as a countercultural person. Very down to earth, there was nothing in the way of your understanding who I am and my understanding who you are. And they didn't like the suburbs, or even other parts of the city. The Village had a certain artist colony quality about it.

Tolerance was the word. People looked to tolerance to be their mark of status. That's what people were judged on. Their openness to not closing themselves off. They would dialogue about anything, and they had a willingness to confront things head on. ◐

Consistently, under the influence of the Quakers, the active

1960s counterculture, and a tradition of liberal political and social values, the Village has developed a reputation in the wider society as being a relaxed area where diverse life-styles are tolerated, if not accepted and encouraged. As issues arise and economic and political conditions change, various interest groups within the Village have become moral communities for a time, defining what they have seen as the proper norms and values of the neighborhood. The Irish and German working-class people succeeded the wealthy first residents and were followed by blacks, the Village Friends, liberal Quakers, and members of the youthful counterculture, which included gay people, aging hippies, and political liberals and radicals. Among the longtime Villagers are college professors, realtors, architects, lawyers, garbage men, cleaning ladies, automobile mechanics, carpenters, dishwashers, taxi drivers, students, and factory workers.

In line with its reputation, the Village has developed a seemingly boundless credo of "live and let live." Over the years, however, its black residents have only slowly come to take part in this collective definition of the situation, and they are thus the ones who probably know best that the openness has its restrictions, the tolerance its limitations, and the espoused egalitarianism its shortcomings.

The Bottom

As changes were occurring among the neighborhood's white residents, equally profound changes were taking place in "the bottom," black sections of the Village. Where the all-black high school now stands, a low-income black enclave once existed. Under the auspices of the Eastern City Redevelopment Commission, exercising the law of eminent domain, that enclave was removed. The blacks, who tended to be lower income to very poor, were offered a presumably fair price for their dwellings and were required by law to vacate. To the outrage of many black and white residents alike, a number of the properties were condemned outright. There were bitter complaints and unsuccessful lawsuits. Initially the residents were told that their land would be used to build low-cost housing, and that they would have the first opportunity to purchase the new homes. Through the condemnation process, approximately one thousand blacks were required to move. A number of black businesses were among the casualties. Although some of the blacks remained in the immediate area, a large number moved many blocks or miles away, often sustaining great emotional and financial loss.

Major service corporations and organizations now are located where black homes and businesses once stood. A significant portion of what was then the black community is occupied by the high school. At one point the land was intended to be used for a science complex, including a "magnet school" that was supposed to draw gifted students from all over the city. Some community groups rejected this idea, arguing that such a school would be all white and thus an insult as well as a disservice to the local black community. The science complex is now almost completed, but because of community agitation the plans for a magnet school were dropped, and a segregated high school drawing from nearby neighborhoods was built in its place; very few white students from the Village have ever attended it.

Across from the school is a row of houses that were spared in the demolition and rebuilding. They are occupied by members of the original black community. Behind the houses is a row of vacant buildings that were also left standing, which once housed small businesses and apartments. After lying vacant and boarded up for many years, those structures were renovated. As the construction workers restored them, a sign reading "Manchester Homes" announced the future of the block. When the work was completed, the apartments and business provided homes and employment for upper-income people, mostly whites. Most of the apartments are at present rented to Eastern Tech students who live cooperatively and can thus afford the relatively high rents. Of course, all this contributes further to the area's social complexity, rising real estate values, and high taxes.

The poor, black and white, and those with fixed incomes are simply unable to afford the taxes and the consequent higher rents that result from these changes. They are thus impelled to sell their homes and move away, and the area becomes even more upper income and white. Those who have to leave may try to remain close by, but in the end they must move to whatever area they can afford. Thus blacks tend to go deeper into the ghetto of Northton, fanning out in various directions. Their choice of residence is often based on chance, but at times it reflects their desire to remain near relatives and friends. They appear to be seeking protection from real estate speculators, but such protection is at best temporary. The process that forced them to leave their Village homes is moving forward and is likely to operate again.

Together the actions of the Redevelopment Commission and the rising taxes effected what amounted to a wholesale amputation of a major portion of the Village's black community. With the exclusion of so many black residents, the Village became wealthier, whiter, and thus more attractive to middle-income whites in search of decent housing close to local institutions and the center of the city. Few whites, including the progressive Quakers, would have moved into a virtual ghetto without very good financial incentives. Thus the removal of the blacks helped pave the way for the present-day development and gentrification. But the process is gradual. It takes a period of living in the area to get a clear picture of real estate activity. One observes that the blacks and the poor tend to move out and white middle- and upper-income people move in. For gentrification to thrive the area must be deemed, sometimes formally, to be "hot"—a place where good deals can be obtained. This is usually accomplished through public relations, aided by news reports, and more informally through encouragement by local real estate agents. Word then spreads, seeds are planted, and houses may be rapidly bought and sold. But occasionally there are detours, roadblocks, and for many of the new residents and local developers and speculators, seemingly interminable delays.

For example, in the late 1970s the radical "back-to-nature" organization ACT, racially mixed but predominantly black, was involved in a standoff with the local police that drew Eastern City into a drama lasting for weeks, resulting in a shoot-out that left one policeman dead. The incident galvanized the community, dividing it along political and racial lines. In some ways the situation brought residents together, and in others it revealed deep strains and opened wounds that have still not completely healed.

Based in an old Victorian house on one of the area's main thoroughfares, the group was a bizarre spin-off of the youthful counterculture of the sixties and seventies. The organization was said to share the "humanitarian" values and ideals of many others in the community, though with loudspeakers blaring and garbage decomposing naturally in the front yard, attracting rats and stray dogs, the ACT group was viewed as highly inconsiderate of its neighbors. Night and day its members would take turns shouting from the rooftop their commitment to "nature" and their generalized hatred and distrust of modern technology and, by implication, of the wider, more conventional society and its institutions.

In the generally "laid back" and socially tolerant atmosphere of the Village, the community seemed at first to accommodate ACT, as it had so many others in the past. Admittedly, the group's members attracted inordinate attention on the streets as they presented themselves in "dreadlocks," a new and provocative (even to blacks) hair style that marked them as outsiders. In public places, where diverse elements of the local population come to "know about" others, the members were generally seen to be civil to others of the community. At Mel's, a handy but overpriced grocery (now Mr. Chow's), ACT members could be seen loading shopping carts with candy, sweet rolls, and soda, and more conventional residents would sometimes snicker about the group's pretensions to "natural foods" and healthful diets. But in their home, or compound, they were determined to do whatever they wanted, without the scrutiny of neighbors.

Other residents tolerated or even supported this newly emerging neighborhood group, particularly since it included so many small children. Indeed, some of the most conservative Village residents would patronize its street car-washing business or hire members to do odd jobs. But this tolerance was short-lived.

The aspect of the group's behavior that drew the attention, and sometimes disdain, of the local community was its treatment of the children: on forty-degree winter days, the ACT people would strip their children naked and in the name of health send them to play out in the front yard in full view of passersby. Most community residents found this behavior scandalous, and it made a poignant and lasting impression. It also encouraged some heretofore reluctant neighbors to take action against ACT.

Although the community was generally able to tolerate the group's often disagreeable conduct, supporting its rights of free speech and independence, it could not sanction behavior it considered harmful to innocent children. A local campaign was begun to have the city health department investigate ACT. But given the group's suspicions and fears—some said paranoia—about local government, it was not about to allow this. To "defend" itself, the group is said to have begun brandishing firearms, including semiautomatic weapons and hand grenades. ACT and the city reached an impasse and approached a violent standoff.

Tension existed near the ACT compound, and many Villagers felt the community was in crisis. After some fruitless pleading and cajoling by local officials, the police were called in. In response the

ACT people barricaded their compound and took up defensive positions. Over a bullhorn, the members continued to shout obscenities at neighbors and passersby at all times of day and night, condemning the wider "technological" society and its institutions. The police response was to cordon off the area for a block around and virtually occupy it. It was during this standoff that various groups and factions of the Village-Northton revealed themselves to be either "for" or "against" ACT.

Because they were viewed as a predominantly black group opposing the local government, which was out of favor with a large proportion of the black community, some local black leaders felt a need to support them, though many blacks were put off by their "nappy hair," their unkempt "hippy" appearance, and their incomprehensible dispute with the city. Many of the "old-time Village people" were sharply divided over the issue; they were generally against violence in any form and abhorred the prospect of bloodshed, and they felt great concern for the ACT children. They tended to fault the city government for escalating the crisis by stationing police and cordoning off parts of the neighborhood, thus contributing to local tension. Many members of the counterculture had mixed feelings as well, but they too generally faulted the city's handling of the situation; they needed to show solidarity with another "oppressed" group, but they too were concerned about the children and about the rumors that the ACT people had guns. But many of the emerging class of local developers and incoming young urban professionals simply wanted the ACT people out and the crisis resolved so they could get on with their lives.

The battle against ACT was waged in the name of law and respectability, reminiscent of the battle waged against the squatters by the more "respectable" residents of an earlier day, who demonstrated by such campaigns that they themselves were decent and law-abiding. But underlying this campaign, particularly on the part of property owners and those whose interests were tied to local real estate, was the question of what effect the ACT people were having on property values. As one resident of the Village during this period said:

◉ *They [many homeowners] had great impatience with the "we have to understand how people feel" approach to all of this. There were just as many homeowners and apartment dwellers who cared little about property values and were much concerned with toler-*

ance. But there has been something of a transformation: the young urban professionals were beginning to arrive around the late 1970s, and they were displacing those who were traditional. ◐

For many property owners and people who cared about living in a trendy area, ACT became emblematic of stasis, if not regression; but the issue also became a kind of litmus test of progressive values for those concerned about tolerance and diversity.

The issue was resolved by gunfire. In the end one policeman was dead, the ACT people were publicly beaten and arrested, and their barricaded compound was bulldozed by the city government.

And the Village, it seemed, was never the same. For many who cared about the neighborhood's "taking off," including an increasing number of homeowners and developers, the "fly in the ointment" had been effectively removed, and the Village could proceed on its way to becoming hot, trendy, or at least more expensive. But development and the anticipated increase in property values did not occur as quickly as some hoped. Perhaps the largest impediment was the proximity of the ghetto of Northton, a presence to which all the various groups in the Village could relate.

Gentrification

When neighborhoods are occupied by middle- to upper-income whites, the associated spaces—including houses, buildings, and parks—generally are considered more valuable by various people. Segregated blacks who live on architecturally similar property pay a racial tax. Their property becomes more valuable on the open market when it is demonstrated that upper-income whites consider it valuable, and the demand for this housing then goes up. Market value is strongly affected by whether such whites want to enter the neighborhood. When this desirability is made widely known it helps an area to become financially "hot," or on the move (see Sumka 1979; Gale 1979).

As well-to-do whites move in, they form a new cultural group whose social status attracts others like them and makes the area even more desirable. But the emerging neighborhood is valued largely to the extent that it is shown to be separate from low-income black communities. In a democratic society it is difficult to completely cut off adjacent neighborhoods, so blacks and others are virtually guaranteed access, often to the dissatisfaction of the newest residents.

As newcomers move in they in effect invest themselves, infusing a certain aura that can be transformed into market value when they sell their property. They thus bargain in part with class status and culture. When they sell, they sell their informal share in the community that they have had a hand in shaping through their residence. The scarcity of these areas increases the cost of such property, while the actual and anticipated increase of individual purchases and of real estate activity helps set their general market value.

In contrast, blacks living in segregated communities like Northton find it difficult to infuse this relatively high market value into their own property. One impediment is the internal change occurring within so many black communities, which often leads to their destabilization and decline and which here threatens to spill over to nearby sections of the Village.

In certain parts of the Northton ghetto, blacks of the solid "manufacturing era" working class of about forty-five years ago purchased homes, kept them up well, and paid them off over time. As such people aged and eventually died, they typically left their property to younger relatives who were generally much less well off and in some cases very poor, and often had numerous small children. When these poorer relatives moved in the house was not painted so often, loose boards and leaky roofs were repaired less promptly, and the yard deteriorated. Neighborhood blight often set in. Such developments, including overcrowding, excessive noise, and sometimes vandalism and street crime undermined the morale of the community and drove the remaining residents out one by one, in the sociological process of "invasion-succession." Eventually the whole neighborhood would turn over, changing from solidly working-class and middle-class to become increasingly poor and blighted. Black residents of Northton speak of having witnessed such developments repeatedly.

Because of racial prejudice and discrimination, such working-class to lower-middle-class blacks have operated in a restricted housing market. Even in the Northton of today, though owners might make numerous improvements to their dwellings, these changes by themselves do not increase their value. Property values increase when the area itself is defined as desirable by those who more readily participate in the general market, including at times upper-middle-income blacks. This trend is consolidated through individual transactions that bring in middle- to upper-income whites.

If lower-income blacks began moving into the Village in droves, very probably property values would decline. One factor that hedges against such an occurrence is the supposed value of the general area.

As the value of the properties rises, lower-income people are less able to afford to buy homes or to rent in areas like the Village. This supposed value is affected by various factors, the most important being the area's desirability. Contributing to this value are the increasing cost of energy, particularly gasoline, the vogue for such city neighborhoods among young urban professionals, proximity to the universities, access to the central city, and the limited availability of acceptable housing stock, but the spillover from Northton in the form of drug addicts and panhandlers has a dampening effect on the desirability of the Village community.

Also important is the potential value of Village property. Part of what fuels the invasion of middle- and upper-income people is the antique nature of the dwellings they seek to own and inhabit. The new residents themselves have a hand in creating the value of such antiques, which is unrealized until such persons "discover" them, apply "spit and polish," and purchase "old things" to re-create a vintage style. Often they congratulate themselves and their friends for having the ability to recognize a good deal and exploit it. Their social status enhances their "finds." The houses and other possessions that they recognize as "valuable antiques" become more valuable through their work, their ownership, and perhaps most important, their claims. In this regard the most effective claim is made by the "done deal." It is through such sales that potential value rapidly becomes transformed into market value.

As well-off newcomers move into the Village, they refurbish the area. With their money, education, and class position, they can return the dwellings to something approaching their original condition. Until now the inhabitants often have lacked the resources—including the priorities, the money, the taste, and the knowledge of just how to go about the restoration—to ensure a high return on investment. As the newcomers move in, they exploit not only the immediate value of the property but its potential, obtaining home improvement loans for thousands of dollars. Hence their real estate claims become all the more believable. And the "antique factor" becomes much more operative in their hands, partly because of their knowledge of the market, confidence, and social status. Following the law of supply and demand, as more people like themselves want what they have made attractive, the amount they can get may increase. And with each turnover the price goes up or down as the market changes. Generally it goes up. In effect, sellers bet on the local market, keeping tabs on what the last house sold for. Thus they work to fulfill their own claims, to make them real, ultimately inflating home prices and rents and contributing to an increase in taxes.

Thirty years ago racial prejudice was a greater motivation for many people than the desire to remain in a comfortable building. Before the community reached the value it has today, many Irish and German working-class and middle-class residents gave in to their antipathy toward blacks and fled. As they left and blacks moved in, property values declined and ghettos formed.

Today whites are moving back despite the presence of lower-income blacks. They are acknowledging the advantages of living close to the center of the city and the university campuses, the quality of the houses, and the quaintness of the community; but most significantly, they anticipate an imminent rise in the status of the general area. Hence property there has attained a value that depends not simply on the racial makeup of the present residents, but on the racial and class attributes of potential residents, and thus on the future of the area.

At present this scenario appears to reflect a nationwide trend toward buying up and appreciating old areas of the inner city (many of the "best" of which are now inhabited by blacks, white ethnics, and the poor). If so, it dovetails with another important development: the change of the employment base of many cities from manufacturing to service-oriented industries. This suggests that a new, white-collar group is likely to be an important part of such areas in the future. As the process occurs and matures, those employed in manufacturing gradually become less prominent and people associated with the white-collar, service industries become more prevalent. This change, though slow, will continue to have important implications for the makeup of the Village-Northton area.

The early battles for the neighborhood and for manufacturing jobs were often fought bitterly by the different working-class ethnic groups that made up so much of the city. Ethnic identity was strongly associated with particular neighborhoods, which were often close to the workplace. This is one of the reasons racial and ethnic struggles were so acrimonious: newcomers threatened the claims to ethnic control not only of the workplace, but of the neighborhood itself. So ethnic tensions rose (see Davis and Haller 1974).

In the Village of today, the old ethnic and racial considerations seem to be much less important for the middle class, since many newcomers work in high-tech or service industries and in education. Whites, often the children of working-class ethnics who fled the city to get away from blacks, now move in right next door to them. In this respect it seems a new day for race relations in the city, as the new middle- and upper-income service-oriented occupations emphasize not ethnicity and skin color but the technical skills a person can provide.

In personal relations, occupation or social class increasingly competes strongly with race. To be sure, many newcomers can hardly wait until "better" people move in to displace the poorer residents, who are often black. But such considerations often go beyond the color of the next person's skin and are strongly interrelated with and complicated by issues of social class and culture.

Generally this process ebbs and flows, but a major current impediment is the variety of social ills now afflicting Northton, including persistent poverty, illiteracy, teenage pregnancy, drugs, and crime. These ills spill over into the Village and work to undermine its quality of life. These effects appear to have slowed down gentrification, but they have not yet reversed it.

Elements of the Present-Day Village-Northton Area

The current residents of the Village might be categorized as the old-time Villagers, the former counterculture group, the "yuppies," the Eastern Tech students, and the blacks.

The old-time Villagers derive in large part from the Quaker element that once lived here in numbers. Such "old-timers" have been in the Village for fifteen to forty years, and their most important primary group is here or nearby. The designation indicates long familiarity and connection with the Village and implies a healthy respect for liberal social values.

The old-timers may be further divided into those who have owned Village property for many years and have raised their children here and those who keep up with their old friends but have moved to other communities. Though many of these individuals are well-to-do, they tend to distrust those they accurately call "speculators" or real estate entrepreneurs, whom they view as "trying to make a killing" by buying and selling property in the Village. They object to such presumed lack of loyalty to the community and fear the effects. Although some of the old-timers own property within the Village that has greatly appreciated in value, many initially gravitated to the community because of its architectural ambiance and its socially liberal and humanistic values, not to speculate.

The old-timer label refers to people like Thomas Winslow, an elderly man who was an early and successful realtor in the area. For much of his life he has been concerned about "making the community a place where all different kinds of people can live" and "keeping the area from becoming a land speculator's paradise." He began his own business through his work with the Village Development Association, and he says that an important part of his involvement in the association was motivated by civic purpose and the good of the community.

The old-timers have had numerous common experiences in shaping local history. Because of this involvement they have grown together, winning or losing on issue after issue that has faced the community through the years. For example, they know about "the Rocks," a landmark that was recently renovated for apartments; a few can talk about the unique history of the building, including its various owners. (For years the building housed squatters in its roomy apartments. A small area of the basement was rented to Mel, who ran a delicatessan there for many years, until he sold it a few years ago to Mr. Chow, a Korean immigrant.) Because they are "in the know," they can talk easily with others who share this history about the numerous stories and rumors surrounding the apartment block. They also "know about" the problems with ACT.

Mr. Winslow used to drive by the ACT compound and sometimes patronized their curbside car wash. People like him can still be found around the Village and the city more generally. They are now about fifty-five to seventy-five or even older. Many proudly acknowledge the "old days" when they lived together in local communes and opposed the Korean War. Some were associated with the socialist movement, while others saw themselves as "economic egalitarian" conservatives. Most held egalitarian values and were especially progressive on issues of civil rights and racial integration. They would rail at any evidence of racial injustice and become outraged at manifestations of bigotry and intolerance. For these people the community of the Village was an experiment in interracial living. Many of these old-timers still encounter each other at parties and social affairs, and they keep in touch generally. Occasionally they reminisce about the old days, telling funny stories such as when the FBI was believed to be infiltrating the neighborhood in search of antiwar demonstrators.

One of the most distinctive features of the old-time Villagers was their tolerance for those different from themselves, racially and socially. They demonstrated their values to their black neighbors in Northton and the Village, helping to establish norms of tolerance for diversity that still operate strongly within the Village.

In certain respects the old-timers anticipated the youthful counterculture of the 1960s, offering support for many of its values, including pacifism and antimaterialism. In line with this, their homes and automobiles understate their supposed financial position:

◐ *On a chilly November evening I visited James Church, a well-known white member of the Village community, at his home on Cherry Street. He lived in an old Victorian house with gingerbread trim. He answered the door and invited me inside. When I stepped into the vestibule, I was struck by how dingy everything seemed. The walls needed paint, cobwebs draped the corners, and the hardwood living room floor was bare and dusty. A forest green overstuffed sofa sat in the middle of the room, well worn in a few obvious places. An old oak rocking chair sat by its end. The maple coffee table was stained, and the house had a general look of clutter. Mr. Church offered me a cup of tea, and we talked about the neighborhood.* ◐ But despite their prominently liberal social and political values, in comparison with the youthful counterculture the old-time Villagers seemed quite conservative.

The former "counterculture" people are now between thirty-five and fifty years old and many were around the Village in the 1960s, living in communes or squatting in East Village near Eastern Technical University. Many of them identified with the youth movement of the 1960s and 1970s, defining themselves in distinction to the more conventional culture, including the "old-time" Villagers. They were outspokenly "antiwar" (Vietnam); many of them demonstrated and marched, and a few were said to be hunted by the FBI. Counted among their number were draft resisters, "hippies," and political radicals; some were blacks.

Decidedly against intolerance, they welcomed diverse associates, but their views tended to be more radical than those of the old-timers. Whereas the conventional old-timers opposed discrimination toward individual blacks, members of the political counterculture would speak in terms of general "racism," more fundamentally condemning the wider culture. And whereas the old-timers were prepared to accommodate the wider culture and work to remedy its flaws, counterculture members argued that the whole structure of society should be changed.

Such counterculture people have now "grown up," and many have stayed in the community, marrying, having children, and buying homes. Over time they have become more conventional, gravitating to many of the social and political positions held by the old-time Villagers. They are becoming professionals and merchants and have grown less insistent about changing society. Approaching the old-timers' social level, some are doctors, lawyers, and architects. Many now accept the system's flaws and concentrate on "brightening their own corner" of the world.

But though they have become more conventional, they retain a healthy distrust of powerful organizations, dominant institutions, and material possessions. Indeed, a number of the problems of the 1960s continue to be an important part of their consciousness. Some of these people, as they age, become community activists, particularly on behalf of Northton. For example, they involve themselves, at times in cooperation with the old-timers, in campaigns to improve local schools. A small but very impressive group has formed the Village-Northton Educational Fund (I was a board member for two years), which works hard to improve instruction and promote desegregation, in tandem with the local school board. Many send their own children to the public schools, which sometimes include at least half black and other minority students, thereby demonstrating their support for integrated quality education.

The decision whether to send one's child to public or private school has become a mildly contentious issue within the Village community. Those whose children attend private schools are associated ever more closely with the new professional group, and the decision confers a certain status on the family but distances them somewhat from those who see themselves as adhering to the "human values" associated with the counterculture of the 1960s. Not only are such parents viewed, at times erroneously, as striving to achieve status, but they are seen as contributing to the segregation of the local schools by sending their children off to predominantly white private schools. Thus they risk being viewed as "racist" by their black and white peers, with whom they otherwise appear to have much in common. In dealing with such implicit, and sometimes explicit, challenges to their integrity as racially tolerant families, they may agonize and feel the need to apologize for their decisions about their children's schooling: a common excuse is that "Johnny has a learning disability and needs the attention he gets in small classes." In the name of civility and tolerance their liberal neighbors and friends "understand" such a position, but they may "talk about" them nonetheless. Essentially, such educational choices are viewed as strongly associated with families' class orientations.

The third group I call the "yuppies"—the young urban professionals. These people range in age from twenty-two to thirty-five. Many hold professional positions with local universities or with organizations downtown or in the suburbs of Eastern City. Single people may live with roommates in the Village's expensive but spacious apartments. Most married couples have no children; if they do the suburbs call, and they tend to move. If they stay, unlike their more liberal counterparts, they send their children to private schools with little hesitation or explanation.

With the incursion of the newcomers, a natural affinity between the former counterculturalists and the old-time Villagers has become increasingly clear. Given the choice of associating with the yuppies, many counterculturalists would rather socialize with the old-time Villagers, and vice versa, since they are much more compatible ideologically.

Yuppies are easy to spot. They are young, and most are white. Early in the morning they may be seen walking their dogs, scooping up behind them, sometimes in business attire. Young women, often wearing suits and carrying briefcases, march along in sneakers. The men, similarly dressed, sometimes walk with the women, guarding them as the team makes its way to the bus or trolley; in the evenings they reverse this trek.

Not all newcomers are necessarily closely associated with the yuppies, but they appear to share their political and social values. Some are live-in landlords and developers, though a few of these have been around for a long while. They look for ways to buy up Village property for investment. These new people threaten to change the community in a way that leaves both the old-timers and the former counterculturalists somewhat ambivalent, alternately upset and pleased by the prospect of change. Many of these new renters and owners seem to have a vision of the Village as homogeneous in social class. Whereas the old-time Villagers actively encouraged diversity, the yuppies seem uncomfortable with it, especially with class heterogeneity. The developers in this group do not promote diversity but are inclined to avoid it. For instance, whereas old-timers and counterculturalists might encourage the presence of a local home for delinquent boys, the yuppies and their associates would want it placed elsewhere, charging that its presence devalues property. They would see it as a blemish on the neighborhood, whereas earlier residents would see it as a testament to brotherhood and assistance for those less fortunate. The newcomers appear to lack a strong social conscience and to be preoccupied with enhancing the market value of local housing stock.

According to community gossip, many of these people hope the Village will one day become a Georgetown (D.C.) on the Tyler, offering spiffy apartment buildings, pastel houses with antique furnishings and fittings, and wealthy neighbors. Consistent with this image, they encourage chic restaurants, trendy shops, and fancy boutiques. In this way newcomers and local developers work hand in hand. A few former counterculturalists and even some old-time Villagers find it hard to object to local development that promises to "improve" the neighborhood and increase their own property values. In the sporadic but ongoing local battles over issues affecting the community's future, the young urban professionals, developers, and others interested in development are likely to prevail.

Generally perceived to be closely related to these groups are the students of Eastern Technical University, along with a few from Ivy University. A complex lot, students are often associated by residents with the young urban professionals. Given the similarity in age and background, the yuppies may serve as role models for the younger students, who are often heading for professional careers.

Most students are undergraduates, but there are also an increasing number of graduate students, particularly since Eastern Tech started encouraging them to live in the local community. The policy has encouraged developers, providing financial support to meet the growing demand for housing, which is increasingly oriented, both in high cost and in style, toward affluent students and the yuppies. To meet this demand, developers buy old Village buildings, further driving up their cost. Thus the students, the developers, and the young urban professionals come together as a group with perceived common interests.

Within the community the students constitute a "use group" in the public spaces of the Village to a greater extent than many other white residents. Not only do they help inflate rents and property values, but they are willing to move to the very edge of the Village, making territorial claims on portions of Northton. In their somewhat marginal role, these young white students will live in areas that the yuppies would never consider. Their numbers help claim the streets for whites. They come in contact with poor blacks, ignoring them socially but having to deal with them in public places. They see them at the grocery stores, on the trolleys, in the laundromats, and on the streets. Living as they do, they often have their cars broken into and their stereos and television sets taken, or are accosted and mugged on the streets.

Given these experiences, they may be easily provoked or intimidated by blacks, often becoming intolerant, particularly of young black males, during fleeting public encounters. At the same time, some genuine friendly conversation occurs between young white students and their black neighbors, and they sometimes play with small children in Northton. However, these good efforts may be undermined by the intolerance shown by other students, particularly fraternity members.

However, many students have as little as possible to do with the local black community, in contrast to the attitudes and values of the old-time Villagers and the former counterculturalists, who went out of their way to know and support their black neighbors, both in the Village and in Northton. Yet perhaps these first activists were simply the front lines of the process known as gentrification—stretching, delimiting, and in effect redefining the boundaries of the Village.

The last and largest portion of the area's population consists of black homeowners and renters living within the boundaries of the Village and immediately across the Bellwether Street boundary in Northton. These residents range from middle class to very poor; but there are relatively few middle-class blacks among their number. Mainly because of distinctions of culture, social class, and color, these people tend to keep to themselves where whites are concerned. Where lower-class status and dark skin color intersect, a sharp social caste line appears and endures, effectively putting blacks in one social place and whites in another—whites as privileged and blacks as poor, whites as trustworthy and blacks as not. In glossing over this line of demarcation, some black residents, particularly middle-class blacks living in the Village, engage in friendly exchanges with their white neighbors, but others are highly suspicious of black-white relations and generally maintain a certain distance, expecting others to behave in much the same way.

Serving as a buffer group between Northton and the Village, some older, homeowning, churchgoing black families live on the Village side of the Bellwether Street boundary. These are generally people who gained some prosperity from the old manufacturing economy, accumulating enough capital to buy a home and by their example inspiring their own children and a few others to "do something worthwhile in life." Now usually in their mid-sixties, the women may be great-grandmothers who have worked hard to raise their own families and now are sometimes drawn into extending themselves to help raise yet another generation of children. In this they may feel a certain frustration mixed with a genuine willingness to contribute what they can. To their counterparts in Northton and other "rough" ghetto neighborhoods around the city, their residential situation may be viewed as desirable; some blacks point to "white" neighbors as a mark of status, noting that city services such as law enforcement and garbage collection are more reliable in a "white" neighborhood. Such people live on what middle-income whites, ironically consider the "edge," the "frontier," or the "bad" section of the Village. Some are the counterparts of the financially stable families of Northton who fled as the community began to "go down," but they saw no reason to leave and remained to see the area "turn around." The white middle-class presence has served as a stabilizing force, allowing such families to remain and perhaps to cash in on their housing investment. They now enjoy a certain tranquility on the tree-lined streets of the Village, amid the students, the young urban professionals, and the older Village residents.

On warm Sunday afternoons the "church ladies," as they are sometimes known in the neighborhood, sit on their porches and take in the sights, suspiciously eyeing certain "strangers" passing on foot, and visiting with friends who have come by after church services. On weekdays they may work as cleaning ladies or baby-sitters for white residents of the Village to augment their pensions, or they may keep busy around their own homes. The men, who may be retired, may hang out at a local "recreation room," where they play checkers and socialize. Some, though they may deny that they "do it for the money," serve as "gypsy" taxi drivers, driving local people around the area or across town for a negotiated fee. For example, James Murphy, sixty-seven years old, is a retired welder who draws Social Security and a pension. He and his wife have "raised six kids." He now owns a new Cadillac and drives various people around for money as "something to do."

These older residents' homes are usually neat and well kept, but with old, heavy furniture and sometimes dingy walls that need paper and paint. In the winter they may sit around a kerosene heater to keep the heating bill down. They are polite to their white neighbors, maintaining friendly but superficial relations with them. They almost universally lament the "ruined" state of the local black community.

Younger versions of the families just described may live either in Northton or in the Village proper, but there is a significant difference: the man is more often missing. One longtime black male resident who knows the area well told me, "Ninety percent of the families around here are made up of single women and children. The men are just not around. That's gone out [of style]." The single mother may have a "good" job as a policewoman, janitor or nurse's aide at one of the local hospitals. Marlene Davis, a nurse's aide at the local university hospital, lives with her mother, her teenage son, and two small children on tree-lined Linden Avenue in the Village. She has been divorced for two years and has a male "friend" who visits her regularly. She and her family attend Bethel Baptist Church regularly, and with the help of her mother she takes her domestic role very seriously, setting particularly "strict" standards for her children. One of her biggest worries is that her son might become mixed up in the drug trade.

But ordinarily blacks living in Northton and some parts of the Village tend to be poor to extremely poor. The family usually includes a single mother on welfare and two or three children, with a man playing the role of father part time if at all. Residents say some men roam from one family unit to another, "playing daddy" to the children to win the mothers' favors. As the children become teenagers, the boys may become increasingly responsible for the family's financial support—or at least may see themselves that way. They work at low-paying jobs and bring home part of their pay to help "Mama and my brothers and sisters."

John Brown lives with his mother and siblings. He is a "high-school graduate, a former halfback for the football team, and has done a lil' boxing." He is about 5' 10" tall and weighs about 170 pounds; he is built like a prize high-school football running back. John works at a nearby pizza parlor and has been looking for a better job for "a long time," to no avail. He likes to dress in a fashionable navy blue or dark green Fila sweat suit, or in designer jeans, T-shirt, and jacket, with expensive white "sneaks." At twenty-one John was the father of four children born out of wedlock to three different women; two sons were born only months apart.

John says of his family life,

◑ *[My father] left seven years ago, and he don't have much to do with us. That's between my mom and dad. That's them. I'm grown now, and I try to help my mom as much as I can, 'cause I'm all she got. I'm her oldest son. My brother is just a baby. He got epilepsy. And my sister, she a woman, so she can only be so strong. . . . I got to help out at home as much as I can. My mom, she don't have a boyfriend, she don't have a fiancé. I'm all she got. I'm her oldest male child, and she depends on me. I'm her backbone. . . . [She] barely making ends meet. We heat our house [a large Victorian] with kerosene.* ◑

Eastern City is said to be a "city of neighborhoods," but beyond this, the young men of many Northton streets organize these informally bounded areas into territories, which they defend against the intrusions of outsiders (see Short and Strodtbeck 1965; Suttles 1972). These territories can become quite extensive, guarded by numerous boys—often from single-parent homes—who then form larger units that lend a certain structure to the general area. Each neighborhood unit is considered responsible for public behavior within its boundaries. Members of these units police the streets, harassing outsiders and strangers. It is not uncommon for a young man to walk up to a complete stranger, particularly a young male, and demand to know his business or ask who gave him permission to use "these streets." If the stranger gives no acceptable answer, there may be a fight. These young men affect the crime rate of the area; at times they commit crimes, at other times they discourage them. If they like their neighbors they may be protective; if they dislike them, they and their homes may be fair game for robbery, assault, or harassment. In the area of John's home, the groups tend to not be formally organized but are simply small groups of neighborhood "young" boys who take a real interest in protecting what they consider their turf. Now the drug trade has established itself in the general area, and some people say it has made use of the local street gang's structure, absorbing many neighborhood boys into the drug distribution network. For young John Turner, this network calls loudly and insistently.

This brings us to the local black middle class. Usually these people have grown up under conditions of racial segregation, either locally or in some other part of the country. Some are the first members of their families to acquire a college education. They range in age from thirty through middle age. Unlike the black working class, they hold business and professional positions at local universities or work downtown among educated whites. When they return home to the Village, they generally seek other blacks for friendship, but sometimes they socialize with white neighbors, who may be eager for such friendship, given the felt scarcity of middle-class blacks in the area. Yet because of lingering racism and feelings of social distance from whites, particularly in public places, blacks may approach these relationships with ambivalence, and they tend not to initiate them. To some degree the emphasis on black ethnic particularism appears emotionally protective and thus is highly persistent.

In this context at least two often competing, highly complicated racial perspectives may be discerned. Essentially these views appear to govern racial conduct in the community while defining individuals to one another. Blacks in this environment may take one or the other position or even both simultaneously. In managing the stresses and doubts that confront them, some move back and forth situationally between the two. For conceptual purposes those assuming these perspectives can be thought of as social types, but in practice the two types may merge.

Type A blacks view the social world mainly in terms of ethnicity and color, emphasizing these characteristics in all important relationships. A central problem for such individuals is retaining their racial identity, or "blackness," in a predominantly white socioeconomic class context that they perceive as threatening. All whites are considered suspect on the race question, and from experience they always come up short. Therefore prejudice toward whites is understandable and tolerable, if not totally acceptable. Type A people are resigned to the notion that whites are unalterably prejudiced toward blacks and are beyond help. Hence they believe that almost any relationship with whites that is not clearly instrumental is fundamentally a waste of time. Moreover, they observe a racial etiquette based on these assumptions.

Consequently, such people's primary group relations are exclusively with other blacks. They decline social invitations from whites or may accept simply out of politeness, curiosity, or "politics," and their own social gatherings are almost always totally black. In support of these actions, they recall the history of the black experience, citing white racism and persistent black social inequality. They perceive racial prejudice as rampant in the Village, particularly noting the treatment of black males in public.

The type B perspective presupposes a somewhat more cosmopolitan outlook, while retaining important elements of the type A position. Confronting the everyday issues of racial caste—on the streets, on the trolleys, and at work—blacks holding this view assume there is persistent racism in society, and because of this, and the etiquette surrounding it, most of their close friends are black. Yet in everyday life social class generally outweighs racial influences; they move comfortably in both white and middle-class black circles. They are prepared to play down the importance of color in their own lives and are open to an array of friends from a variety of ethnic backgrounds. At local social gatherings they mingle with middle-class Jews, Italians, Irish individuals, and others—people estranged from their ethnic ghettos. Ethnicity is ignored, not emphasized. In these settings type B blacks find themselves reasonably at home.

Moreover, they are inclined to see themselves as "individuals" and thus to choose their friends not so much by color as by apparent social attitudes, interests, and affinities such as tennis, community organizing, Home and School participation, and politics. On political issues these people are moderate to liberal, but they may surprise some of their white friends, particularly former counterculturalists, with "pro-life" stands on abortion, conservative views on the work ethic, or intolerance toward individual members of the local underclass.

A class component may be seen operating in the distinctions noted here. Generally, type A attitudes are strongly associated with the ethnic particularism of the working and lower classes, whereas type B attitudes are more readily found in the emerging middle class, people who may expect a cultural payoff from adopting dominant cultural and behavioral codes that let them move more easily in the wider professional society. Yet both types are represented in the local black middle class.

Moreover, as individuals with the "courage of their convictions," people may be fiercely independent, believing strongly in their right to be conservative, liberal, or radical, defying stereotypes commonly held by both blacks and whites about a socially and politically monolithic black community. In this sense such individuals seem at odds with the earlier "race man" (type A) ideology identified by Cayton and Drake and appear consistent with a more cosmopolitan "color blind" ideology (type B) (see DuBois 1965; Drake and Cayton 1962; Wilson 1980).

Because they work in technical and service-related jobs, blacks of either type A or type B gain exposure to the wider culture and may come to accept the need to get along with professional peers. Moreover, because of their middle-class position, the child-care arrangements of both types, including their children's play groups, tend to be predominantly white. And because of such associations they may come to know the parents of white children socially, as individuals and not simply as members of a racial category. On occasion they may attend the symphony or the theater with white friends; some even take up "white" pastimes like golf or tennis. But because of the social complications alluded to above, particularly the etiquette of the color line and the limited number of middle-class blacks in the community, at parties and social affairs given by their white friends they may be the only blacks present. To be sure, a large number of blacks live in the general area, but most are working-class people who might be acceptable to some middle-class whites as neighbors but problematic as friends.

The Village School

Perhaps no place are the values of social tolerance and harmony more fully expressed than in the neighborhood elementary school. The school was established in 1962 through the campaign of a middle-class, highly committed racially and ethnically mixed group of progressive community activists, a number of whom were Quakers. They wanted a racially mixed school where they could send their children. One woman who was active with this group described it this way:

◑ *They favored progressive, high-quality, "integrated" education, and they were determined to have a school in the area that would serve local needs. They were progressives, and they wanted a school to reflect their life-style. They wanted an integrated urban school, and they really cared about this. And they did a superb job in getting the facts and figures together and making their case to the school board. They had maps, they had graphs, they had statistics galore to show that there was a need in this neighborhood for an elementary school. It was really impressive.*

There were [in the group] Jews, Gentiles, blacks, biracial couples. It was a multiracial, multiage group. In those days there was a special ambiance in the Village that cut across class lines. It was a real neighborhood school. I guess it was that a lot of us were from small towns, and our childhood school memories were related to that. We just wanted the Village school to be the same, and we achieved it. I gather it's still being achieved. The middle-class people who lived there at the time chose to live there because they wanted an integrated environment. They did not want their kids fleeing to the white suburbs; that was a big issue at the time. They just didn't want that phony environment for their kids to grow up in. There was this wish to just get rid of these racial structures, to move beyond that, and that was done by a certain nucleus of the group, and it was a real point of view. ◐

Although the school began as integrated in terms of both class and race and has maintained much of this character, over the years it has become increasingly black, though at present the racial makeup has stabilized at about 60 percent black and 40 percent white. The newer Village residents tend to send their children to private schools, while poorer blacks send their children to the Village school. Projections were for the school to become increasingly black, and this imbalance was addressed by local parents who successfully petitioned the school board to declare it a "desegregation magnet school." To accomplish all this required vigilance, campaigning, and sometimes bitter fights with reigning itinerant principals. In an effort to desegregate the school, the board allowed for white students only who lived outside the regular school-district boundaries to attend the Village school, thereby angering black parents who looked forward to sending their children there. But the school board's action has brought some stabilization of the school's racial makeup.

Until this past year, however, classes were labeled "open" and "traditional," and this led to a kind of de facto segregation within the school. Among the black parents, even those who are middle class, there is much concern over a need for "structure" and a distrust for "open" learning situations, which they fear will not prepare their children to compete and succeed in the real world. Hence black students are overrepresented in the traditional classes, while the white and middle-class students fill the "open" classes. At the beginning of each school year there is much parental anxiety, particularly among the middle-class parents, over classroom assignments, since they associate "open" with superior instruction and traditional with imposed limits and dullness. Over the years the Village school has enjoyed a well-deserved and growing reputation for excellence, and numerous teachers there are "child centered" in their philosophy and enthusiastic about their teaching. Until two years ago the school went to sixth grade, and by this level the white students would trickle out, going to private schools or the "magnet" schools within the local system. The result was a school that was predominantly black, especially at the upper grades. Now, under the guidance of a new principal, the school has discontinued the upper two grades and taken a firmer hand in assigning students, with an interest in desegregating the classroom, sometimes to the dismay of white parents from outside the district who were drawn to the Village school because of its reputation for "open" classrooms and academic excellence. This policy has led to more racially balanced classes, though proportions fluctuate from year to year. As a long-term Village schoolteacher concluded:

◑ *One important value that we [at the Village school] hold is that children look at each other as, you know, all valuable and begin to be able to live together with children who are different physically and culturally and intellectually and all kinds of ways. On the other hand, children who have come to this school because their parents want them to have a certain kind of education should also be given some support, and we certainly want to keep the white population, so we have to give them some kind of support. [The white population comes from the Village, but also from other areas of the city, including the general area that has certain attributes in common with the Village.] We stress that every child can learn and that there are many ways to approach learning—that each of them is legitimate and they should be all supported. And that they can learn and can be responsible, happy kids together. I think there is a spirit here that is unique. It shouldn't be, but it is. I think that—and I'm just looking at the playground now—they can be happy with themselves, and they can be children.* ◑

The following fieldnote portrays a typical Village event:

◑ *On a Tuesday evening in late April, the spring concert was to* occur at the Village school. Outside cars were passing, people were coming and going, and children and their parents were arriving for this big annual event. The setting was the small gymnasium, which opened onto the Village Avenue entrance of the school. Folding chairs had been set up in rows; at one end was an elevated platform that would be the stage. It was just the beginning of the warm season, and the gym was already stuffy. People sat and fanned themselves. There was much coming and going. A middle-aged Asian man in shirt sleeves sat on a railing, his camera in hand. An elderly black man in coveralls and cap strolled in. A young urban professional, dressed in a light business suit, walked in with his wife and five-year-old daughter. All kinds of people were there: white people, black people, Asian people, single fathers with their children, single mothers and their "girlfriends," and children who were alone. They came from all over the Village and nearby parts of Northton to see their friends, sisters, brothers, sons, and daughters perform. David Jameson was in charge, but there were other teachers all about, with some of their aides. They looked over the growing crowd with anticipation. The spectators took their seats, and soon it was standing room only, with people lining the walls and standing in the doorways. A dull roar of sound filled the place, but one could still hear the cars and trucks outside or an occasional "kid" passing by with his radio. I saw John Davis, a professor at Ivy University, and Jenny Murdock, an attorney—her daughter and mine went through first grade together. Irene, a social worker, was there, and Jimmy Lee, a local taxi driver. It seemed the whole community had come to take in this show, though in fact this was only a microcosm.

Mr. Jameson welcomed us all and described the program. First we heard the recorders. The little children filed onto the stage and stood facing the audience, ready to flee, it seemed. But then the pianist began and they played along, their shrill tones sounding in unison. The adults indulged themselves, trying to pick out their own children's performances, feeling for them, giggling a little, but always appreciating their effort. Then came the bells, with the fifteen or so children of the second grade. They knelt in rows, their eyes on Mr. Jameson, who moved his hands slowly, giving them clear directions. The audience was riveted. No sooner was this finished than the chorus appeared. They were ready, and with the pianist, they gave a soothing rendition of "Autumn Leaves." The parents were impressed and responded with loud applause. Finally Mr. Jameson appeared, *thanked us all for coming and told us to drive home safely. With that the concert was over and people began filing out into the night, where they would become strangers—but not quite such strangers as before this concert.* ◑

The Village-Northton Entity

The residents of both Northton and the Village impose on their environment similar boundaries distinguishing the two neighborhoods. Bellwether Street is the primary one, defined and maintained in different ways by each community. Street corner groups of black youths defend the Northton side of the boundary from unknown blacks and whites who may venture near, including members of the local college fraternities. Through expressive public behavior, which may include rock throwing, loud talking, name calling, and hostile looks and gestures, outsiders are informed or reminded of exactly where the boundaries lie. At times a middle-aged black—usually a man— informs a white person walking the streets of Northton that he may be going the "wrong way" and politely asks if he needs directions.

Although the Village is not a "defended neighborhood" in the sense that certain ethnic communities are, the white fraternities of Eastern Tech serve the same purpose that gangs do in other neighborhoods. The following narrative is by a twenty-two-year-old black female college student, who was raised in Northton but now lives in the Village:

◑ *One evening I was walking down Thirty-sixth Street toward the trolley, and I saw these white fraternity boys playing Frisbee with their dog. I wasn't paying them much attention, but then I heard this voice say, "Come here, nigger. Nigger! Get over here." I looked over at them, puzzled. Then one of the boys said, "Oh, I'm sorry. Our dog's name is Nigger, and we were just calling him." I knew what they were up to.* ◑

The resulting informal boundaries are consummated through the routes people take in meeting an average day's basic needs and desires. The newsstand where one buys the Sunday paper, the store one runs to for a quart of milk, and the streets one travels to visit a friend express one's sense of the boundaries. The people encountered along the way and the quality of interaction, whether hostile or hospitable, carry weight in the decision whether to take a particular route again.

Through such experiences, one learns where one can and cannot go without receiving an unfavorable reaction. Thus whites tend not to stray into Northton, and young black men and women may think carefully before walking the streets of the Village at certain times of day or night, though in general the anonymous black male is accorded informal hegemony in public. By choosing to use or to avoid a given street, one either claims it as safe or abandons it. Because boundaries are set through collective public action, they are not static; rather, they are created by social habit, situationally shaped and determined by those who share the space (see Katz 1988, 252–53). This conception indicates how much background knowledge and work may be required of ordinary passersby just to make their way through the streets. The following interview with a twenty-eight-year-old black resident of Northton illustrates this:

◑ *Once you cross Bellwether Street it's the Village, or Northton. . . If you cross one side it's the Village; if you cross the other side it's Northton. . . . The Village consists of a lot of college kids, students, a lot of people that want to get away from the ghetto and find a nice spot. The only thing about that that messes up the Village is that the people over in Northton, the young ones who have nothing to do over there . . . go over there [to the Village] to rob, steal, find old ladies to mug—that's bad. Most people go over there to have a good time, which you can. You come over to the Village and have a good time, meet the right people. But people from the Village, they can't find too much of a good time over in Northton. They feel different. They act different, really. They're from different atmospheres, different surroundings. They're not used to certain people.*

Most of the time this is good. People in the Village like to meet people; I make a lot of friends on that side. I'm not really a prejudiced type myself; I like anybody. That's the way I was brought up.

The whites and the blacks, they mingle. Say, whites have a party. There's a black family across the street. They say, "Won't you come over to our party?" You can see whites and blacks, [even though] it's a white person's house. I know a guy on the third floor, he's white. The neighborhood's so quiet. . . . Too many cops over there, undercover cops. Four men walkin' down the street, you think eight blacks gonna mess with 'em? All four of 'em cops. Northton don't have that much trouble. A lot of cops hang out in the Village. I know a couple of policemen who live over there. They're Caucasian. I know them. I even know where they live at. See, they got police protection over there. Only protection we got over here is our friends. You stay where you live at, they stay where they live at. A black move over there [to the Village] in an apartment, nothing happen to him. A white move into Northton like on Friday or Saturday, and he's in trouble. ◐

A second set of crosscutting boundaries exists in the minds of many Villagers and Northtonians. These perhaps operate at a less conscious level than boundaries of defense, but they are meaningful in determining what kinds of people deserve trust. This second set of boundaries is suggested by Gerald Suttles's (1972) use of the term "ecological units" and has a conceptual history in the work of such early human ecologists as Robert Park, Ernest Burgess, and Louis Wirth.

In his essay "Human Ecology," Park (1936) used the concept of the "natural area" to divide the city into units for study. Reacting against the use of arbitrarily imposed administrative units such as census tracts and borrowing ideas from the work of Darwin and Thompson, Park suggested the natural area as a sociologically sensible way of imposing boundaries in studies having an areal dimension. Since in strict biological ecology the term denoted a territory within which relations of competition and cooperation were relatively self-contained, Park's metaphor brought into relief the economic as well as the social and cultural organization of ecological areas.

Although the apparent continuity of physical structure in a city tends to blur the presence of natural areas in Park's ecological sense, competitive and cooperative relations are discoverable within more or less physically distinct areas of the city. Take the most factual rendering of the area north of the university in greater Eastern City as a map showing only streets and parks. If one were to lay a transparency over this with a boundary line falling along the train tracks on the east, along the main thoroughfare of the area on the west, along the edge of the university campus on the south, and along Northton Avenue three blocks beyond Bellwether on the north until it intersects the tracks, these borders would encompass both Northton and the Village. One might call this encompassed space a "natural area" in Park's sense.[2]

2. Park and Burgess (1967), in a discussion of human ecology as a branch of sociology, remind readers that the strict biological metaphor is limited in value for guiding research into human social organization because, unlike other organisms, humans partake of cultural institutions that influence processes of competition, invasion, and succession. Park goes on to write, however (p. 93), that "ecology conceives society as fundamentally

In physical quality Northton's housing does not vary greatly from the average housing of the Village, though there are relatively few grand old houses in Northton. But the residents to the north and south of Bellwether Street tend to live according to very different traditions. They inhabit distinct though overlapping cultural areas. Northton is almost exclusively black and lower income to poor; the Village is much more culturally heterogeneous, while becoming increasingly white and middle to upper income. In the long run, the culture of upper-income residents appears to be displacing that of lower-income dwellers. Such factors counter any tendency to lump the areas together.

But it is precisely because so much of the residents' boundary-maintaining and status-oriented behavior involves distinguishing the areas from each other that the whole can be viewed as a single system within which at least some residents compete for resources and status. As the buying and selling of local housing accelerates, the two neighborhoods are likely to become increasingly indistinguishable in terms of value and name. Already residents who move to the very edge of the Village and beyond glibly refer to their area as the Village, not as Northton. Although the contrast in neighborhood identities can be used to explain their separateness, one can also use it to explain their relatedness, even their ecological convergence, particularly where large sums of money are involved.

What, then, might reasonably be considered the combined physical features of the Village-Northton area, and how do these features encourage or discourage cooperation and competition? For one thing, the size of the buildings and their suitability for conversion into either one- and two-bedroom apartments or large single-family homes help govern residential density and the socioeconomic status of each population. The greatest concentration of grand old townhouses and

---

a territorial as well as cultural organization. So far as this conception is valid, it assumes that most if not all cultural changes in society will be correlated with changes in its territorial organization, and every change in the territorial and occupational distribution of the population will effect changes in the existing cultures." The Village, as a physical habitat, with its mansions and apartment buildings, has caused certain kinds of people to gravitate to it and remain. One way these "successful" inhabitants can be classified is by occupation, such as "young" professional, developer, landlord, craftsman, and unskilled "handyman." The neighborhood might thus be viewed as a natural area in the human ecological sense.

mansions is to be found in the eighteen-square-block heart of the Village, but this is only a minor exception to the general rule.

On blocks well north of Bellwether Street, old mansions resembling those in the Village are dotted here and there. The careful observer soon perceives that what was once a sparsely settled region of huge old homes has been disrupted by the two-story brick row houses that one associates with Northton. Northton is generally thought of as more run-down and crime-ridden. Although true, this view converges with the observation that it is more uniformly inhabited by low-income blacks, who until very recently have had no real political influence to attract the municipal services that other areas take for granted. It is hence more easily defined by middle-class people, black and white, as an undesirable place to live.

Since Northton has been defined as a low-income, high-crime ghetto, its mansions have more frequently been left to rot. Major speculators, gentrifiers, and ambitious Village landlords have been more likely to identify a three-story twin on the main street of the economically and racially mixed Village as ripe for quick conversion into a six-unit income property. In fact, however, the same gingerbread facades exist in vacant, decaying Victorian townhouses just six blocks away in Northton. Now there are signs that these places will be bought up and developed in the not-too-distant future as land values continue to rise in the Village.

Until about ten years ago, many considered even the Village too much of a slum for investment, though many others thought of the neighborhood as a well-kept secret. A few of its large homes are still in a state of blight, but they may soon be refurbished, if only to secure or protect an investment. These places draw white middle-class families, some black middle-class families, and landlords and developers. Among the last group, it is a status symbol to live in one of the big old Victorian townhouses. Even landlords with no families retain prize properties for their own residences, thus sparing the Village from irresponsible absentee landlords.

These buildings have spacious rooms, leaded-glass windows, and abundant yard space with century-old wrought-iron fences, and they are suitable for conversion into either apartments or showplaces. The materials with which this housing was originally constructed figure into the relationship between landlords and workmen; they require both highly skilled craftsmen and unskilled manual laborers who can be hired on the street corners. People skilled in the relevant crafts have gravitated to the Village, and along with them have come architects who step in and change a feature here or there, making the practical areas of a home or apartment (such as the kitchen or bathroom) more appealing to gourmet cooks, plant growers, and other modern-day tenants.

Though a few modern apartment buildings have crept into the Village—primarily on the eastern and western fringes, where the middle-income black homeowners tend to cluster—the residential heart of the Village retains its original Victorian appearance, owing to the efforts of local craftsmen and the capital invested by landlords. Such skilled craftsmen and unskilled handymen constitute a neighborhood labor force. Most of the workers who maintain the homes of the Village are self-taught craftsmen who make do as best they can between jobs. The case of John Feewell, a white Village landlord, exemplifies the responsible-owner ethos that characterizes landholding on some of the main blocks in the Village; it also illustrates the landholder's relationship with the neighborhood labor force.

Feewell, a fifty-year-old amateur architect and professional landlord, owns five or six multiple-unit dwellings in the residential "heart" of the Village. He hires various "kids" to fix this or that broken fence, to sand a floor in some building he is currently renovating, or to clean the yard surrounding one of his biggest properties, a twelve-unit twin townhouse on the main street. The "kids" he hires are usually young black men he knows from previous jobs or those recommended to him by other workers. Occasionally he hires a bona fide carpenter or tradesman, but usually the renovations he makes are simply cosmetic, involving a couple of coats of paint or a new sheet of linoleum. The workers are sometimes given projects in Feewell's own yard. For example, one sunny day they were visible and very audible, using hand sanders to refinish lengths of an old bowling alley that Feewell had bought to make the "modern" kitchen countertops he uses to divide living and eating areas. Usually his renovations involve knocking out walls built by former landlords to provide separate kitchens for apartment dwellers who wanted more than just one long room. Now the trend is toward larger, more open spaces, so the "fake" walls come down and bar-height counters are installed. An illusion of space is thus created, and chrome-armed, frosted-glass globes spread light through the white-walled, "spacious" one-bedroom apartments. Also the price goes up, especially as more Eastern Tech students live off campus in the Village.

Feewell's own home and yard are impeccably restored to their Victorian proportions. His three-story gray brick house received a local renovation award and wears the sticker on the heavy oak front door. The yard is one of the Village's largest, a space where another house might easily fit. Most of it is hidden from the street by a tall hedge, but from a second-floor window of the house directly behind one can glimpse the suburban lawn and patio. Especially in the summer, when Feewell brings his giant houseplants outdoors and arranges them around the patio furniture and the barbeque, one can admire private outdoor space at a high level. A redwood picnic table on the brick patio is sometimes used for repotting and at other times is a lounging platform for Feewell's well-fed dogs. The expanse of lawn is deep green all summer long. The flowerbeds are meticulously weeded and are watered with built-in sprinkler heads. The wood trim at the back of the house is neatly painted in a rich federal blue, a color that is gaining popularity among the renovators of the Village. The wrought-iron scrollwork around the windows is a satiny black. Storm windows go up in the winter, screens in the summer. Walks are swept. In many ways Feewell's home could qualify as a suburban showplace.

Surrounded as they are by sycamore trees, hundred-year-old shrubbery, and twenty- to thirty-foot grass borders, Village apartment buildings and homes often require more than the average janitorial staff. Black street corner men and teenage boys from the Village and Northton are drawn into the Village economy as they take on odd jobs for various landlords. Usually unskilled, these males constitute a work force as well as a residential group, for they often rent from the same landlord they work for and are known from face-to-face interaction on the streets and in the public places of the Village. Occasionally Feewell comes to trust one or two of them enough to let them drive his Peugeot, a much-valued show of prestige among the workers. One such trusted employee, a black man of about thirty named Jim, has since become a union carpenter and now shuns "odd jobs for low pay" like the ones Feewell provides. He now talks about him with resentment:

◐ *You know, that man used to live in a one-bedroom apartment over on Cherry Street, but he just saved and saved his money, man, and lived like a recluse for all those years and started buyin' up places, and he owns like half the Village now, man. Him and McCall [another Village landlord].*

When questioned about where Feewell finds men to work for him, Jim replied:

He hears about 'em through word of mouth, you know. He gets a lot of 'em through McCall, but he don't hire no one he don't know personally, man. You gotta know someone who worked for him before, and that way he just keeps funnelin' 'em through, you know? Indeed, Feewell (whom his men refer to as "Mr. Feewell" in a show of deference) keeps a tight rein on his workers. He can be seen and heard in the yards of his properties bossing the crew around, trying to shape them into a professional-looking team, which they are not.

"Cut this! Now that!" he shouts in the manner of a drill sergeant. The men comply in the way any team would—football team, army platoon, or whatever. In his presence they work very hard, mowing and cutting and picking up trash in the yard. But the moment he leaves, sometimes in his Peugeot, sometimes walking around the corner to see about another property, the men sit down and resume their conversations, shooting the breeze under the green canopy of sycamores. It is during these times that they must often explain their presence to residents of the building and passersby. ◐

Usually these men, especially the least known and the least skilled, have little commitment to the owner of the building where they are working. Their wages are just enough to encourage a semblance of caring and of taking the job seriously. But this stake is often too small, for some have no qualms about "ripping off" the buildings or telling their buddies about them for future rip-offs. Thus, when they come into a yard or a house and are confronted by tenants—especially white tenants, who tend to make few distinctions among the local blacks—they feel the need to explain themselves, even though they may have already been explained by their sweeping up or painting and by the loud orders given them by Feewell. A sort of plantation mentality arises as white landlords make use of local black men for jobs in Northton and the Village that might otherwise cost them more. Black-white relations thus appear to be unequal but still mutually beneficial.

Although these laborers are chiefly black and male, some are now having to compete with newly arrived Asians, who form labor cooperatives, hiring themselves out as teams and workng for relatively low pay as painters, plasterers, concrete masons, and general maintenance crews. This situation has created some tension between blacks and Asians.

Many of the young black craftsmen grew up in their parents' large homes on the fringes of the Village and have learned Village home maintenance firsthand. One such craftsman is a forty-year-old black ironworker who is also a successful local artist. He now creates large municipally funded sculptures for other areas of the city, but the history of his progress as an ironworker is preserved in nicely crafted gates and grilles tucked away near Village homes. "I taught myself everything I know," he says. Other less successful craftsmen make up a skills network within the Village, which homeowners and landlords know how to tap when a fence needs repair or walls are to be replastered or stripped of many layers of wallpaper. Also, the scale and details of the buildings have attracted a good number of professional architects who choose to renovate buildings and live in their own creations; members of this group tend to be white and middle class.

Although it is true that Bellwether Street exists as a color line between what residents think of as Northton and the Village, many blacks live south of this line in the Village. These residents are much better off economically than those living north of Bellwether Street. But strange young blacks in the Village are often assumed—by blacks and whites—to be from Northton unless they provide evidence to the contrary. Thus unknown blacks are considered to be from the ghetto, and their very visible role as janitors and sweep-up crews for the white landlords supports an oversimplified public view of status arrangements between blacks and whites in the area.

Many blacks and whites measure themselves in reference to each other, a process that involves enduring conceptions of both neighborhoods and thus links them in a single ecological entity. Although their divergent traditions countermand mindlessly lumping them together, the two neighborhoods do affect one another significantly. The status and identity of one are inextricably tied to those of the other, and thus one community cannot be adequately assessed without considering the other. The two have similar architecture and were established near the same time, though the Village has many more grand old mansions and Northton has many more small row houses on narrow streets, reflecting the social class of earlier residents.

First came the old-time Quakers, followed by the Irish and German working classes, followed by African-Americans from the South, followed by the progressive Quakers, followed by the youthful counterculturalists of the 1960s, followed by the young urban professionals of the 1980s. Today, many types of people appear to coexist in relative peace. The area is considered "racially mixed" or "integrated" and is one of the most diverse communities in the city. But the Village promises to become increasingly homogeneous, in social class, if not in race. The remnants of the Quakers, the counterculture, the middle-class blacks, the yuppies, and the students all become frustrated by crime, which lowers their tolerance for those who are less fortunate. Many people long for a crime-free and harmonious public environment. Unsafe streets give the well-off residents a common problem to solve, helping them coalesce into a group of haves who are increasingly wary of the have-nots.

Northton is black and predominantly poor, while the Village is racially mixed and becoming increasingly white and upper income. In some respects, segments of Northton depend on the Village for income. Black women sometimes do housework or baby-sit there. Young black street corner men are drawn into the Village landlords' economy, doing janitorial chores and other projects. Some may canvass the Village for odd jobs. After heavy snowfalls, the sidewalks are populated by young black men carrying snow shovels, offering to clear walks for a fee. Some poor people beg door to door. And the criminal element of Northton sometimes looks to the Village for new victims, a reality that makes some Villagers have serious doubts about living there. Drugs are bought and sold in both communities, and crack addicts make the public spaces worrisome.

As wealthy whites extend their territory, the market value of housing rises. At present the yuppies and the Eastern Tech students seem to be in the vanguard of this movement. As they occupy marginal properties, the nearby areas become defined as more civilized, inspiring the interest of other middle-class people. Hence these groups become an economic and social force; their presence encourages investment by developers who are then able to obtain financing. The refurbished buildings, though they are sometimes across the Bellwether Street boundary, are still referred to as the Village. As wealthy whites slowly move in on Northton, black activists fear that housing prices will escalate and drive poor blacks out. But it is the proximity of Northton, with all its social ills, that for the moment slows down neighborhood change and gives pause to its agents.

2

o

The

Northton

Community

Northton was first settled before the turn of the century by well-to-do industrialists and working-class Irish and Germans, who wanted to be close to their workplaces. Because of the important social and territorial link between the traditional ethnic neighborhood and the factory, residents took a proprietary interest in both living and working spaces, often physically defending them against outsiders. Protecting such territorial interests gave rise to intense feelings of group solidarity that were readily expressed as racial prejudice, particularly toward invading black migrants from the South.

The first blacks began arriving around World War I, when workers were needed for the railroad and the small factories of the area. But the most impressive migration occurred during World War II, when great numbers left the South in search of social and economic opportunities in northern cities. Because of a labor shortage and ongoing strikes by white unions that excluded black members, the companies were able to use blacks as strikebreakers.

These developments enabled blacks to penetrate the industrial workplaces. To be close to their jobs, they looked to nearby white working-class neighborhoods and settled in areas that began as enclaves but soon turned into ghettos. Racial conflict ensued, resulting in the gradual but steady flight of the whites. The ghettos spread until blacks succeeded whites in virtually all areas of Northton, not only in homes, but also in the schools, churches, and small businesses. For instance, throughout the Village and Northton, formerly white churches began ministering to black congregations as the growing black community was able to support these institutions. Over the years of neighborhood change, many middle-class blacks have moved out but remain connected to their old churches, commuting back for Sunday services, sometimes from many miles away.

Black social life in the Northton of the 1940s and 1950s appears to have been highly cohesive compared with the present situation. Some of the changes may be viewed as indirect consequences of the civil rights movement, the urban riots of the 1960s, and various government remedies for racial exclusion, including the civil rights legislation of the 1960s and 1970s. Fair housing, affirmative action, and various "set asides" for blacks and other minorities have made a tremendous difference in the lives of great numbers of black Americans. These programs have affected Northton, but mainly by expanding opportunities for housing and status for a minority of residents who were poised to take advantage of such "openings" in the wider society's occupational and class structure. Some of them have in fact risen socially and economically, approaching upper-middle-class status.

But as members of this group move socially and economically, they also tend to move geographically, becoming more distant from the ghetto and leaving it without the leadership from which it has traditionally benefited. If those who are better off do remain in Northton, they tend to become socially disengaged, thinking their efforts as instructive agents of social control are futile and may in fact bring them trouble. Consistent with this, current high rates of teenage pregnancy, rampant drug use, a lack of motivation to work in certain jobs when they are available, a desire by some to "get over" on fellow residents, and a prevalence of black-on-black crime may reflect the increasing absence of the black middle class as a stabilizing social force within such ghetto communities.

At the same time, opportunities for poorer blacks to participate in the regular economy are limited, as evidenced by recurrent high levels of black unemployment and underemployment. With severely limited education and skills, numerous Northton blacks are caught in an employment bind. Low-skill Eastern City manufacturing jobs have declined, and jobs in the emerging service economy that are available to young blacks are low paying or far from the inner city, constraining many to a life of poverty.

To many young inner-city blacks the underground economy of drugs and vice appears attractive (see Anderson 1980). This economy pervades Northton, in many instances augmenting or replacing the regular one. As it expands, it undermines the interpersonal trust and moral cohesion that once prevailed. Young men without legitimate job opportunities become especially vulnerable. And law-abiding people who remain in or near the neighborhood, particularly the elderly, fear crime and personal injury. An atmosphere of distrust, alienation, and crime pervades the community, segmenting its residents. These changes, indirectly effected by wider social and economic forces, alter the social organization of Northton (see Wilson 1980, 1985, 1987).

Changes in the Black Community

In the past, blacks of various social classes lived side by side in segregated Northton, a "Negro" section of the city. They shared racially separate neighborhood institutions, including churches, schools, barber shops, and even liquor stores and taverns (see Cayton and Drake 1962; Lewis 1955; Clark 1965). For instance, on a visit to a local barbershop, it would not have been unusual to see a black doctor, dressed in coat and tie, follow a black factory worker, still in his overalls, into the chair. Living close together, the children of working-class blacks attended school with the children of black lawyers, doctors, and small businessmen; the black churches often worked to help such disparate individuals coalesce into a single congregation.

Successful people in Northton carried local reputations as big shots and were treated as pillars of the community. Their behavior, mannerisms, and habits were studied, discussed, and imitated; young people paid especially close attention. For instance, people knew all about Dr. Davis: where he lived, what car he drove, how he walked; they knew the same things about the lawyer, Mr. Willis. They knew Mr. and Mrs. Jones, the proprietors of the corner grocery store, who "raised" so many children of the community; highly respected, they served as stand-ins when parents were not around, chastising and disciplining those who needed it, and Mrs. J was an usher at church. Residents also knew Reverend James, a moral force and human institution of the community; he was always ready with a word of advice to those who sought it—and often to those who didn't. He could be counted on to help people, particularly young men in trouble with the law. Until recently, these leaders had to live in areas like Northton because of widespread residential segregation, but they served the black community well as visible, concrete symbols of success and moral value, living examples of the fruits of hard work, perseverance, decency, and propriety. Because of their presence and the honor accorded them, there was more cohesion among individuals and the various classes of the black community than is generally seen today. They were effective, meaningful role models, lending the community a certain moral integrity.

But it was not solely black professionals and small businessmen who led the community. There were also construction workers, factory workers, and others who had "slaves"—jobs that required hard physical labor. Some men would hold two jobs or have a "hustle" on the side, in the form of odd jobs or handyman work, in order to get ahead. Not only did such men set an example for others, who at times would compete with them, they actively encouraged the young to follow their lead. Imbued with a strong commitment to the work ethic, they generally viewed working hard for a living as a positive value. Their wives often worked as domestics, hairdressers, nurse's aides, or storekeepers, setting an important example for young women. In those days people generally regarded having children out of wedlock as serious deviance. To be single and pregnant was generally frowned upon and considered a sign of being "messed up." Moreover, being "on welfare" was a stigma in many circles.

Because of recent openings in the opportunity structure of the wider society, as well as a widespread belief that the local community has changed for the worse, Northton has experienced an outflow of middle- and upper-income people such as Dr. Davis and Mr. Willis, as well as some church leaders. Many have died, and others have moved away; their children have been educated and have joined the professional class of blacks away from their original community. With legally enforced "fair housing," for the first time blacks are theoretically able to move into any housing they can afford. In this social climate, even some of the construction and factory workers have moved to "better" neighborhoods, though some still meet strong resistance in entrenched white areas of the city. Many of their children, too, are becoming better educated and hoping to join the middle and professional classes.

When students used to leave segregated communities like Northton for college, they would often go to institutions such as Howard, Spelman, Fisk, Wilberforce, Central State, Southern University, or Virginia Union, the traditionally black colleges and universities. After graduation many returned to the black community, perhaps to work as schoolteachers, social workers, dentists, doctors, or undertakers. They did this not so much because they preferred to as because of widespread discrimination and the fact that social rewards and economic opportunities for educated blacks were in the black community.

But today, when many black students are educated in major, formerly all-white universities and colleges, they tend not to return to urban black communities like Northton. In pursuit of bright futures in big corporations, law firms, and universities, these young educated blacks gravitate to suburbia or to trendy areas of the city. As they move into leadership positions in the wider society, they leave the poorer, uneducated blacks without tangible role models or instructive agents of social control. As it was described by a black minister who is a part-time taxi driver:

◐ *The [black] community needs these people. I know, they've worked hard for what they got. [Black] people don't resent them for it. They worked for what they got, and they're still working to keep it. They're well qualified for their jobs. But people, black children, need them. They need to be around them. How many of these kids have met a Mayor Johnson, you know? They see him, you know, just sometimes. How many of these kids get close to a black businessman? Or a black lawyer, or somebody? None. They need these people right around them who will guide them and show them how to take hold of life. To teach them how to behave themselves and to teach them that they care. That's the big thing, too. People don't care. See, time was when the big people had distinguishing features about them, and they made you feel like "here's someone who is a leader of the community" and "I want to be like him" or "I want to be like her."* ◐

To be sure, newly mobile members of the black middle class may have close kin in Northton. In a unique manner, they serve as culture brokers, linking the new black middle class with the ghetto and, more generally, the black community with the wider society. Occasionally there are family reunions that may include relatives from diverse backgrounds, ranging from members of the lower class to successful medical doctors and business executives. Such reunions may be related to trouble of some sort, such as sickness or death in the family or legal difficulties. During such occasions, when old ties are renewed, those in need may make outright requests for financial help, and the successful members of the family may feel some obligation to render at least token assistance. But repeated requests can discourage intimacy between well-off and poorer relatives, or at least strain the relationship. The successful members of these families may also feel a duty to serve as role models for younger sisters, brothers, cousins, and other kin. It is at this family level that the new black middle class may have an effective social connection with the Northton ghetto.

But in general the newly educated groups appear increasingly distant and formal in their relations with ghetto residents. Involved in careers ranging from doctor to investment banker to lawyer, this new middle class appears much less a merchant and service class, financially dependent upon the black community, than the middle class traditionally has been (see Frazier 1957; Landry 1987). Members do not aspire to own a restaurant, tavern, or barbershop, and they seldom operate the local grocery, clothing, and furniture stores. In Eastern City other ethnic groups, including Jews and Koreans, tend to dominate in these commercial areas of Northton.

On the streets of Northton, race-conscious blacks at times complain bitterly about the recent incursion of Asians and wonder aloud "who helped them out." Some fail to distinguish among the Asian groups, assuming they are all "boat people who just got here." A common view is that the federal government has made loans readily available to Asians, helping them to establish businesses in Northton. Yet Jews, who have long run similar businesses there, provoke little hostility; the community is used to Jewish merchants. The hostile reception the Asians get has to do with the way residents perceive them as a new competitive group bent on taking opportunities from blacks and establishing itself within Northton. But generally the working class does not have the capital or the inclination to take over local businesses, and the upwardly mobile blacks have their sights set on careers far beyond Northton. The following narrative by the middle-aged proprietor of a barbershop in Northton illustrates these points:

◑ *Yeah, look like the black man always gets the raw deal. Now the Vietnamese are coming in. Course, I can't tell 'em from the Koreans, ha-ha. One time I called a Korean lady a Vietnamese to her face, and she like to had a fit. She said, "No! No! I'm Korean." I guess it's kinda like the blacks and the Puerto Ricans. The blacks don't want to be mixed up with the Puerto Ricans. But the Koreans are moving in strong. They taking over businesses left and right, and they move the blacks out and bring in they own people. Now take what happened up on the corner. That big cleaners was just taken over by a Korean. It had been owned by a Jew. . . . Well, the Jew first offered it to a black man who had been working there for many years. He knew the business well, too. He could run it himself, knew how to mix all the chemicals himself. Well, he was gonna get it, but his family got together and discouraged him, told him it was too much responsibility, and he listened to them. Well, then the Koreans came along, and the Jew sold it to them. The Koreans invited this black man over to their home and treated him real nice and everything. And he then continued to work for them and taught them everything he knew. Showed them how to mix the chemicals, how to do everything. Then after they learned it from him and had the business moving along, the black fella found his paycheck short a hundred dollars. He say, "There's some mistake here." And they say, "No, there ain't no mistake. That's all you worth, now." Boy, was he ever mad. It took him a while to get straight over that. He started drinking a lot. Man, he was mad. He wanted to do something [violence] to them, but I talked to him. I told him how he had his whole life in front of him, that he should just try to forget it. It took him a long time, but he finally settled down. Then he went on and got himself another job, and tried to forget about it, but I know he never will forget that. ◑*

But it must be pointed out that not all black residents feel hostility to the Asian newcomers. Some working people admire them, comparing their apparent successes with the financial "failings" of local blacks. As one sixty-seven-year-old, now retired, formerly "hardworking" (twenty-eight years as a welder) black man said:

◑ *See, I have no objection to them people. They hardworking people. See, the blacks have that same opportunity. See, look here. See this man's car. [He walks me over to the recently broken-into car of one of his friends.] See here, this is all they wanta do. See here. See this man's car. They went in there, right where my car parked at right now [he points across the street to his car]. They went there night before last and ripped that man's radio out of his car. Now, you would never hear tell of a Vietnamese [tendency is not to distinguish among Asians] doin' that. What they make, they make their money honestly. Now you see how they ripped that man's car up. See, today, everybody is prejudiced against everybody. But see, I don't have no objection to them people. If they hardworking people, come over here and build a foundation for themselves, God bless them. Understand what I'm saying? These niggers have the same opportunity, but that's all they wanta do. Ripped the man's radio out, and he caught him doing it! He run him down and tried to catch him, and he outrun his shoes. The man come back and throwed his shoes in the trash. See, that's all they wanta do. About an hour later, he caught him with the radio. But I noticed these people have come over here, and stores have been empty for twenty years and they get together, and two or three months later, they got that whole place stocked off. Colored folks got the same opportunity to do that, if they want to. They don't wanta do that, though. Onliest thing they wanta do is sell crack, stand on the corner, sell ten bags.* ○

On "the avenue," the central business street of Northton, Asian shops proliferate, filling a void left by the Jewish merchants who owned family businesses in Northton for many years; they are now prepared to move on, but generally they seem to prefer to sell their businesses rather than pass them on to family members. The Asians run family businesses as well, but with a somewhat different twist. They seemed somewhat crude at first, but they are now catching on to the art of doing business in Northton. In any number of instances a Korean, for example, would buy out the owner of a particular store and set up for business with all his family, relatives, or friends in his employ. The common picture, then, in grocery, clothing, fish, produce, or hoagie shops, was of two teams of different ethnicities: the proprietor and his staff were conspicuously Asian, and the customers were exclusively black. Initially these changes caused some black people to grumble and threaten to boycott the stores. No effective boycott ever materialized, but certain militant and race-conscious blacks expressed resentment toward the storeowners, at times physically harassing them. To deal with this, Korean businessmen began to hire more blacks. Now the common picture of the Asian-owned establishment is of a number of trusted blacks performing certain functions, from armed guard to grillman at the hoagie shops, being supervised by an Asian, usually male, who invariably stands at the cash register and takes the money:

○ *At one of the primary intersections of Northton there sits a large old brick structure with a newly remodeled facade and eating area that serves hoagies and other fast foods as well as providing check cashing and other financial services. Until two years ago, it was simply one more crumbling and unused building. Today it is a true market center, drawing customers in search of both legal and illegal items from many parts of Northton and even from the Village. Out in front is a newsstand run by an elderly black man "who's been here for twenty years and knows the community like the back of his hand." Black people pass by freely or stop to chat with the news vendor or other friends. It is the site of much camaraderie and heavy foot and vehicle traffic. A large bright yellow sign proclaiming Hoagies invites the hungry to step inside, where there is almost always a line of black people standing at the long counter, waiting to be served cheese steaks, hoagies, fried chicken, french fries, and various sandwiches.*

Off to the left is a Plexiglas booth with the sign Check Cashing above it. A stern, no-nonsense black woman cashes checks, sells lottery tickets, and transacts business for Western Union. The place is packed with middle-aged black men, young men, little girls and boys, and young women with babies in their arms. After getting their food, they go over to the booths along the back wall or out on the street. In the booths may sit one or two intoxicated men.

Behind the counter taking orders are Sammy, Joe, R.D., and two other black men. "Hey, baby, what can I do for you," is the usual question from Sammy. Someone opens the front door and hollers in, "What's up, Joe?" Everyone turns toward the door. The person is acknowledged, "Yo, baby, see you tonight!" The workers are clearly from the neighborhood. Sammy resumes his work, in view of the black clientele. Sitting at the cash register at the end of the counter is a small Korean man, busily taking money. ❍

A black minister who was unfamiliar with the changed community had the following reaction:

❍ *Yeah, I visited a variety store, you know, where they sell all this junk and sandals and stuff. Well, I bought comb and umbrella and hair products. I bought me a pair of sandals, for a dollar, from China, you know. Ha-ha. I bought a little scarf for a dollar, you know. Nothing over two dollars—hats, umbrellas, and they had a kinda built-up counter with a glass booth. And there stood two Asians back there taking the money. Then they had two black male employees waiting on folks and watching them. Like one Asian kinda floated back and forth. And the brother [black man] would say, "Now what's the price on this?" And he would answer, "Chie chei dit che che," you know, so and so. But they were very much in charge, using blacks ironically as fronts. It was so shocking, because I had never seen this in the area before, you know, close up.* ❍

Members of the emerging black middle class, people who might have the business and organizational skills, and also the financial resources, for small business enterprise, tend to be uninterested in such pursuits in Northton. Such people find their futures in the private and public professional sectors of the wider society. The new middle class tends to gravitate to residential areas of second and third settlement, as did the upwardly mobile Irish, Italians, and Jews who preceded them (see Wirth 1928; Shaw and McKay 1942). Ostensibly they are motivated by concern about crime, drugs, poor public schools, run-down and crowded housing, and social status. They are attracted by the prospect of good schools, "crime-free" suburban neighborhoods, good real estate investments, and the status requirements of their professional and corporate careers. A few find their way into the Village, but for many there may be a deep emotional desire to get as far as possible from poorer blacks. The black middle classes increasingly send their children to private schools. Although their black peers sometimes chide them about remembering where they came from, they generally offer no apologies for leaving the ghetto, believing it is their right to enjoy success.

Advanced education and connections with professional and corporate America thus contribute to gradual social, economic, and perhaps political estrangement between the black middle and upper classes and the poor urban black communities. As these processes mature, the socially mobile group is likely to be slowly transformed from separate individuals ambivalent about their connection with places like Northton into a class increasingly concerned with itself.

The prospect is for the lower-income residents of Northton to become increasingly isolated, sharing neighborhood institutions with the financially desperate and the criminal element. Great numbers of Northton residents appear mired in poverty and second-class citizenship reminiscent of the castelike system of racial exclusion described by Cayton and Drake (1962), Myrdal (1944), and Clark (1965) more than a generation ago. In this situation crime, drugs, and general antisocial behavior serve as social forces that underscore status lines drawn within the community. With the massive introduction of drugs and the correspondingly high incidence of black-on-black crime, fear and distrust abound, particularly toward young males. It is this feature of the present situation that has such fateful implications for the way the community is related to its erstwhile leadership class. Many of the better-off people simply want to get as far away as they can. And what they do not achieve by moving physically, they work to accomplish socially: they distance themselves from others who do not meet their standards of behavior. Yet through such conduct they in fact contribute, however unintentionally, to the construction of a local underclass.

The Underclass

This underclass of Northton is made up of people who have failed to keep up with their brethren, both in employment and in sociability. Essentially they can be seen as victims of the economic and social system. They make up the unemployed, the underskilled, and the poorly educated, even though some hold high-school diplomas. Many are intelligent, but they are demoralized by racism and the wall of social resistance facing them. In this context they lose perspective and lack an outlook and sensibility that would allow them to negotiate the wider system of employment and society in general.

Emerging from the ghetto's crippling educational experience, often lacking even rudimentary skills but scorning subsistence jobs, they also tend to be discriminated against by prospective employers, who find it difficult to trust them. In part this is because of their inability or unwillingness to follow basic rules of middle-class propriety with respect to dress and comportment, but it is also because of their skin color and what this has come to symbolize.

Though one may argue that the institutions of both the wider society and the local community have failed members of the black underclass, local working-class and middle-class residents often hold the people themselves to blame. Such a stance allows those who are better-off to maintain faith in the wider institutions, particularly the work ethic, thus helping to legitimate their own position in the local system of stratification. Hence, by many employed and law-abiding blacks who live in the inner city, members of the underclass are viewed, and treated, as convenient objects of scorn, fear, and embarrassment.

In this way the underclass serves as an important social yardstick that allows working-class blacks to compare themselves favorably with others they judge to be worse off, a social category stigmatized within the community. Included in this category are the local residents who threaten the financially more successful blacks who remain in Northton and thus incur their wrath or condescension.

To the stable working class remaining in Northton, those fitting the stereotype of the underclass symbolize "how low a black person can fall from decency." On the streets, the members of this class are viewed as "trouble" and are avoided, but residents often have difficulty accomplishing this, for the conditions and cultural manifestations of poverty and blight are all around. For example:

⊙ *Walking the streets of Northton at midday on a Saturday in April, one gets a striking impression of the neighborhood. Back streets are lined with small three-story, crumbling brick houses. The old buildings have not been well maintained, and cracks often line the bricks to the foundations. Signs of past fires are everywhere. The third floor of a building is windowless, and another nearby has its windows covered with galvanized iron. Another building looks on the verge of toppling over, as it seems to totter in the wind. Now and again an intact structure shows definite signs of life, for people come and go and children play nearby. At one house white-painted automobile tires are used as planters for geraniums, and a bright green-and-red awning shades the front porch, where ancient but recently used metal porch furniture sits undisturbed. On other occasions I have noticed residents sitting out on the stoops or porches, watching the traffic pass. They generally watch carefully over the street, at times attempting to quash bad conduct before it goes too far.*

Most automobiles are at least ten years old, but now and again late-model cars turn up, including BMWs and Mercedes and Lincoln Town Cars driven, though rarely, by boys of nineteen and twenty. The young men drive with their stereos booming, and the windshields vibrate to the beat. They nod in time to the music, as though they were in another world.

On the sidewalk little girls run, laugh, and jump rope. Little boys play cops and robbers or basketball; some ride makeshift scooters. In this block the streets are alive with noise and life, with familiar eyes noticing everything.

A middle-aged man dressed in blue jeans, a jacket, and a baseball cap, his hands dug into his pockets, makes his way with a demonstrative style and walk. Two women follow, undisturbed, unafraid; they move with aplomb, for they know the neighborhood and it knows them; they know where they're going, and everyone else knows it too.

Down an alley, teenage "young boys," eight or ten of them, are shooting dice, gambling in broad daylight. An expensive portable radio sits nearby, blaring a "rap" song; a couple of the boys nod with the beat, which sounds almost military. They are dressed in bright-

colored athletic suits of green or red or gold, their bodies accentuated by the white stripes down the arms and legs. Some wear baseball caps, and others proudly "go bareheaded," sporting waves or close-cropped hair with two or three lines shaved into it. It is the latest style in "cuts." A few of the boys wear gold chains and rings, testifying to their worth and lending a measure of self-esteem. The group is abuzz with talk back and forth, getting the dice game right and awaiting the next throw.

All eyes are on the dice. Some of the boys work at local businesses, including the recently opened Korean-owned hoagie shop up on the avenue. Another works at McDonald's. But some of these boys are known drug dealers and can make, some say, hundreds of dollars in a single day. **◐**

This element of the local community is often perceived as having a "street" orientation, generally known—and feared—as "slick" and dangerous, with few moral compunctions against engaging in "wrongdoing" and "mistreating" others. In the minds of the law-abiding, decent residents these young men have a claim to "hipness," and they are believed to sell drugs and commit most of the local street crime to support their habits. Those who are trying hard to achieve a more conventional life readily lump such people with the pimps, hustlers, prostitutes, destitute single mothers, and anonymous street corner men. The easy stereotype is that they "think nothing of making two or three babies with no way to care for them. They don't want to work, and have no get up about themselves." People who develop this street orientation are thought to begin their careers in early childhood, and if they are not controlled and "trained," the parents and families are believed to run a good chance of losing them to "the streets."

In Northton, the homeless and others who are very poor are seen to be "out there." They live on the streets or in abandoned houses and automobiles and from time to time may be seen rummaging through refuse, thus fueling the community's negative conception of them. But they usually draw little sympathy from the stable working class. Ghetto residents themselves seldom use the term "underclass" when referring to the poor and others who have trouble surviving by conventional means. The category referred to by that term is in effect socially constructed through public observations of relatively better-off residents concerned with their own status and identity. The local underclass is a highly stigmatized group, and residents refer to them by terms of derision, working socially to distinguish such people from themselves. Common terms are "lowlife," "street niggers," "tacks," "zombies," or "pipers."

Of "Old Heads" and Young Boys

The relationship between "old heads" and young boys represents an important institution of the traditional black community. It has always been a central aspect of the social organization of Northton, assisting the transition of young men from boyhood to manhood, from idle youth to stable employment and participation in the regular manufacturing economy. The old head's acknowledged role was to teach, support, encourage, and in effect socialize young men to meet their responsibilities with regard to the work ethic, family life, the law, and decency. But as meaningful employment has become increasingly scarce, drugs more accessible, and crime a way of life for many young black men, this institution has undergone stress and significant change.

An old head was a man of stable means who was strongly committed to family life, to church, and, most important, to passing on his philosophy, developed through his own rewarding experience with work, to young boys he found worthy. He personified the work ethic and equated it with value and high standards of morality; in his eyes a workingman was a good, decent individual.

The old head/young boy relationship was essentially one of mentor and protégé. The old head might be only two years older than the young boy or as much as thirty or forty years older; the boy was usually at least ten. The young boy readily deferred to the old head's chronological age and worldly experience. The nature of the relationship was that of junior/senior, based on the junior's confidence in the senior's ability to impart useful wisdom and practical advice for getting on in the world and living well.

The old head was a kind of guidance counselor and moral cheerleader who preached anticrime and antitrouble messages to his charges. Encouraging boys to work and make something of themselves, he would try to set a good example by living, as best he could, a stable, decent, worry-free life. His constant refrain was "Get yourself a trade, son," or "Do something with your life," or "Make something out of yourself." Displaying initiative, diligence, and pride, as a prime role model of the community, he lived "to have something," usually something material, though an intact nuclear family counted for much in the picture he painted. On the corners and in the alleys of Northton, he would point to others as examples of how hard work and decency could pay off. He might advise young boys to "pattern yourself after him." In these conversations and lectures, he would express great pride in his own outstanding work record, punctuality, good credit rating, and anything else reflecting his commitment to honesty, independence, hard work, and family values.

The old head could be a minister, a deacon in the church, a local policeman, a favorite teacher, an athletic coach, or a street corner man. He could be the uncle or even the father of a member of the local group of young boys. Very often the old head acted as surrogate father for those he considered in need of such attention. A youth in trouble would sometimes discuss his problem with an old head before going to his own father, if he had one, and the old head would be ready with a helping hand, sometimes a loan for a worthy purpose. The following interview with a twenty-nine-year-old Northton man gives a glimpse of the relationship between an old head and a young boy:

◑ *Yeah, I got three of my boys in the service right now, and another is on the way. Just the other day, a young boy come up to me in the neighborhood and say he need twenty-five dollars to get some underwear and toiletries so he can get ready to leave for the army. We talked for a while, and then I reached into my pocket and came up with two tens and a five and handed it to him. He said "Thanks." And I said, "I'm gettin' ready to go downtown; you want to come along? We can pick up that stuff you need." He said, "OK." We got the trolley and went on downtown. We got his stuff and come on back home. I was glad I could do that for him, help him out. Now he gone to the army. He's one of my young boys. I been knowin' him since he was very young, and now he's nineteen. I don't worry 'bout my money. He'll pay me. I don't worry 'bout it.* ◑

Through this kind of extension of himself, the old head gained moral affirmation that would be his reward, an important if subtle incentive for helping other young boys.

It may be that such rewards are related to what Cayton and Drake (1962) called the "race man." In the days of the traditional segregated black community, the race man was one who felt an intense responsibility to "the race," to the point of viewing most events, especially public ones involving white society, as having definite implications for the well-being of blacks. To such men it was important to present their race in a positive light, particularly to whites. The traditional old head in the present-day black community embodies a significant amount of the race-man ideology. His attempt to help young boys is also a way to help the black community. It demonstrates to whites that black people are decent, law-abiding, and respectable.

In the old days young boys would gather around an old head on a street corner or after Sunday school to listen to his witty conversation and moral tales on hard work and decency. They truly felt they were learning something worthwhile from someone they could look up to and respect. One of the primary messages of the old head was about good manners and the value of hard work: how to dress for a job interview and deal with a prospective employer, how to work, and how to keep the job. Through stories, jokes, and conversation, the old head would convey his conception of the "tricks of the trade."

On occasion he might be seen walking through the streets with one or two of his boys, showing them how to "hustle"—to make money by doing legal odd jobs. An old head might bring some of his boys over to the Village to help him with yard work, snow shoveling, or general household chores for white residents. The boys then might attempt such jobs on their own, meeting strangers at the supermarket door and offering to carry groceries to the car for money, or standing around the self-service gas station and offering to pump gasoline for a small fee. There was often an old head in the background, encouraging the boys to earn spending money through honest work. If the old head owned his own business, in auto repair, general hauling, cleaning services, or yard work, the boys might serve as his apprentices.

The old head sometimes affectionately referred to his recruits as "my boys." Some would become runners, taking the lead in being publicly responsible for the neighborhood, but under the control or direction of an old head. Whenever the old head needed a favor done or an errand run, one of his protégés would be eager to carry out his wishes. And he would keep an informal record of how well they had learned their lessons—which ones had gone on to college, to successful employment, to the military, or to jail.

Within the traditional black community, the old head served as an important link to the more privileged classes. Often he could be seen pointing out the big shots and speaking about them in glowing terms. Through his example, he offered support to both the local and

71

the wider systems of social stratification and inspired his boys to negotiate them through legitimate means.

Today, as the economic and social circumstances of the urban ghetto have changed, the traditional old head has been losing prestige and credibility as a role model. One of the most important factors in this loss is the glaring lack of access to meaningful employment in the regular economy, resulting in more and more unemployed and demoralized black young people. When gainful employment and its rewards are not forthcoming, boys easily conclude that the moral lessons of the old head concerning the work ethic, punctuality, and honesty do not fit their own circumstances. (For the provocative "social capital" position, which may be applicable to the situation here, see Coleman 1988; Bourdieu 1986; and Wacquant and Wilson 1989.)

In turn, the old heads' attitudes toward young people have been modified to reflect current employment realities, particularly the youths' adaptation to them. For instance, Harry Hamilton, a seventy-year-old wallpaper hanger who has taken on young black men as apprentices over the years, laments the way things have changed with the young boy/old head relationship and says that he cannot find honest, hardworking young men the way he used to. He begins his day at about 6:30 in the morning, arriving at his job promptly at 7:30. He wears a brown work uniform spotted with paint and stains and a beat-up white hat, and he carries his lunch pail. He works steadily until lunchtime, rests for about thirty minutes, then goes right back to work. Some nights it is 6:30 before he has cleaned up and is ready to go home, and he follows this schedule every day, regardless of the weather. At times he makes as much as $100 a room, and he has more than enough work. He fails to understand why there is a youth employment problem, saying simply:

⊙ *These young boys today just don't want to work. They could work if they wanted to. There's plenty of work to do. Today they just want somethin' give to them, wanta get on welfare, I think. I did it [made a living], and they can too.* ⊙

The following interview with a forty-year-old black man who works two jobs to make ends meet follows the same lines:

⊙ *This used to be a heavily industrialized nation, but now all that's done changed. Now it's technology. There's a lot of unemployment, but the statistics just give one picture. I think that's overblown, 'cause there are a lot o' guys out here who just don't wanta work. There are cats who can barely read and write, and they wanta come in and take over. There's a lot o' young men doing the dope thing. They sell it, get high on it. But I'd rather work hard on a grind; the money's better. That dope money is fast, quick money. And you know, easy come, easy go. Can't depend on it. When they doing good, they doing real good, but when they doing bad, they doing real bad. I still try to talk to the youngsters that I run into, but it's hard to talk to these young boys. I tell them to go and try to learn something, but they don't wanta listen. There's a different kind of black man today. And I'll tell you something, as quiet as it's kept [between you and me]. There are some old heads out here selling that dope, and they know better. They sho' know better.* ◐

Female Old Heads

If old heads were important for boys, they were also important for girls, in similar ways. The female old heads were seen as mature and wise figures in the community, not only by women and girls, but also by many young men. The term "old head" usually refers to males; their female counterparts were and are often called "Mama," "Big Mama," "Moms," "Mis' Lu," or "Mis' Dawson," to show deference and respect.

An important source of social control and organization for the community, such a woman operated through bonds of kinship and friendship. She might have been someone's aunt or grandmother, but if not, she played the grandmother role. Like the male old head, she was someone others could "talk to" or "lean on." But unlike the male, she was and still is capable of meting out advice, discipline, and at times corporal punishment to both boys and girls. With this role as her warrant, she takes such actions and offers guidance without condemnation, all with a sensitive appreciation of the child's situation and needs as she interprets them, filling an important fictive kinship role of extra parent or surrogate mother.

Like the male old head, her role is often played out in public places. Supportive of the family, she serves as a third party to publicly augment the relationship between parent and child. Needing a good deal of wisdom, sensitivity, candor, and trust, she is an important source of instruction and social sanction within the community. To play the old head role effectively, a woman must possess what blacks call "mother wit," an earthy wisdom that is readily apparent through her actions, material possessions, and relationships, all of which make up her public biography.

Though declining in influence and authority, these women still serve the community as beauticians, church ladies, and more recently community organizers. They are usually very popular and well respected, and they know everyone. At the same time, they are viewed as successful in a way that makes others defer to them in their presence and say complimentary things about them when they are not around. They might have a number of other women working with them, and together they make up a core group in the neighborhood.

One of the main credentials for serving effectively as such a role model is having lived a "good life." The visible expression of this is involvement "in church" or with "the Lord." The female old head attends church regularly and displays in her home pictures of Jesus and other symbols attesting to her moral worth. She is generally known as a "good" and decent person.

Although these women tend to be rather proper, they also form a social group that "talks about" others, imposing social sanctions through gossip. Taking the lead in the community, some also act as psychologists and advisers for other women.

In Northton the female old head usually has been quite serious about taking care of young girls, attempting to protect them from abuse at the hands of males, but also trying to help them achieve a better material life. Such is the nature of her traditional role, and to some extent it is a role many continue to play, though, with the proliferation of so many "street kids," less and less effectively.

As is shown in the following interview with an elderly black woman, the primary ingredients of the female old head role are motherly love, concern, and wisdom:

🔾 *They call her just a mother, a real mother, not a mother who don't care for children from the bottom. The way I feel about it, the way I tell these children, is "I love all children: If you don't love somebody else children, you really don't love yo' own."*

This is when you see any child out there doing wrong, you goes to him and you corrects him, just like he is yo' child. And that's what I do. I don't care what I'm doing, if I see somebody fighting, arguing, or whatever. I have taken care of all the kids in this street going backwards and forwards to school. They come through here, get in a fight, I get out there and stop it.

And if they wanta be strong with me, I get stronger. I let them know that they not gon' outdo me. I tell 'em, "If you want me to take you in the house and give you a good spankin', I will do it."

And they listen. A lot of kids come back and visit me. There was one boy. About twenty years ago. He went up on the fire escape, way up on the third-floor fire escape, and he almost fell. And I told him, I say, "If I catch you again, I'm gon' take you in my house and I'm gon' tear you up good." He said, "Alright, Mis' Porter." He came down. But then another day, he went back up. And I was just lucky enough to catch him. The wind was blowin' so hard. And he got on top of the rail and he sat there, rocked, he almost fell.

And I say, "OK, Eddie, come on, come on." He walked on in the house and sat down. I said, "You know what I promised you for that." I said, "I promised you a whuppin'. Now, I'm gon' whup you." So I said, "Take off the coat." So he took off the coat. And he said, "You gon' tell my mother that you beat me?" I said, "Yes, I am. Soon as she get home, I'm gon' have your mother and father to come up here, and let them know what I done to you, and let them know why." So I whupped him. So, when they came home, I had 'em to come in and sit down and talk with 'em. And they said, "Well, he gets another whuppin'." It was so funny. When I got finished whuppin' him, and he finished crying, and all, he said, "Mis' Porter, now you already whupped me and all, can I have some of them collard greens and cornbread you cookin'?"

I said, "Yeah, you can have some. You can have all you want." I say, "I don't mind doin' or givin' you anything that I have." I say, "But you must not do wrong things to hurt yourself. I say, "When somebody tell you not to go up such steps as those, way up there, and you are only eight years old, you shouldn't go." I say, "You should listen. Yo' mother and father are both gone to work." I say, "I don't know them that well. And it doesn't matter if I don't know them. Long as I save they child. You just get down and remember to do what I tell you to do. And I'll always look out for you."

So one day I went out to the doctor's here. And I guess I hadn't seen him in about twenty years. I was sick. And this tall boy reached and grabbed me round my waist and he hugged me and he hugged me. He say, "Mis' Porter, you can't forget me." He say, "You don't know who I am, do you?" I said, "Yes I do!" We called him Eddie spaghetti for a funny name. And he say, "Mis' Porter, like you whupped my behind; you made a man out of me! I've been to the army, and everybody in the army knows that you whupped me. I told 'em. Ha-ha." He reached down and he just hugged me. He said, "I will never forget you. You gave me a good start, that I had to lis-

ten. And I'm listening right on. And I'll never forget to do that for my kids." And I said, "OK, fine." ◐

To gain greater appreciation of this narrative, I interviewed various residents of the ghetto. Many of those I canvassed said the woman's behavior is not so likely to occur on the streets today. Their responses suggest a breakdown in feelings of community. Residents say people tend to keep more to themselves now, that they no longer involve themselves in their neighbors' lives as they did as recently as ten years ago. As one middle-aged mother pointed out,

◐ *A grown person takes a real risk when she corrects someone else's child. And if she puts her hands on another's child, that's asking for trouble, unless she knows the family real well.* ◐

While a spanking might once have been generally approved of, and perhaps welcomed as an affirmation of love and caring, today the issue of child abuse looms, and the authorities might be called. Possible legal action or out-and-out verbal and physical retaliation constrains many from actively playing such old head roles.

But there are other constraining influences as well. The old head often exercises authority in public places. As the community has experienced the coming and going of so many residents, social life has become less stable. But the really important factors complicating public life are drugs, community perceptions of increased crime in the streets, and the virtual abandonment of the neighborhood by the middle class. In a word, the area is experiencing segmentation, and residents feel especially distant and wary around strangers. Public spaces have become increasingly complicated and dangerous, or at least they are perceived that way.

These developments make the roles of male and female old heads, in part because of their public nature, all the more difficult to enact. Declining in influence and authority, the would-be old heads tend to disengage. And the community becomes even more vulnerable to a variety of social ills, from teenage pregnancy to rampant drug use.

3

○

The

Impact of

Drugs

With the massive introduction of drugs into Northton, both a drug culture and a drug economy have proliferated. The attendant financial opportunities and possibilities for "getting high" compete effectively for the minds, if not the hearts, of boys and girls. The roles of drug pusher, pimp, and (illegal) hustler have become more and more attractive. Street-smart young people who operate in this underground economy are apparently able to obtain big money more easily and glamorously than their elders, including traditional male and female old heads. Because they appear successful, they become role models for still younger people. Members of the older generation, many of whom are not doing so well financially, find it hard to compete, and in frustration some accommodate the younger people.

Further, the working residents of the community have become very cautious and have begun to shy away from young people they do not know well, believing the young are the primary source of drug-related street crime. These general perceptions have contributed to the flight of many from Northton and have deflected others who considered moving there. The black residents who might serve as upright role models for youth often hesitate to become involved or do so reluctantly. Many simply say, "The young boys have changed" or "I can't take the chance." Their general tendency is to define boys pejoratively as "mannish" and girls as "fast." Growing up prematurely, many cannot handle the stresses of adult life and thus become crime-prone, aggressive, and generally unpredictable. Having reason to think that many of the unknown girls and boys they encounter are mixed up in the drug and alcohol culture, older people disengage.

They believe, perhaps rightly, that a person on drugs is dangerous and out of control and is thus capable of robbing his own family and friends or turning on them violently. The following are the stereotypical comments of a self-employed carpenter who lives in Northton:

◉ *Oh yeah, the hardworking men used to be free with time to help anybody they could help, help 'em to gain a skill or a trade. Even now, we'll sometimes get some of 'em through OIC [Opportunities Industrialization Center] or somewhere. At least then we know they into it [serious] and not just messin' around. These young boys, they all into the drugs, that's all they do. I get so I don't even want 'em around me. They'll be doing drugs right on the job.* ◉

On the streets of Northton, the concern about the drug culture, mixed with a general distrust of anonymous young people, has augmented the atmosphere of estrangement, segmentation, and social distance. Since so much of the criminal element lives in the community, neighbors feel vulnerable to a host of criminal assaults and incivilities that require effective personal management. For instance, the perpetrator of a crime might be a nephew on drugs, one's best friend's son, or simply a young man "down the street." Though neighbors in Northton are cautious, they cannot keep secret their work schedules, sleep habits, appliance deliveries, physical frailties, and aloneness. An out-of-work youth living down the street can sit on his mother's front porch steps and watch old Mrs. Brown leave for the market each day at 3:00 and return at 3:30.

To deal with the prospect of crime, residents may try to manage their public environment by "making friends" with their neighbors in an effort to "be known," to ingratiate themselves with potential criminals. Here a young black man tells how his mother managed to keep from becoming a victim of crime in Northton:

◉ *My mother goes through a lot of changes, just to live from day to day. I mean, just like when she gets a new appliance, she would make sure she was there on the day it was delivered. When they [the store] would call in the morning and say when they would come, say between 10:00 and 2:00, she would always be there. To make sure they got the right house. Or she would leave the light on, saying, "Mine'll be the one with the light on," so they wouldn't have to look for the place and find the wrong house. They would deliver it. I remember when she got a new fridge one time, she just cut the box up and put out a little each week; she'd put it in a big Hefty bag and just put it right out. She didn't want her neighbors to know she'd gotten something, because that meant either she had money or there was something in there to steal.*

And whenever she'd go to church, she would put her pocketbook over her shoulder, and then put her coat on over the pocketbook. She'd never carry her pocketbook hanging out. That was her strategy. And no jewelry. Even if she was gonna get a ride. Sometimes when she'd be picked up and taken to church, she wouldn't wear the jewelry out of the house. She'd wait till she got in the car, and then on the way to where she was going put it on. On the way back, she'd take it off. It's a hell of a way to live, but that's how she avoided problems.

My mother, when she died, was sixty-four. She lived alone. And she had to maintain a low profile. It's like walking a tightrope. She was sort of a mother [fictive kinship] for so many of the youngsters of the community area. They knew her as a church lady, but still she had to be very careful. Certainly a lot of 'em [young boys] respected her, and they knew her, but some just didn't care. Now there are all the young guys of Northton. And she would go to the Northton Community Planners group meetings and things like that. I have an aunt and uncle still living in the community, and they live pretty much the same way. They are just careful. They have to be.

Usually, if they see you, your presence is somewhat of a deterrent, if they know you. It's a deterrent for some, but for others, even that don't matter. They'll snatch your bag. They'll run around the corner, and they live around the corner. And they know damn well you know them, 'cause you see 'em sitting on the steps. They don't care. 'Cause they need that money right now. She [mother] was always leery about carrying large sums of money. And she always walked fast. Walked very fast. Was unobtrusive as possible. She'd speak, but she was always on the move, never breaking her stride. She'd say things like, "Aw, how y'all doing, I'm fine."

And she'd bake cakes for some of the young boys, if they had a birthday. And when she'd pass by and see a bunch of guys on the corner and they'd be coughing and sniffing [implied cocaine habit] or whatever, she'd have these Hall's cough drops. She'd reach her hand in her pocket and say, "Here, son. Take this for your cough." She got to be known as "the lady with the cough drops." And she'd just walk up and hug him [a local street corner youth] and say, "How's your cold, son?" She knew all the time that the cough and sniffles were from drugs.

And there's been times when they've [young boys on the corner] tried to catch her by surprise. One time in particular she was going to work. She was standing right at the bus stop, and he [a youth] approached her, but she caught him off guard and said, "Son! Where's your coat? You're gon' catch your death of cold out here." He was wearing a sweatshirt or a sweater, and she started raisin' hell with him for not having on a coat. "What would your mother say?" She caught him off guard. She knew that he was behind her for no good reason. She was always aware of what was going on. He came up behind her very slowly, but she caught him totally off guard. "Where do you live, son?" She would act like his aunt or his mother. "What's your name? Take better care of yourself." She had to scold him but stroke him, too. Man, she used to spend a fortune on cough drops, ha-ha.

Another way she survived was by calling out their kin's names. Or just acting like she knew them. She'd say things like, "How's your sister?" or "How's Bea?" or whatever. Out of ten young guys, if you can just connect with one, then the whole group will be cool. "You can't talk that way, man." They would say, "Oh, hi, Mrs. Brown. We just talking." "OK, son." All the time, she's steady moving, with no jewelry, no pocketbook. She didn't want to tempt them at all. ◐

As this narrative illustrates, there are areas of Northton that are beleaguered by the youthful criminal element living there. To survive, many residents, old and young, respond creatively, inventing any number of tricks and scams to get past the foreboding groups of young men who hang out on the street corners. They try to negotiate with such young men, who become a kind of informal police force that protects, defends, or simply does not "bother" those who are deemed deserving of such consideration, while accosting or even robbing those who are not. Hence one senses the superficially tight-knit quality of neighborhood relations through the etiquette of cake baking and public shows of familiarity. No specific act of endearment, such as Mrs. Brown's baking a cake for a teenager next door, can be reduced to cold, self-interested calculation, but it is a peculiar combination of neighborliness and self-defense.

The need for such defensive actions grows more urgent as residents attempt to cope with the proliferation of drugs and the attendant crime. They must be on guard even against people they have known over many years, which attests to the community's state of desperation. Whereas the older generation of local men were able to work in the regular job market and earn wages that allowed them to live much like the American middle class, the changed economy has made this extremely difficult for the younger generation. Largely unskilled and with serious educational deficiencies, the youth of today are left to participate only at the lowest levels of the emerging service-oriented economy. In response, many have become attracted to the underground of crime and drugs, while others have become so demoralized that they are ready candidates for alcohol and drug addiction. This social context of persistent poverty becomes a fertile field for the growth of the drug culture, as described in this account by a former dealer:

◐ *The way I see it, there's top dogs, middle dogs, and low dogs. In the neighborhood, right? The top dogs are the guys with the money, dudes with the cars. The majority of them sell drugs. They got the big money. They drive Caddies, El Dorados, Rivieras. They selling their drugs in the bars. There's not many of them that work at regular jobs. They dress casual. Then on weekends they go on out, they can show off their suits, walk in the neighborhoods. They sell cocaine mostly and heroin. They're in their late thirties, thirty-six to thirty-eight range. They make big money. They have a little war here and there, when they sell bad stuff; they get their cars shot up. They stand on the corner and someone come shooting at them.*

Mostly you see top dogs at after-hours spots, after the bars close. I went to one, they had a gambling spot upstairs. They go to them all morning. They're located in somebody's house, one of the top dog's houses. They sell food, and they have liquor at a bar upstairs. They have a little whore room where the whores give you a little action. To me it was nice, but I knew everybody in there, just about. Everybody want to be tough; they got guns. But as long as you mind your own business, you're cool. All of them are black people. They had a couple of white guys in there one time; they were nice. They sat around, talking shit. Nobody went up to them and say, "White motherfucking shit!" like that. All was cool. I spoke to them, laughed, talked shit with them, take a hit from their smoke. That's the way it was. They knew the top dog. Someone starts in with them, well, they knew they came with a certain person. You don't fuck with them. He told me, "You have no problems with them. They with me." That's the way it was. They was nice people. That's the top dogs.

The middle dogs are the ones who sell drugs for the top dogs. They're trying to be like them, trying to get like the top dogs, selling drugs for them, shit like that. They range from seventeen to late twenties. They get their supply from the top dog. They're selling drugs. When they sell out, they give him the money, they get their half, and they give them some more drugs to sell. You get the drugs first. Then you bring in the money when you sell the drugs. He gives you like ten or fifteen bags of cocaine to sell. That's $20 a bag. So you make from fifteen times $20. When he gets out there, he give you $5 off a bag, the middle dog. And they make pretty good money, I assure you. You know, the top dog, he'll take care of you. You say you owe money here, he trusts you and he'll give you money. But don't burn him, shit like that. 'Cause he'll burn your ass. He'll get you shot. But it hasn't happened lately; they don't want to go through all this shit [trouble with police].

He'll get a bunch of gang boys together and they'll sell drugs. There are certain bars. There's one gang be in a bar. Another gang member can't come in and sell drugs. I saw a guy go in one time and try to sell drugs in the wrong place, wrong turf. They said, "Hey, you can't sell that shit in here. Go to your own space. You want to sell, get to your own space. We sell the shit here." There was a big fight. And I knew the guy. I swung around and said, "Hey, this is their territory. It ain't yours. They my allies. You can't do it. You do and you'll get hurt, I assure you."

The middle dogs ask or the top dog asks the guy, "Do you want to sell for me?" Everybody knows the top dog. The guy wanted me to sell for him. He knew I knew a lot of people. And I said, "No, that's not my style." I used to sell speed pills, but I can't go through that shit. People can knock on your door and they can't give you the money they owe. "You buy me out. I need you this time." Then they want more and you say, "You still owe me." It got tiresome. I told my top dog, "You can have this shit. I don't want it no more. I don't need you in my shit, and I don't want to be in your shit." So, I was poof. So the middle dog gets a lot of the young boys who come out of school and want to make some money. They can make $150 a day selling that shit. And they sell it to the low dogs, 'cause the low dogs are the guys that want to buy it. They buy the shit from the middle dog. Then they become middle dogs, a majority of them do. Some of them even become top dogs. That's the way it is. Just like climbing a ladder. They got these jobs at McDonald's, places like that, or they may be unemployed, getting money from their father and mother, or they're stealing. Stealing money, ripping people off, going around town snatching pocketbooks and stuff like that. That's the low dogs for you. They hustle downtown. They steal gold chains and sell them. They steal shit and sell it. They want some cocaine. They get the money together, they get half a gram of cocaine, get it from the middle dogs.

When I see a transaction, I just sit back and laugh. 'Cause I buy from the middle dogs sometimes, too, when I want something. I want a joint and I don't know nobody to go to so I go to the middle dogs and they make a bag. That's all I need. I get some grass, some cocaine. They make a bag of cocaine. No selling nickels [five-dollar bags], just twenties. Sometimes they're nice. If the guy knows you are good and he likes you, you can get it for ten. Like a half a gram will cost you $50. You know, you're five dollars short: "All right, man, here." Only if he likes you, if he knows you're good. A gram costs a hundred. If you're a good friend of the person or you grew up with the person, he'll say, "OK, give me $90."

Crack is out there, too. I took that shit one time, almost killed my damn self. If my friend at home had not poured milk down my throat, man, I woulda been gone. That costs $10 a bag. That's some nasty stuff. That shit'll turn your keys green. We snort that shit. That will hook us up. And I took too much of it. I realized that I was on my way, but my boy Steve saved me. He's in jail now for shooting two guys already. Well, he knew I was fucked up. He said, "Come on, Bird, where you going?" I took too much, and I'm lucky to be alive. But he knew I was having a hard time. He knew something was wrong, 'cause he'd used it before. So he ran to the corner store and snatched the guy at the counter, grabbed a half pint of milk and poured the shit down my throat. You see, if you drink milk, the shit brings you down. Milk brings you down like that. I was fucked up. My heart going real fast, you know. That shit could bust my heart. I never fucked with any more of that stuff since. No more. You call it crack, call it crank, monster, or beast. Them four names. They take them pills for downers. I can't take that shit.

The low dogs never get completely off that shit. When they like it, they like it. Some of them will get off crack maybe and do regular cocaine. You know, I had these boys, eight, nine, ten, eleven, twelve [years old], ask me for rolling [cigarette] paper. I was shocked. I said, "How old are you?" He said, "I'm ten." I said, "Man, you're crazy. What are you going to do with paper?" "Smoke a joint, man." Eight, nine, ten years old. I was shocked. I didn't know they did it that *young. Ten years old? Man, that freaked me right out. Cute little guy. Dressed nice in his Fila sweat suit. Nice. I'd say he was wearing $200 worth of clothes, easy. Shit, a Fila sweat suit is $200. Fila sneaks on, they $70 a pair. Fila hat, another $5. Ten years old, smoking a joint, had over $300 worth of clothes on. He comes with a sixteen-year-old guy and a fifteen-year-old girl. He got the shit from a middle dog. They don't care who they sell that shit to. You got the money, you can have it. Tiny dog, I call him. That's a lot of money for a little boy like that, a ten-year-old boy. I didn't believe it, I looked at him. He had to be selling something or he had a good mother and father, one or the other. I didn't picture him selling drugs really. I just pictured him. Young guy. You should have seen him sitting like this [pretends to roll a joint], rolled that shit like a pro, two hands and tongue in it. I said, "Jesus. Oh, my God." That freaked me out, that did. Street kid.* ◐

The Drug Culture

Tales like these, related through a network of associates, friends, and relatives, help interpret and define the drug culture in the Northton ghetto. The culture is further objectified by the proliferation of "crack houses" sprinkled through the neighborhood and by drug-related violence, including killings and crimes on the streets in which innocent people, including bystanders and children, are victims. When an unexplained murder or break-in occurs, residents often conclude that it was drug related.

Among young people there is sometimes a strong desire, induced partly by peer pressure, to experiment, to try a certain type of "high" just one time. But in such peer groups there are individuals, users and nonusers, who have an interest in "beaming up" or "hooking other people up." In the crowded situation of camaraderie and sociability, one dealer's approach to prospective users is, "Everybody else is doing it, why not you?" There may be mental coercion bordering on strong-arming, and when mixed with peer pressure it can be deadly. For instance, a young woman may have a boyfriend who deals in drugs and needs customers. He might "hook up" his girlfriend, convincing her that "there's nothing wrong with gettin' high." Giving him her trust, she may follow his line and try "the pipe" (crack), since it is said to be "what's happening" (the latest and most wonderful thing). These people often have the notion that "one time can't hurt you" or "I'll try anything once." But one night on crack is enough to get a person "hooked up" or addicted for what may be life. One drug dealer told me, "I've never seen a person walk away from the pipe." Another approach to initiating new addicts is to be "out of stock" of the weaker drug the buyer is used to, but to offer the crack free until the person is hooked.

Dealers tend to have certain corners and spaces "sewed up," marked off as their own territory, and may prevent other dealers from selling either at a particular corner or even in the general area. At times these corners are bought and sold, leading to turf disputes and violence to decide who owns them. A "king of the hill" competition may ensue, awarding the corner to whoever can claim it. The one who controls the corner determines the types of drugs bought and sold. Thus, if only crack is easily accessible, drug users who need something may use it.

Addicts may gravitate to a crack house, usually a nondescript dwelling where drugs are easily purchased. Neighbors know about it, mainly because of the steady stream of traffic passing in and out at all times of the day and night and from the way others talk about it. Streetwise passersby can also recognize a drug house by the telltale discarded crack vials or "works" strewn nearby.

The house may be owned by a private person or may be an abandoned, boarded-up building that has been taken over and perhaps fortified by dealers. Or it may be just a shell where addicts hang out and get high. If the building is owned by an individual, it may operate in much the same way as a "speakeasy," where not only drugs but also liquor, food, and sex may be for sale. The owner might rent out rooms for sex. Drug dealers then pay a fee for the right to market their drugs to the steady stream of customers, who buy everything from rock cocaine to marijuana.

Inside, a visitor sees people getting high, in various states of undress, or simply standing around or sitting at tables lining the walls as in a restaurant or bar. The opium den quickly comes to mind. Depending on the proprietor, people may lie around on the floor with needles stuck into them; in full view of new visitors, they search for a vein, hitting or missing and spewing out blood. Clutter and dirt are everywhere. Used matches litter the floor, testifying to the many "tokes" or "hits" off the crack pipe. Some people sit around in a stupor.

People from the community may queue up with television sets, videocassette recorders, food stamps, or anything the drug dealers will take. Some women wear no underwear, prepared to engage in all types of sexual acts in exchange for drugs. They eventually leave the place not with money, but with a number of highs to their credit. Sex is sold for the pleasure of the drug, not to make a living, as was common in the past.

When addicts deplete their resources, they may go to those closest to them, drawing them into their schemes for getting high. The process may go something like this: Unable to fully appreciate what is happening, the family may put up with the person for a while. They provide money if they can, but a pattern of begging usually develops. They come to realize that the person is on drugs, though at first this may be very hard to believe. But reality sets in, and family members begin to accept the fact of addiction as they put together the person's past actions and repeated, increasingly desperate demands for money. Still not fully accepting the situation, some may continue to give the addict money and other kinds of support. Arguments may ensue as family members try to make sense of the person. Slowly the reality sets in more and more completely, and the family becomes drained of both financial and emotional resources. Although quitting is not a simple act of volition, relatives often act as though it were, and they may hopefully cajole and plead with the addict to quit. If this is of no avail, many are prepared to "blame the victim."

The addict, generally young to middle-aged, is usually on crack. During more lucid moments, he or she promises relatives and other supporters to "do better." But it is very difficult to do better. The first time the father or mother or other relative gives the addict $30 for an errand to the grocery store, he or she returns hours later with no groceries and no money, despite starting out with good intentions. After a number of times, close relatives lose faith and begin to see the person as untrustworthy and weak. Eventually the addict begins to "mess up" in various ways, taking furniture from the house, perhaps a lamp, a toaster, or anything of value. Despite stories about thefts and burglaries, the others can see through these tales.

On the streets, this complex of events is known as "backstabbing." When it is engaged in often enough, when faith is found to be misplaced and irretrievable, even parents will put the person out. At this point the addict may become very contrite, but often it does little good. Relatives and friends begin to see the person from a different perspective, as "out there" in the streets, and the length of time spent "out there" underscores the distance they feel and create between themselves and the addict. Some begin to speak of the addict in the past tense, as though a death had occurred, and in a certain social sense the person has died.

The evicted young woman or man may then gravitate to the home of a sympathetic relative or a friend and be allowed to stay awhile, but the backstabbing repeats itself. The person may then visit a number of acquaintances, begging for money with sad tales. The possibilities are quickly exhausted.

Pipers and Zombies

One deviant act leads to another. Crack addicts may become closely associated with a drug dealer who has a steady supply. They smoke the pipe, which the dealers and others call the "glass dick," particularly when they see a woman on it. She cannot help herself. The first-time high is "just incredible." Then comes the crash, in only ten to fifteen minutes. The person gets it, then wants it, gets it, wants it. Pursuing the euphoria of the first-time high is said to be like "chasing a ghost," for there is no satisfaction. Residents, at times jokingly, call these people "pipers."

After leaving the crack house, addicts may roam the streets looking for yet another "blast." Their eyes are cast down, scanning the ground for anything of value. If they spot a penny, they stop abruptly to pick it up, then linger to look for more. Local residents, who sometimes "see and don't see," have spotted them down on their hands and knees, inspecting something they think may be dope; they finger it, taste it, then get up and move on. Members of the drug culture call this "fiending." Those who are so seriously addicted that they engage in such behavior are called "zombies."

The zombie is a recent addition to the streets. Although having much in common with earlier drug addicts, including what were referred to as "dopies," "junkies," or "addicts," the zombie has a distinctive difference: addiction to crack, a cheap but highly addictive drug that brings about a brief euphoria, then a sudden "crash" that leaves the user with an intense craving, or "jonesing," for more. While smoking the drug, "all they can think of is where they gon' get the next blast." One pursues it until one's resources are depleted. Addiction is widely believed to be instantaneous and permanent in effect, rendering the addict "a fool for crack."

At night, community residents say, the pipers and zombies come out. Stories have emerged about the hapless zombies' antics, but also about the very real threat they pose. In Northton, zombies scavenge for drugs at night. They beg, and they commit robberies, break-ins, and assaults.

In some ways this behavior is not so unlike what has come to be expected of more conventional drug addicts. One important difference is the new boldness with which pipers or zombies approach criminal activity: they seem to lack a sense of reality and of the immediate consequences of their behavior. In their agitated state, zombies do things even other drug addicts would think twice about and perhaps resist. For instance, they beg aggressively from passersby, they are known to engage in hand-to-hand combat with the police, or they may break into a car or house in full view of others who might call the authorities. With their sense of reality drastically diminished by the drug, they will take greater risks than other criminals, who are generally believed to be more sensible. Indeed, it is this presumed sensibility of the common street criminal that has allowed residents to travel about the streets with some feeling of protection from crime. The presence of the zombie introduces a strong element of irrationality, further complicating public relations among anonymous passersby.

The Coke Whore

The dealer's object is to place his available drug in the hands of users. For some the primary goal is to inspire customers to try the pipe. As one dealer said:

◑ *The girls like "the girl" [crack], the boys like "the girl." That white bitch [cocaine]. That glass dick [the pipe]. They puffin' away for the genie in the glass bottle. Ha-heh.* ◐

Hence, on the ghetto street a new pimp emerges. Unlike the traditional pimp, who might wine and dine and "sweet talk" the girls to get them to "turn tricks" and at times used physical violence to force them to continue in prostitution, a new style of coercion has developed. It appears more sophisticated, in that drugs are more centrally involved in social control. In behaving as a type of pimp, the dealer may get the young woman to try the highly addictive crack, then encourage her to prostitute herself to get more, sending her out on the streets in this manner.

"Coke whores" have a characteristic look. They are typically gaunt, the skin drawn tight over their facial bones, and they have narrowed, glassy eyes. When seriously addicted they eat what is easiest to digest, which limits their choices, and they become emaciated from loss of appetite. Often they force down handfuls of dry noodles, which are cheap and easily digested. They have a dazed look, their attention always focused elsewhere.

Those who sell drugs laugh about the girls who become hooked, for they are capable of doing anything for a "blast" of crack. Dealers sometimes compare these addicts with who they used to be and take pride in bringing them down. They sneer about the decent, "good-looking girls who were so hard to get next to" sexually in high school, but who are "now doing everything in the book."

Some young women become agents for the drug dealers, hooking up unsuspecting or "weak" men. During the sexual encounter, drugs are introduced, and at times the couple may remain in a hotel or drug house for days, having sex and getting high on cocaine or crack. After this initiation they may part company, but in a few days she may call on the man again, asking him to repeat the sexual encounter. Remembering the good time they had, he may say yes. They meet and again get high, but this time he draws money from his bank account or some other source, spending a huge sum on drugs. In these sessions the couple may move back and forth between cocaine and crack. She acquires more money from the man, goes to her dealer to get drugs, returns, and they continue to get high. Through all of this, he becomes addicted. Later a direct contact is made, and the dealer becomes the man's source for drugs. This accomplished, the woman may move on to other men, hooking them up and being used by her pimp/dealer. She may do this less for the money than for the "good time," as a cheap way of supporting a very expensive drug habit. All the while, the drug dealer's pockets are being lined with cash. As I was standing on a Northton street corner, an elderly old head commented on this situation, saying:

◐ *I just saw a girl go down there while ago. Beautiful girl, used to be a beautiful girl. Beautiful family. Look at her, she walking up and down the street, a crack user. What good is she to society? She just passed by there. When she meets people, she begs for money. She sells her body. There she goes, see her going there. [An emaciated twenty-year-old black woman runs across the street, holding her head in her hand.] That's her, educated girl, she got three and a half years in college. That crack got her that way, on that crack. That's all she live for now.* ◐

Meanwhile the young children of such women suffer extreme poverty, including hunger, homelessness, and sometimes a total lack of supervision. Without the aid or support of the grandmother or other relatives, the children may become "street kids," at high risk to repeat their mother's career in some form. As one male old head commented:

◑ *If it wasn't for grandmom, the kids wouldn't survive. The grandmoms have to take over from the mom. See, I talk with a lot of grandmoms, and they be tellin' me, "Lawd, I got to take care of my grandchild since this thing." Some of 'em don't want to go into detail about it, and some of 'em go right into detail. They tell you, "I got to take care of my grandchild, 'cause somebody got to do somethin'. My daughter, I don't see her half the time. She done got her mind messed up, or she out there." Or some of them say, "My daughter, she ain't doing nothin'," so then you know what's happenin', you know. Anytime a grandmother, a mother tell you a child ain't doin' nothin' for the child, then you know what she doin'. She got to take over. And if it wasn't for a lot of the grandmothers, a whole lot of kids wouldn't be able to eat, or sleep neither.* ◑

As one black taxi driver told me:

◑ *I've had my share of run-ins with these women on crack. They get in the cab, and wanta give you sex instead of the fare. I've had 'em do that to me. They got their stories, now. I'll tell you. One night a woman flagged me down over there [in the general area of Northton], and I could tell right away that she wasn't right. She looked like a broomstick, and I knew she was a piper. But she had this little baby with her, and I felt sorry for her. She said she had no place to stay, and I told her I'd take her to the shelter. So she gets in my cab, then she says she knows a woman a few blocks down who'll let her spend the night for ten dollars, and she wants me to give her the ten dollars. No way I'm gonna give her money for her drugs. I told her I'd get her to the shelter, but nothing else. The little baby stank like piss, and the Pampers hadn't been changed for a long time. All they [crack addicts] care about is getting that pipe. They're bold. And they can get very creative on you [concoct schemes] to get money. They don't have any feeling. And they'll do you in for your money. But she looked so bad, dragging that little baby around.* ◑

The Family and the Peer Group

The young woman who becomes addicted to "rock cocaine" or crack often comes from an unstable family. The economy and drugs are often implicated in this instability. In sharp contrast, the strong ghetto family, often with both a husband and a wife, but sometimes only a strong-willed mother and her children who have the help of close relatives, seems to instill in girls a hopeful sense that they can reproduce this strong family or one even "better." Such units, when they exist, are generally regarded as advantaged. The father usually works at a regular job and has a sense that his values have paid off. Both parents, or close kin, strive to instill in the children the work ethic, common decency, and social and moral responsibility.

Young girls growing up in such situations, strongly encouraged by their mothers and fathers and other kin, are sometimes highly motivated to avoid habits and situations that would undermine their movement toward "the good life." They are encouraged to look beyond their immediate circumstances; they often have dreams of marriage, a family, and a home. The strict control their parents exert, combined with their own hopes for the future, makes them watch themselves and work hard to achieve a life better than that lived by so many in the ghetto. Because of such interests and concerns, these young women tend not to follow the social track leading to drug addiction, though even they can become victims of crack, since because of its highly addictive nature one behavioral lapse or seeking an "experience" can fundamentally change a person's life.

By contrast, young girls and boys emerging from homes that lack a strong, intact family unit, usually headed by a single mother working or on welfare and trying desperately to make ends meet, become especially vulnerable to drug addiction and unwed pregnancies. The process leading up to such events usually begins in early childhood with full participation in play groups on the streets. Children who become deeply engaged in the drug culture often come from homes where they have relatively little adult attention, little moral training, and limited family encouragement to strive for a life much different from the one they are living.

Coming from a single-parent household, often headed by a nearly destitute mother, children may have almost no effective adult supervision. As some people in the community say, "they just grow up." Many become "street kids," left largely on their own, and by the time they are preteens some are becoming "street smart," beginning to experiment with sex and drugs. The local play group may become something of a family for youths who lack support at home.

The ghetto street culture can be glamorous and seductive to the adolescent, promising its followers the chance of being "hip" and popular with certain "cool" peers who hang out on the streets or near the neighborhood school. Often such teenagers lack interest in school, and in time they may drop out in favor of spending time with their street-oriented peers.

To be sure, most adolescents dabble in the street culture, including experimenting with sex and drugs; for status and esteem, they must learn to interpret and manipulate its emblems. Those who are most successful may become invested in such pursuits to the point of becoming overwhelmed and socially defined by them. Such definitions contribute to the formation of a street identity, which then gives such youths further interest in behaving in accordance with the peer-group's norms—or even inventing them.

The morally strict and financially stable intact nuclear families, on the decline in the underclass neighborhood, with their strong emotional and social ties and their aspirations for their children, must engage in sometimes fierce competition with the peer group. With a variety of social supports, including extended kin networks and strong religious affiliations, such families can often withstand the lure of the street culture, but even they may succumb and lose control of their offspring, sometimes permanently. The much less viable family headed by an impoverished young woman who has her hands full working, socializing, and mothering stands little chance in the struggle for a child's allegiance and loyalty and often does not prevail.

Though stable families possess an outlook that considers upward mobility a real possibility and try to instill this outlook in their children, such value transfers are difficult to accomplish. One important reason is the street culture's very strong and insistent attraction. But also important is the fact that the wider culture and its institutions are perceived, quite accurately at times, as unreceptive and unyielding to the efforts of ghetto youths.

Resolving this situation depends to some degree on luck. Youths from the most socially "promising" domestic arrangements sometimes become fixated and invested in the ghetto street culture, but they may have a chance to grow out of it (see Matza 1964). Those from the poorest families, with the least control over social resources, appear to be most vulnerable to the street's seductive draw.

Vulnerability to the street may be manifested in a variety of ways, from adolescent pregnancy to street crime to serious drug abuse. One may approach "hipness" through good looks and grooming, nice clothes, dancing ability, sexual activity, crime, and drug use—which may be more or less important depending upon one's particular crowd or peer group.

On the streets of Northton many young people drink alcohol, and a significant number smoke marijuana and engage in moderate use of cocaine. Something of a drug and alcohol culture has emerged, and limited participation is acceptable and even encouraged. It may be that mindless experimentation with thrills like smoking marijuana predisposes one to crack addiction. Many crack addicts report that they moved from smoking "reefers" (marijuana) to smoking crack.

Given the drug culture and the association of hipness with indulgence, it is common for young people to "get high." Perhaps the generalized acceptance of such indulgence leads to the quest for "better and better" highs, as one person says to the next, "Try some of this." In this context, in which young people get high by passing around "smoke," sometimes engaging in elaborate rituals that include the "hip" and exclude the "lame" and "square," the one-time user may become seriously addicted to crack.

The following conversation I had with a twenty-four-year-old black woman crack addict supports and illustrates the description above:

◐ *I'm not well really at all. I just try to convince myself that I am, but when I get alone I think 'bout all these things . . . I just know I need help, and give myself a will enough to ask for it. Later, five minutes, ten minutes from now, I just get messed up, you know. I don't want nothing to happen to me. I want to save myself. I don't have no kind of medical assistance, no anything at all. Because the person who I used to stay with, right, took me through so many changes. I could just tell somebody all my problems. Two years I could break down into two hours.*

I grew up in the projects around drugs and everything. I went to the tenth grade. I ain't got no mother, no father, my son had a death from drugs, and I have a little girl and my sister has custody of her, and my sister let me see her sometimes. I even had enough will that when I knew I was gon' go back [to the pipe], I had my baby 'bout a couple hours, and I took my baby and I ran [took] her to my sister so fast, 'cause I refuse to let her [the baby] go through what I been doin'. So I just left her with my sister. And my sister thinkin' 'bout just takin' her back to the home [social agency] and all that stuff, and it's really bothering me. I say she better off there than with me.

But my sister's a slimy somethin'. She not really tryin' to help me. I think she want me to stay on it deep down inside. Certain things she say, certain things she do. She never was really too proud of me. She was jealous when I got myself together. So I really don't depend on her too much. I have to respect her because she takes care of my kids, but she gets on my nerves so bad. Now she talking about putting my baby in a home. I won't be able to see her. I want to get my self together, but I can't. ◑

I asked, "When did you get addicted?" She answered, "Two years ago, off and on, but I always had the will to stop." Then I asked, "How did you first get involved with crack?" The rest of the interview has been edited to reflect only the answers to questions I asked her.

◑ *A boyfriend. And now that person is nowhere around. I don't even know that person no more. He was nice and he convinced me that he wouldn't take advantage of me. I was strong, but I had too many problems. We used to smoke reefer [marijuana]. And after I tried the pipe, I didn't need the reefer no more. He said it was a better high, and I did both. You try one thing, and it doesn't do enough, and then you go on to another. All I ever wanted was love and under-standing. My boyfriend [current boyfriend] don't do it [crack], and he tried to keep me off it, and I don't do it when I'm with him. But he took me through changes so much lately that I found out it [trouble] just made me run back [to the pipe].*

If I just had the will of my own like the will of God, I would just stay off it forever, 'cause I shouldn't let no one make me run back. But that was the problem. Depending on someone else. And I was going pretty good. And my friend [current boyfriend], the changes I took him through, all he think [about] is violent retaliation [against me]. And I'm scared, and I think if anything bad happens for what-ever . . . And if anyone come to me, I feel real violent [defensive]. And I know I am [capable of violence], 'cause when I gets real mad, I punches windows and be ready to go crazy, and I don't have good sense. And I don't want to waste my life like this. But just up to a week ago I was alright for a month and a half. I have a big [crack] problem, and I have to learn to stop on my own. I used to stop for my friend [current boyfriend], and I used to think he was the only one who helped me get off [the drug], which he did. But then when he did so many rotten things to me that I had to hide my babies, and now his [new] girlfriend found out that my two kids was his and all.

And I know that he probably mad, and I know everybody just turned against me, and I know that all I want is just to get my life together.

I'm so ashamed of what I do, but I enjoy it at that time. But I know it's hurting me at the same time. And while I'm doin' it, I say, "Damn, you see all this shit, what it's doin' to me." And I know right from wrong, and it hasn't took my mind away, but it's really startin'. . . . So anybody out there can hear me. If anything happen, I can be dead.

I knew that I wanted to make it [to be drug-free]. 'Cause I believe in God. OK, that's what has helped me. I believe in God. And if you commit suicide, you go straight to hell. And I don't want to go to hell, 'cause I want to see my son and my parents and brother [deceased relatives]. Like right now I'm high, but not as high as I normally be. But I'm talkin' with sense. It [the high] doesn't last at all really, doesn't last long. It last for as long as you smoke it. When the light [fire] go out, you need more. That's how I feel about it. It's [crack] no damn good, and I know it. Right now, I just can't stop it. I get high all day long. And the price never end. Five-dollar cap last about five minutes, and then I'm up for a couple minutes. You know what I do now, I be going up and down. I'll smoke a joint [marijuana] or drink liquor, and I now I even drink [straight] alcohol.

This is embarrassing, but sometimes you have to talk to somebody who don't know you. The people who know you don't realize [your desperate situation], especially if you hurt them before. They don't really realize how much, what you really saying, and how much you really need their help. My mother's dead. I don't have no mother, no father no more [begins to cry and whimper]. My baby brother and my son, all the people who really love me, they dead. And that's botherin' me too. I was on the drugs before my mother and dad died.

Right now I'm all out of breath and all, and my heart is hurting. I know my lungs is probably as black as hell. I was doing so good until a couple of months ago, and I'd get into the Bible and right now it helps me to forget about it. I went to church two Sundays ago, the first time I went. I was doin' real good. Right now, I'm really disappointed in myself, in what I'm doin' to my babies. I lost my babies. I have three kids; none of them are in my custody. I voluntarily gave them up to my sister. I told my sister that I don't want to see my baby no more, because she don't deserve to see me for what

I'm doin' right now. It's hurtin' me that I said that, and I want to go see her, but I can't let her see me like this. That's my baby. And she still livin', and I don't wanta die. And I don't want her to go through it [begins to cry]. But I just can't take no more of this, 'cause as long as I'm out here [in the street] all I want to do is keep gettin' high, keep gettin' high. I wanta go away. I wanta get away from it all. I just have to get away.

My problems were ones I grew up with in a family full of problems. And I always tried to run, and I always depended on someone to take care of me, and then I'd take care of myself. Now I'm just trying to make it on my own. And the place where I'm stayin', I even stole money and ran out and got stuff, and the person didn't even know. I stole money for what I got [high feeling] right now. I stole it from people who trusted me to do certain kind of work for them. My daughter, I don't want nobody to see me. I done got so [physically] small. And the last few days . . . I hate myself when I look in the mirror and say, "This ain't you." Like right now, I thank God for talkin' with you. See, tonight, what's gone happen is like . . . Later, if I don't get help, every place I call, you got to have a medical card. You got to have this and that. I say, "Darn, do I have stab myself or shoot myself to get to a hospital so these people can help me?" Do I have to really do that? I'm startin' to have trouble with my heart. ◐

"Do you turn tricks [engage in prostitution] for drugs?" I asked.

◐ *Naw, I don't wanta have to do that. I never will do that. [Begins to cry.] I'd rather steal than go sell my body. You know, talkin' helps and all. I just hate the people who gave it [crack] to me, that's how I feel. Even when I'm doin' it, I look at them and I say, "Damn, as much as I want to stop . . ." And I can do it [stop]. It's just that I'm on my own. I lost my home. I lost everything. I was stayin' with certain people, and they found out about me. And now I don't have no place to go, you know. I don't have no place at all. I just have to get myself together. I don't want no more [crack], but I just don't have my willpower.*

Last night I got violent, because nobody would give me any money, and I got really violent. I started throwin' things around and just went off. I came and I laid down and just started cryin'. You won't go off [go crazy] if you know you can go out and sell your behind [engage in prostitution]. You know, I just got mad. There are a lot of slimy broads around the street [she cries], and I hate that. Let me tell [mentally agitated], I did that one time [engaged in prostitu-tion], and ever since I did that, I just felt so low. I wanted to kill myself that first time. I could never do that again. 'Cause I always been like a one-man woman.

The love for my man [current boyfriend] is very strong, and you feel very bad when you feel like they betrayed you. All my sisters are that way. We'll give you the world if you just love us the way we love you. I just gave up. I said, "I don't want no man. I want my kids." That's why I want to kick. Right now I'm not eating right. I know I'm killin' myself. I'll take and mix some eggs up with some milk and drink it. I can't eat nothin', and my stomach done shrunk so bad. Can't eat nothin' now. In the past three of four days, I haven't ate no more than a one-course meal. That's why I feel so bad and weak and everything. ◐

Community Reaction

In some long-term residents of the community, reports of the drug culture bring about feelings of deep frustration and an impending apocalypse. As one retired black man related:

◐ I'm very disturbed about things going on in the community, especially with this dope going around; it's bothering me so now, it's something that is aggravating me. I'm gettin' like some of the white folks do. I don't want to be bothered with some of us neither. Drugs done gone out of control.

Aw, man. You can just sit around on this corner [we were sitting on a street corner], or better than that, just get in yo' car and ride up Warrington Avenue, and I'll bet you before you get to Forty-fourth and Warrington, 'bout four or five of 'em'll try to stop you. Three dollars, four dollars, just enough to try to get some crack. They beg-gin' you.

I usually tell 'em, "Look." Now, they black. They my peoples. I used to try to talk, be nice, say, "Hey, doll. I don't have no money." They say, "Hey, whatcha got? I know you got somethin'." I say, "No, I don't. I ain't got no money." She say, "You ain't got three dollars?"

It's pitiful, you know, 'cause I got three daughters myself. It's pitiful to see this kinda stuff goin' on. Look like it's gettin' worse. You see these young girls out there. Pretty girls, you see some of 'em, that used to be pretty, and they gone down. I'll tell you, I've seen girls last year walking past here weighing 280 pounds, ha-heh. This year, they look like they weigh 120 at the most. That's how far I seen one

destroyed. You look and see 'em standin' up there on the street cor-
ner. Some are just gettin' started.

    And the later at night it get, the worse it get. Right now
[3:30 P.M.] we be doin' good, now. Only a few [women hustlers] out
right now. It just get very bad at night. We call. . . . The fellows got
a tendency to call 'em head hunters, heh-ha. Late at night, every
other block, you standin' or sittin' here, they coming by. Well, they
know us, basically. The ones in the neighborhood that know us don't
usually say that much. They'll come by and wave and go on. But if
you get in yo' car, you go up the street, they'll literally try to pull
you out yo' car sometimes. I've had 'em come up to. . . . They gon'
insist to open yo' door. "Hey, com'on, baby." I say, "Ain't nothin'
happening, sugar." They say, "Well, you can open the door and let
me talk," and she tryin' to open the door all the time. I'm telling
you. But not me! Man, this AIDS. I was listening to a radio program
that said AIDS is gon' spread so much in the next few years, and
can't understand it. Because they are out here in such a force, they
dealin' [having sex] with everybody and anybody, you got to catch
something. And if they jump in bed with me, that means I'm gon'
catch somethin', heh-he-ha. You see what I mean. So the number
gon' increase. Now, I believe in religion. I'm a religious type person,
believe in God. But I'm just sayin' the truth. A lot of these peoples
out here, now, for this habit [crack], they'll go to bed with a fly, if
you got five dollars, you understand what I mean. They don't care.
And it's pitiful. It's really pitiful.

    And a lot of 'em is intelligent. I know one particular girl out
here. Was a teacher. She had all her master's, BAs, all that in school.
I seen her 'bout six or seven months ago. She came by here. I said [to
the fellows], I know that girl. And somebody said, "She's on that
pipe." I said, "Yeah?" They say, "She used to teach." I said, "I knew
her. Ha. Very smart. Very intelligent. She used to teach out in south-
west. And she was very intelligent." But I look at it like this. When I
look at the pipers, now, I'm thankful. I'm thankful for one thing.
That sometime we all want to experience something for a high or
enjoyment. But it makes me thankful to know not to never try that.

    Because I've seen so many people that is good, that is in my fam-
ily, in-laws, nieces, some distant cousins, that went from "s to s," as
the old folks used to say, from sugar to shit. I mean this done happen
to intelligent peoples. They were well kept, smart. And it's pitiful,
'cause they probably just say, "Well, I wanted to try. I just want to

have an experience." They went out there. And this thing [crack] is so devastating that, wow, look like once you get into it, you just can't get away from it. Most of the peoples I seen, like I've known people that says, I don't wanta bother with this stuff, and they went out and got in a party, next thing you know they with the group. They say, "Oh, I can handle it. I can handle it." Every last one of them that I've seen that I've known personally got on it. When they first started, they say, "Oh, I can handle it. I can handle it."

The next thing I see them in the street. They don't have anything left. They job's gone. Everything is gone. And they don't have. . . . Their integrity is gone, ha-ha. They don't have nothing left. And if it's a female, guys walking up and down the street stealing all night, trying to get something to support their habit. The girls walking up and down the streets hustling [selling their bodies] all night, you know what I mean. So it's one of those things that is bringing the peoples down as a whole. It's just so bad when I see my peoples coming down this way. Only thing I can think—and I look forward to that the Almighty must be got a plan down the road that he gon' turn this thing around or something gon' happen. If something don't happen soon as bad as this thing is now, I often say, Russia ain't gon' have no problem, they can come over and take over the country 'cause all the young folks gon' be somewhere high. Or be walking down the street looking to get another cap [crack]. So really, they'll ain't gon' have no problem. They can come right in and take over, you know. 'Cause all the people gon' be somewhere high. That's our young people.

But the bad part about it is just like when they had the other drug thing, with the heroin and all that. And the attitude was nowhere like this [at present], you know. But it's how it looks like it's mostly in the black thing [community], but if the people down in Washington don't get off they butts, and I believe a lot of them is got money invested and making money out of this, after while it's gon' be all out in the surburbs. All out there. It's going out there. Now a lot of them [suburban whites] come in town and buy it. You see 'em comin' in here [Northton] and all around, staggering on the corner and asking somebody to give little tips [information], giving some of the addicts a few dollars so they can go get some dope so they can carry it back to the suburbs. And they [whites] know who to ask. They ain't gon' ask me, ain't gon' ask you, ain't gon' ask him [pointing to another corner man]. They gon' stop the type of person who they *think is dealing with this stuff. They say, "Com'on, I need such and such." Sometimes it be the man [police], but they don't give a shit. "I'll give you five dollars if you go. . . ." Sometimes I seen 'em get ripped off. Peoples come in and give a guy $20 to go get something and you know sometime they get ripped off, you know.*

But what I'm saying, the stuff is going out to the suburbs, to all these neighborhoods, out in Mr. Charlie's [white] neighborhood. And if they don't hurry up and get something did, it's gon' destroy—like a great disease—this whole country. It's bad these peoples [government] is waiting to get to that point 'fore they decide to do something. Me personally, I think it's too many big peoples is backing this stuff, in big places. They arresting a few peoples, but the few people they arrest is just little guys trying to superfly [show off] around the streets in a BMW so he can make a fast dollar. And he goes out there, he goes into business. But that little guy with the fancy car and whatever he bought he bought; he didn't bring that stuff into this country. It got here through some other means. Some big man brought it into this country and know it's coming in and under control. And until they [government] start waking up, they ain't gon' do no good. ◗

The fear and concern about drug-related behavior discourages the traditional old heads from assuming the roles they played in simpler times and alters their relationship with young boys and girls. With limited employment opportunities, the old heads assume young men are likely candidates for selling drugs. As another old head lamented:

◗ *These drugs are ruining the community. They done ruined it. People break in other people's cars, they walk the streets, might knock you in the head. They trying to get that dope. And the money's going back to the dope dealer, that's what it's doing. Then they [dealers] drive Mercedes, BMWs, and Lincoln Town Cars, and ain't working nowhere. You understand what I'm saying.*

We can't get through to the young boys anymore. They call us names like "Pop" and try to make fun of you, all that kind of stuff. Nothing you can tell 'em. But you got a few you can talk to. Like I got a guy, a couple of guys out here on the corner, you can talk to 'em. But very few. You can count on one hand. See that group of boys across the street, you can't even go down there and talk to one of 'em right now. They might cuss you out. If you don't believe it, you try it out. And all of 'em will be in jail before—I'd say, in the next two and a half years, every one you see over there will be in jail. They don't want nothing. Won't listen to nobody. Can't tell 'em nothing.

Nowadays, these young boys set the church up and rob. Two churches up there on Bellwether Street got robbed a couple months ago. They went in the broad open day and robbed the church. Yes, on a Sunday morning! When they was talking up collection. Guys come running in there with sawed-off shotguns and robbed the church! Now you tell me what kind of young mens that we got coming today? You understand what I'm saying. We got nothing! ◐

Many conventional residents adopt this attitude and offer the advice, "I just see and don't see, watch my back, and mind my own business."

Traditional old heads seem puzzled by their changing relationship, or lack of relationship, with young boys and girls. When observing the community effects of unemployment, they are more than prepared to blame the victim for "not wanting to work." So strong is their own commitment to the work ethic and their belief in the infinite availability of traditional work that many have great difficulty understanding how anyone could be unemployed for long. But while some people may not want jobs, the overwhelming majority would work if they could find gainful employment. As the elders approach young people with their views, they are patronized or ignored. In response, the traditional old heads sometimes accuse the young of "sassing" them and being arrogant. One detects hurt feelings among many old heads, who openly complain that the boys and girls of today fail to listen to them as they themselves listened to their elders and the old heads who raised them. An old head of fifty-eight said this:

◐ *I was sitting in the back of the bus the other day down on the South Side and three young boys [anonymous] were sitting across from me. We had stopped, and a crippled man was getting on the bus. I looked over at these young boys and said, "Now, y'all watch this man." They look at me and then they look at him. I said, "Now, just watch. I'm gon' show you something." We all watched the man get on the bus. It must've took him seven or eight minutes. Then I said, "Y'all see that? That man is independent. He ain't got as much as you got. You got all yo' health and strength, and what y'all doing, huh? That man is independent, he's taking care of himself. That ought to give you some inspiration to go out and do something worthwhile. If he can do it, why can't you?"*

You know, them young boys just looked at me and laughed. That's what they did. They weren't listenin' to anything I said. I could tell by the vibes that they weren't studyin' me [paying attention]. They were being disrespectful. Now in the old days, they, at least one of 'em, would have stopped and come over to me and heard me out, and listened to what else I had to say. But today, I just don't know 'bout these young boys. They don't care. They don't listen to their elders. ○

In the traditional black community, old heads had such legitimacy on the ghetto streets that they could chastise unknown boys and girls and expect the parents' support, as was graphically illustrated in the earlier interview with "Mis' Porter." But today, given the high degree of mobility, segmentation, and anonymity within the local black community, which has been exacerbated by persistent poverty and crime combined with an elaborate drug culture, the young people are viewed as unpredictable and threatening. All of this encourages a very cautious approach to strange young people in Northton, if not total avoidance. As one middle-aged old head told me:

○ *I have to watch what I do today, because you just don't know what you gettin' into when you speak to these youngsters. You could get cussed out or cut up. You just don't know, and many of the old heads are not sayin' anything.* ○

The greatest complaint of female old heads is that young girls "don't listen" or that "they've changed so." So many young girls, they say, fail to ask advice or to heed it when it is offered gratuitously by "square old ladies." When rebuffed, they are inclined to call the younger women "fast" or "children who think they're grown." Such derisive comments seem warranted when they see girls on the streets with children in tow or answering a young man's call of "Hey, baby!" from across the street. Indeed, the female old heads know all about such young women, and they affirm their own identities as they discredit others. Likewise many of these young people, in self-defense, work to discredit older people at every turn. They tend to be socially disconnected; they may lack a father in the home or simply have an ineffectual family unit. Thus they have little sense of the values the old heads so badly want them to learn and adopt.

So female old heads have also become more reticent. They keep out of the business of others. And where there is such disengagement by people who could be important role models, there is an even greater tendency for young women to lose their constraint against seriously deviant behavior, from having babies out of wedlock to experimenting with drugs.

The New "Old Heads"

With the influx of the drug culture, new role models are being created. Engaged in fierce competition with the traditional old head—the standard-bearer of yesterday who worked hard in the factories and mills, and in the homes of the well-to-do, coming to value that way of life—the emerging old head is younger and may be the product of a street gang, making money fast and scorning the law and traditional values. If he works, he does so grudgingly. He makes ends meet through the underground economy, dabbling in the drug trade or participating full time. As far as family life goes, he shuns the traditional father's role. His is a "get over" mentality, and as the traditional old heads comment, he is out to beat the next fellow.

The new model for girls is often involved in the "high life" and hangs with her daytime group of friends, occasionally "getting high." She spends her meager income mainly on herself, buying fancy clothes, drugs, and alcohol. Like other members of her peer group, she may have one or two young children, whom she may dress up expensively as they compete over whose baby is the cutest. The babies' fathers may not be immediately involved in their lives, or they may be around part time. The woman may work at a local hospital or fast-food restaurant or she may be on welfare, but she generally has her hands full with child care, social activities, and men.

These emerging figures are in many respects the antithesis of the traditional old heads. The man derides family values and takes little responsibility for the family's financial welfare. He feels hardly any obligation to his string of women and the children he has fathered. In fact he considers it a measure of success if he can get away without being held legally accountable for his out-of-wedlock children. To his hustling mentality, generosity is a weakness. Given his unstable financial situation, he feels used when confronted with the prospect of taking care of someone else.

For him women are so many conquests, whose favors are obtained by "running a game," feigning to love and care for them to get what he wants, only to discard them at the slightest adversity. Self-aggrandizement consumes his whole being and is expressed in his penchant for a glamorous life-style, fine clothes, and fancy cars. On the corner he attempts to influence others by displaying the trappings of success. Eagerly awaiting his message are the young unemployed black men, demoralized by a hopeless financial situation but inclined to look up to this figure and, if they can, to emulate him. But for them broken lives and even early death may be in store. As one traditional old head commented:

◑ *See, when these young kids, especially these thirteen- and fourteen-year-olds, see, we got to get to them to let them know that that drug dealer you see riding down the street today in the Mercedes-Benz, next week you might read about him going to the cemetery, or in prison. We got to get to them and let them know this. Because what is happening is, we find these drug dealers, these kids on the corner, ten, twelve, they come from poverty-stricken families, things are going bad, they don't know half the time whether they gon' eat, what not gon' happen. So they see Joe Doe come by, maybe five or six years older than them. Joe Doe driving a new car. You know, he coming around, a group of guys coming around, and they look at 'em, and they say, "Wow, there go so and so there." He's down [hip], he got all the gold chains, and he got a big role of paper [money] on him, so they thinking, hey, I can do some of this too. And they go into it.*

Now, I know, in a particular neighborhood, the young boys got a drug house in the area. So what the young boys doin', the young boys not selling dope, right? His father don't know this, but a lot of people had to get together and tell his father what was happenin'. The drug house got him watchin' and directin' company [customers]. He standin' on the corner, they payin' him like $50 a day, and that's big money to a kid like twelve or thirteen years old. Stand on the corner and tell somebody to come down to this house down here, that we dealing here. Stand on the corner and tell us when the police is coming. Now, this the kind of stuff that is happening. ◑

For females the high life, welfare, prostitution, single parenthood, and crack addiction await. The high life holds out thrills for young girls, many of whom also seek independence from households with their mothers and sisters and brothers. Involved in sexually active peer groups, many settle for babies and participate in status games for which a "prize"—a cute baby—is the price of admission. They often act like adults too soon, coveting the grown-up life but unable to handle so much of it.

Awaiting them are the young male hipsters, who are there to

trick them into "adulthood," into having "my baby," and leaving home and "be on your own." But this notion of success is little more than a dream that is seldom realized; it gets worked out in the local tenements among young children, meager resources, sometimes drugs, and a further need for "a good time." As such role models proliferate on the streets and in the homes of the community, they blur the line between themselves and the traditional old heads. Many of the young people fail to draw a distinction, having never known any attractive old heads other than those they now see, who provide a limited outlook. Consequently those who are looking for direction to achieve a more conventional life have little direct personal support.

An Old Head's Reaction

But within the Northton community Tyrone Pitts, a traditional old head who has lived there for more than twenty years, is determined to make a difference. He lives on the boundary of the Village and has been much involved in local community life. Like other traditional old heads, he is concerned about his neighborhood; but Mr. Pitts has become so concerned that he has begun to engage in direct action against drugs in the local community. The following account is based on my interview with Mr. Pitts, edited and condensed into a narrative:

⊙ *I had five teams, see. My football team. I was losing my players. Quarterback on crack, and I didn't know it. He didn't know what he was doing. See, I'm standing there one Saturday, telling him to do a running play, and he passing. I thought it was me. So I call it again, same thing happen. I call him over and ask if he's out of his mind. And one of the guys on the team says, "You know, Mr. Pitts, he's on that crack. He don't know what you talking about." That was in the winter. Then in the summer my baseball team, we gettin' ready to have a championship baseball game. And one of my best players, he came but he was bombed out. My baseball pitcher got hooked on it. He was one of my best pitchers. This was my fourteen- to sixteen-year-old group. And this was what made me really start looking around. And then it start dawning on me, you know, what kind of problem I had.*

So I went and started after-school drug and alcohol awareness [programs] and an after-school AIDS awareness, and after-school tutoring. I began to feel these things going on. So I began to start these things in the high school.

Then I looked around, and three or four of my nieces and nephews got hooked. And they got to robbing the family, you know. Yeah, I started to become very aware that it was just such a terrible problem all over. It was just frightening, all through the family, all over. It really got to me. And I didn't see no other leadership. No nothing. Nothing else happening. You know, I had decided I'd do something about this. I couldn't just let it happen like that. So, I'm gon' turn this energy to doing something, instead of just talking about it. Business to be done now. Ballplayers, nephews, nieces. Everytime I look up I say, "Hey, wait a minute. This was one of my favorite kids here." I just had to just admit to myself that if you don't do nothing about it, then you gon' have to take the consequences.

I said, "Where's the leadership?" No one was around. Seem like the youth have taken on false opinions, like gold, funny TV shows, and dancing with any kind of myths. No concerns about education or survival of race. No recollection of history at all. Then on top of it all, drugs. To me this is more frightening than anything I've seen, you know, I mean like what's been dealt to us [blacks]. Lynchings, you know, we could deal with. That inspired us to fight more. That got us together. We weren't taking it. We could handle open affronts to us. But this thing [drugs] has everyone doing things that are really opposite to all we've ever been about.

Northton against Drugs is total reaction. It is a reaction out of frustration at seeing that nobody is in charge, and that somebody has to take charge again. We waiting on young people to say, "We not gon' involve ourselves [with drugs]." We looked up and seen they were being very passive about all this. From an older adult point of view, we had to take over the fight. Old heads had to reappear again. They had normal old heads in the sense of being ten to fifteen years older than the kids. Well these [Northton against Drugs] activists are almost thirty years older. See, the new [traditional old heads] batch didn't appear. There is a gap. A whole group did not appear. They didn't take the baton; that group [cohort] would now be about thirty years old. But they are the problem, see. The new old heads are these hoodlums. There is a gap in the leadership. The new old heads are not doing their parts. They are not doing anything. So the old old heads in fact have to do a double stint.

This was about two and a half years ago. First we were just try-ing to get them [drug dealers] off the corner of Spaulding Street. We had to get the neighbors to see there was no need to fear them, to get rid of the myth that we [the community] are afraid of them. You have to show them how tough we are. The little frightened fifth-grade dropout kids [grown up to be drug dealers]. They are using people's [neighbors'] fear as one of their weapons. We had to stop that.

The second thing is that you have to get everyone who has any gumption left in them to get out and fight. We have to get them [drug dealers] off the corner. You must force the police to do their job. See, the police who know that taxpayers are there [on the corner watching] have to behave differently. See, they were under the impression that didn't nobody black care. I've heard them [police] say that. They say, "What the heck? Don't seem like they care. Their own race don't care." But now we got the senators, the governor. See, all them people have come in. See some black people care. They really have started to react to our tactics. So we've been able to get really enthusiastic. The district attorney, U.S. senator, the governor was out. We've shook them all up.

There are old heads, and then there are bald-head old heads. We have to do the same battle we fought before. Before, we were doing it with anger and enthusiasm [1960s], with hope for the future. Now we are doing it because we ain't got no choice. We are the last line of defense. After this there's pure death [of our community]. That's why we don't mind stepping into the teeth of it. If we don't do that, then there is no hope for anything else. In our group, they come from all walks of life. Every one of them has a job; they know how to keep a job. Eight hours on the job and then seven more in the street, at night [vigils]. They range from semiprofessional to some who are grandmothers [female old heads] who have to work and take care of grandchildren too [because daughters are on crack]. Bus drivers, parking-lot attendants, engineers, teachers, barbers, ministers, and restaurant owners, Village people, and we got Catholic sisters, priests. All kinds of people. The [drug] problem brought all kinds of people together. Black, white, Spanish, and Chinese together. It's a total rainbow coalition. We got a few yuppies in it too. We got some [white] factory workers from Arrington [Irish working-class neighborhood], some police officers, vets. You name a profession, and it's probably represented. Because we got over a thousand people [city-wide]. See, this is what we do. We have about forty-five people. We have policemen. We [Northton against Drugs] pick a drug area that's really heavily infested. We go from our list and find a typical crack house. [We] block the corners, block the streets. Citizens and neigh-

bors. *We stand out there and shout. We have on our white hats [hard hats], our flashlights and bullhorns. We really dressed like a army. We [with the police] lock up the people coming by in cars buying [drugs]. We let some [our] people buy in the car. Then we have walkie-talkies and we call down the street and give the next person the license number. They stop the car. Take the car and the driver. That's been a big tactic. We just did one last night. We had nine cars last night. We lock up dealers that are selling. We stand in front of crack houses and shout 'em down. Tell 'em to come out. We gon' stay there until they stop selling poison to our children. We stay all night. Inside the crack house we find filth, dirt, no kind of living order. Piss in a bucket. Shit in the bucket. No running water. They steal the lights [electricity] from next door; it's usually an abandoned house. Matches all around.*

In some cases we find small children, from one year to eight or nine. The mother brings them because she's on crack. The kids are out there. Hungry. It's just one of the worse sights you ever seen. Sometimes we catch them in the act, laying out, engaging in sex. It's unbelievable.

Then after we raid it [the crack house], we board it up. Soon as the police take them away, we start nailing it up. We put two-by-fours up and plywood boards, and we cement it. We seal it up right away, that night. And when they [drug dealers and customers] get back, they can't get back in there. Police arrest people on the spot. We bricked up twelve crack houses in Northton so far. When we finish with one, we look for the next one. We have a list. Now we teaching other neighborhoods to do the same thing. People think we supposed to stand by and just let them [drug dealers] do it, you know. I won't say it [drugs] won't win, but it won't win with me doing nothing [to fight back]. Its gon' have to catch me. We bust corner guys, alleys, houses. We search them out. We put heat on them. And they never seen no one come after them. They used to cops backing up from them. They teenagers up to thirty years old. This the group that was raised and never had to worry about discipline—you know what I mean. They didn't have any old heads telling them what to do. See, we had old heads [in the old days]. They took an interest in us. All that's gone now. The [young boys] try to go for bad, thinking teachers are afraid of them. They think everybody's afraid of them.

The old heads used to make us play ball, go to school, and tell us about athletes that made it, about jobs, and then take us to their jobs. But that left. They made us take responsibility for the community and one another. They showed wisdom when they talked to us. And I'm just doing what they showed me. I'm doing what they taught me to do. But see, after me, didn't none come around. We missed the other batch. I'm just doing the old head job, making as many as I can. I'm one of the dinosaurs, out of step with everybody. ◖

Tyrone Pitts and others like him may manage to curb some of the drug activity within Northton and other areas of Eastern City. Northton against Drugs has even attracted elements of the Village community, people who might find themselves at odds with Mr. Pitts on certain issues; but they agree profoundly on the issue of drugs. These are positive relationships. Together, through their direct actions, they put drug dealers and users under increasing pressure, driving the drug dealing from one area to the next. As they organize the heretofore passive old head contingent, including numerous frustrated and tired grandmothers who are pushed into service to raise a new generation, certain segments of the community become energized. They hold night vigils, and public officials begin to show interest in their activities, at times perhaps simply looking for publicity photos, at times delivering substantial resources to help such organizations help themselves.

In response to such campaigns, great numbers of local youths pause and think twice about trying drugs or other self-defeating behavior. But drug dealers also become more creative, responding to an important need of the local underclass—employment. The drug dealers promise money and the material "good life" where for many there is little hope. Hence there seems to be an endless supply of youths who are attracted by an often deadly game of "follow the leader." As one goes out of commission, another is more than ready to take his place.

But, with the aid of the Tyrone Pittses of the world, traditional old heads, many of whom have taken their leave over the years, become emboldened. They come out of the woodwork to encourage once again a value system that emphasizes hard work, family life, and church. And this turn of events is positive indeed.

But regardless of their own values, many disadvantaged young blacks living in the ghetto of Northton find themselves surrounded by a complex world that seems arbitrary and unforgiving. Major changes in the regular economy, including cybernetics and the automation of industry, the decline of high-paying industrial jobs, and the rise of a service industry whose lowest levels pay only subsistence wages—combined with the massive influx of drugs into the local community—have exacerbated social breakdown. As inner-city manufacturing jobs have declined, the poorest segments of the community have yet to make an effective adjustment to this reality, and the underground economy competes effectively with the regular job market. All of this has undermined traditional social networks that once brought youths into the world of legitimate work and family life.

A good job is important to anyone, but particularly to someone trying to establish a family and become a productive citizen. What constitutes a "good job"? Thirty years ago, a black migrant from the South could find a job in a factory and take home about $100 a week, amounting to some $5,000 a year. This is equal to approximately $22,000 in today's dollars. In those days a man of the working class could look forward to raising a family with little financial strain. Today unskilled jobs with salaries even approaching this figure are scarce. Good jobs do exist in offices, hospitals, factories, and other large institutions that provide not only good pay but also increasingly important health care and other benefits. But since these jobs require training and are increasingly located in the suburbs—far from Northton and other inner-city areas—many young black men instead work at fast-food restaurants and make $5,000 to $8,500 a year, an amount that would not encourage any responsible person to try to establish a family.

When no good jobs are available the work ethic loses its force, for there is a basic incompatibility between theory and reality. However, some leaders in Northton continue to believe in the infinite availability of work in the traditional sense—high-paying jobs that require little training and skill. These are the words of the minister of a local congregation, who is a part-time taxi driver:

◐ *There are jobs out there for people who want to work. It may not be just what they want, but there is work to be done if you want it bad enough. Honest and honorable work. Something has happened to our community. Now you see a lot more violence than ever before. The drugs are everywhere, taking over our neighborhoods. A lot of our young people don't respect themselves today. Many of them don't know the value of work. Why, when I was growing up, the grown-ups taught us the value of work. I have a deep respect for it. Any man should want to work hard, for dignity comes with a job that enables a man to provide for his family.* ◐

But because of the lack of jobs and the seductive pull of the underground economy, the youngsters the minister preaches to do not believe him. His message falls on deaf ears, and his example is not trusted. Unemployed young men say, "You have to know someone." The common story is that you put in your application, but "you don't hear anything." But even when he knows "someone," the employment problems of a black youth are complicated by prejudice and by distrust about whether he will be a good worker who can be effectively managed. If the worker proves unmanageable, erratic, or unreliable, then the sponsor, who is likely to fit the traditional old head model, "looks bad" and worries about being "messed up" by his own helping efforts. Sponsors thus husband their reputations and limit their recommendations of those who seem the least bit marginal. Hence, increasing numbers of hard-core unemployed black youth have little use for the traditional old head, and the old heads have even less respect for them.

To be sure, there are varying conceptions of work in Northton, and whether a person holds one or another of these conceptions may very well relate to his own place in the world of employment, particularly whether or not he holds a good job. Many of the employed consider the jobless to be personally at fault, their condition the result of their own character flaws—a comfortable perspective. Those without jobs, on the other hand, are inclined to talk about how tough it is for young black men and women. These varying conceptions are voiced in charges and countercharges at local barbershops, taverns, and street corners, pitting one segment of the community against the other. Northton suffers from a host of strains, one being the profound incompatibility between the newly emerging service economy and its potential workers. One strongly related and devastating effect is the perceptible breakdown of the family structure of poor people in Northton. Nowhere are the human consequences of persistent ghetto poverty better illustrated than in the social dynamics of teenage sexual behavior and pregnancy.

4

o

Sex Codes
and Family Life
among
Northton's
Youth

*T*he sexual conduct of poor Northton adolescents is creating growing numbers of unwed parents. Yet many young fathers remain strongly committed to their peer groups. They congregate on street corners, boasting about their sexual exploits and deriding conventional family life. These interconnected realities are born of the difficult socioeconomic situation in the local community.[1] The lack of family-sustaining jobs denies many young men the possibility of forming an economically self-reliant family, the traditional American mark of manhood. Partially in response, the young men's peer group emphasizes sexual prowess as proof of manhood, with babies as evidence. A sexual game emerges as girls are lured by the (usually older) boys' vague but convincing promises of love and marriage. When the girls submit, they often end up pregnant and abandoned, yet they are then eligible for a limited but steady welfare income that may allow them to establish their own households and at times attract other men who need money.

This situation must be viewed in its social and political con-

1. The literature on black family life includes Rainwater (1960, 1966, 1969, 1970); Liebow (1967); Hannerz (1969); Furstenberg (1976); Hammond and Ladner (1969); Green (1941); Arensberg (1937); Whyte (1943); Williams and Kornblum (1985); Schulz (1969); Stack (1974); Staples (1971, 1973); Edelman (1987); Allen (1978); Ladner (1973).

text. It is nothing less than the cultural manifestation of persistent urban poverty. It is a mean adaptation to blocked opportunities and profound lack, a grotesque form of coping by young people constantly undermined by a social system that historically has limited their social options and, until recently, rejected their claims to full citizenship.

The basic sexual codes of Northton youths may not differ fundamentally from those of other young people, but the social, economic, and personal consequences of adolescent sexual conduct vary profoundly for different social classes. Like all adolescents, inner-city youths are subject to intense, hard-to-control urges. Sexual relations, exploitative and otherwise, are common among middle-class teenagers as well, but most middle-class youths take a stronger interest in their future and know what a pregnancy can do to derail it. In contrast, many Northton adolescents see no future to derail—no hope for a tomorrow much different from today—hence they see little to lose by having a child out of wedlock.

This sexual conduct is to a large extent the product of the meshing of two opposing drives, that of the boys and that of the girls. For a variety of reasons tied to the socioeconomic situation, their goals are often diametrically opposed, and sex becomes a contest between them. To many boys, sex is an important symbol of local social status; sexual conquests become so many notches on one's belt. Many of the girls offer sex as a gift in bargaining for the attentions of a young man. As boys and girls try to use each other to achieve their own ends, the reality that emerges sometimes approximates their goals, but it often brings frustration and disillusionment and perpetuates or even worsens their original situation.

In each sexual encounter, there is generally a winner and a loser. The girls have a dream, the boys a desire. The girls dream of being carried off by a Prince Charming who will love them, provide for them, and give them a family. The boys often desire sex without commitment or babies without responsibility for them. It becomes extremely difficult for the boys to see themselves taking on the responsibilities of conventional fathers and husbands in view of their employment prospects. Yet the boy knows what the girl wants and plays that role to get sex. In accepting his advances, she may think she is maneuvering him toward a commitment or that her getting pregnant is the nudge he needs to marry her and give her the life she wants. What she does not see is that the boy, despite his claims, is often incapable of giving her that life. For in reality he has little money, few prospects for earning much, and no wish to be tied to a woman who will have a say in what he does. His loyalty is to his peer group and its norms. When the girl becomes pregnant the boy tends to retreat from her, although, with the help of pressure from family and peers, she may ultimately succeed in getting him to take some responsibility for the child.

Sex: The Game and the Dream

To many inner-city black male youths, the most important people in life are members of their peer groups. They set the standards for conduct, and it is important to live up to those standards, to look good in their eyes. The peer group places a high value on sex, especially what middle-class people call casual sex. But though sex may be casual in terms of commitment to the partner, it is usually taken quite seriously as a measure of the boy's worth. Thus a primary goal of the young man is to find as many willing females as possible. The more "pussy" he gets, the more esteem accrues to him. But the young man not only must "get some," he must prove he is getting it. Consequently he usually talks about girls and sex with any other young man who will listen. Because of the implications sex has for their local social status and esteem, the young men are ready to be regaled with graphic tales of one another's sexual exploits.

The lore of the streets says there is a contest going on between the boy and the girl even before they meet. To the young man the woman becomes, in the most profound sense, a sexual object. Her body and mind are the object of a sexual game, to be won for his personal aggrandizement. Status goes to the winner, and sex is prized not as a testament of love but as testimony to control of another human being. Sex is the prize, and sexual conquests are a game whose goal is to make a fool of the young woman.

The young men describe their successful campaigns as "getting over" young women's sexual defenses. To get over, the young man must devise a "game," whose success is gauged by its acceptance by his peers and especially by women. Relying heavily on gaining the girl's confidence, the game consists of the boy's full presentation of self, including his dress, grooming, looks, dancing ability, and conversation, or "rap."

The rap is the verbal element of the game, whose object is to inspire sexual interest. It embodies the whole person and is thus extremely important to success. Among peer-group members, raps are assessed, evaluated, and divided into weak and strong. The assessment of the young man's rap is, in effect, the evaluation of his whole game. Convincing proof of effectiveness is the "booty": the amount of sex the young man appears to be getting. Young men who are known to fail with women often face ridicule from the group, having their raps labeled "tissue paper," their games seen as inferior, and their identities devalued.

After developing a game over time, through trial and error, a young man is ever on the lookout for players, young women on whom to perfect it. To find willing players is to gain affirmation of self, and the boy's status in the peer group may go up if he can seduce a girl considered to be "choice," "down," or streetwise. On encountering an attractive girl, the boy usually sees a challenge: he attempts to "run his game." The girl usually is fully aware that a game is being attempted; but if the young man is sophisticated or "smooth," or if the girl is young and inexperienced, she may be duped.

In many instances the game plays on the dream that many inner-city girls evolve from their early teenage years. The popular love songs they listen to, usually from age seven or eight, are imbued with a wistful air, promising love and ecstasy to someone "just like you." This dream involves having a boyfriend, a fiancé, a husband, and the fairy-tale prospect of living happily ever after with one's children in a nice house in a good neighborhood—essentially the dream of the middle-class American life-style, complete with nuclear family. It is nurtured by daily watching of television soap operas, or "stories," as the women call them. The heroes and heroines may be white and upper middle class, but such characteristics only make them more attractive. Many girls dream of being the comfortable middle-class housewife portrayed on television, even though they see that their peers can only approximate that role.

When she is approached by a boy, the girl's faith in the dream clouds her view of the situation. A romantically successful boy has a knack for knowing just what is on a girl's mind, what she wants from life, and how she hopes to obtain it. The young man's age—at times four or five years older than the girl—gives him an authoritative edge and makes his readiness to "settle down" more credible. By enacting this role he can shape the interaction, calling up those resources he needs to play the game successfully. He fits himself to be the *man* she wants him to be, but this identity may be exaggerated and temporary, until he gets what he wants. Essentially, he shows her the side of himself that he knows she wants to see, that represents what she wants in a man. For instance, he will sometimes "walk through the woods" with the girl: he might visit at her home and go to church with her family, or even do "manly" chores around the house, showing that he is an "upstanding young man." But all of this may only be part of his game, and after he gets what he wants, he may cast off this aspect of his presentation and reveal something of his true self, as he flits to other women and reverts to behavior more characteristic of his everyday life—that centered on his peer group.

The girl may refuse to accept reports of the boy's duplicity; she must see for herself. Until she completely loses confidence in him, she may find herself strongly defending the young man to friends and family who question her choice. The young woman may know she is being played, but given the effectiveness of his game, his rap, his presentation of self, his looks, his age, his wit, his dancing ability, and his general popularity, infatuation often rules.

Aware of many abandoned young mothers, many a girl fervently hopes that her man is the one who will be different. In addition, the girl's peer group supports her pursuit of the dream, implicitly upholding her belief in the young man's good faith. When a girl does become engaged to be married, there is much excitement, with relatives and friends oohing and aahing over her prospective life. But seldom does this happen, because the boy, for the immediate future, is generally not interested in "playing house," as his peers derisively refer to domestic life.

While pursuing his game, the boy often feigns love and caring, pretending to be a dream man and acting as though he has the best intentions toward the girl. Ironically, in many cases the young man does indeed have good intentions. He may feel profound ambivalence, mainly because such intentions conflict with the values of his peer group and his lack of confidence in his ability to support a family. At times this reality and the male peer group's values are placed in sharp focus by his own deviance from them, as he incurs sanctions for allowing a girl to "rule" him or gains positive reinforcement for keeping her in line. The group sanctions its members with demeaning labels such as "pussy," "pussy whipped," or "househusband," causing them to posture in a way that clearly distances them from such characterizations.

At times, however, a boy earnestly attempts to be the "dream man," with honorable intentions of "doing right" by the young woman, of marrying her and living happily ever after according to their version of middle-class propriety. But the reality of his poor employment prospects makes it hard to follow through (see Anderson 1978, 1987; Wilson 1980; Anderson and Sawhill 1980).

Unable to realize himself as the young woman's provider in the American middle-class tradition, which the peer group often labels "square," the young man may become even more committed to his game. In his ambivalence, he may go so far as to "make plans" with the girl, including house hunting and shopping for furniture. A twenty-three-year-old woman who at seventeen became a single parent of a baby girl said this:

○ *Yeah, they'll [boys will] take you out. Walk you down to Center City, movies, window shop [laughs]. They point in the window, "Yeah, I'm gonna get this. Wouldn't you like this? Look at that nice livin' room set." Then they want to take you to his house, go to his room: "Let's go over to my house, watch some TV." Next thing you know your clothes is off and you in bed havin' sex, you know.* ○

Such shopping trips carry important psychological implications for the relationship, serving as a salve that heals wounds and erases doubt about the young man's intentions. The young woman may report to her parents or friends on her latest date or shopping trip, describing the furniture they priced and the supposed payment terms. She continues to have hope, which he supports by "going with" her, letting her and others know that she is his "steady"—though to maintain status within his peer group, she should not be his only known girl. But for the young man, making plans and successive shopping trips may simply be elements of his game—often nothing more than a stalling device to keep the girl hanging on so he can keep her social and sexual favors.

In many cases, the more he seems to exploit the young woman, the higher is his regard within the peer group. But to consolidate his status, he feels moved at times to show others he is in control, which is not always easy to accomplish. Many young women are "strong," highly independent and assertive, and there may be a contest of wills between the two, with arguments and fights developing in public over the most trivial issues. She is not a simple victim, and the roles in the relationship are not to be taken for granted but must be negotiated repeatedly. To prove his dominance unequivocally, he may attempt to "break her down" in front of her friends and his, "showing the world who's boss." If the young woman wants him badly enough, she will meekly go along with the performance for the implicit promise of his continued attentions, if not love. A more permanent relationship approximating the woman's dream of matrimony and domestic tranquillity is often what is at stake in her mind, though she may know better.

As the contest continues and the girl hangs on, she may seem to have been taken in by the boy's game, particularly by his convincing rap, his claims of commitment to her and her well-being. But in this contest, anything is fair. The girl may play along, becoming manipulative and aggressive, or the boy may lie, cheat, or otherwise misrepresent himself to obtain or retain her favors. In many of the sexual encounters informants relate, one person is seen as the winner, the other as the loser. As one male informant said:

 ◐ *They trickin' them good. Either the woman is trickin' the man, or the man is trickin' the woman. Good! They got a trick. She's thinkin' it's [the relationship] one thing, he playin' another game, you know. He thinkin' she alright, and she doing something else.* ◐

In the social atmosphere of the peer group, the quality of the boy's game emerges as a central issue, and whatever lingering ambivalence he has about his commitment to acting as husband and provider may be resolved in favor of peer-group status.

In pursuing his game, the young man often uses a supporting cast of other women, at times playing one off against the other. For example, he may orchestrate a situation in which he is seen with another woman. Or secure in the knowledge that he has other women to fall back on, he might start a fight with his steady to upset her sense of complacency, thus creating dynamic tension within the relationship, which he uses to his own advantage. The young woman thus may begin to doubt her hold on the man, which can bring about a precipitous drop in her self-esteem.

The boy may take pride because he thinks he is making a fool of the girl, and when he is confident of his dominance he may "play" the young woman, "running his game," making her "love" him. Some young men will brag that they are "playing her like a fiddle," meaning they are in full control of the situation. Though his plan sometimes backfires and he looks like the fool, often the young man's purpose is to prove he "has the girl's nose open," that she is sick with love for him. He aims to maneuver her into a state of blissful emotionality, showing that she, not he, is the "weak" member in the relationship (see Short and Strodtbeck 1965; Horowitz 1983).

During this emotional turmoil the young girl may well become careless about birth control, which is seen by the community, especially the males, as being her responsibility. She may believe the boy's rap, becoming convinced that he means what he says about taking care of her, that her welfare is his primary concern. Moreover, she wants desperately to believe that if she becomes pregnant he will marry her or at least be more obligated to her than to others he has been "messing with." Perhaps all he needs is a little nudge.

Yet the girl may think little about the job market and the boy's prospects. She may underestimate peer-group influences and the effect of other "ladies" that she knows or at least suspects are in his life. If she is in love, she may be sure that a child and the profound obligation a child implies will make such a strong bond that all the other issues will go away. Her thinking is often clouded by the prospect of winning at the game of love. Becoming pregnant can be a way to fulfill the persistent dream of bliss.

For numerous women, when the man turns out to be unobtainable, just having his baby is enough. Sometimes a woman seeks out a popular and "fine," or physically attractive young man in hopes that his good looks will grace her child, resulting in a "prize"—a beautiful baby. Moreover, becoming pregnant can become an important part of the competition for the attentions or even delayed affection of a young man, a profound if socially shortsighted way of making a claim on him.

Pregnancy

Up to the point of pregnancy, given the norms of his peer group, the young man could be characterized as simply messing around. The fact of pregnancy brings a sudden reality to the relationship. Life-altering events have occurred, and the situation is usually perceived as serious. She is pregnant, and he could be held legally responsible for the child's long-term financial support. If the young couple were unclear about their intentions before, things may crystallize. She now considers him seriously as a mate. Priorities begin to emerge in the boy's mind. He has to decide whether to claim the child as his or to shun the woman who has been the object of his affections.

To own up to a pregnancy is to go against the peer-group ethic of "hit and run." Other values at risk of being flouted include the subordination of women and freedom from formal conjugal ties, and some young men are not interested in taking care of somebody else, when it means having less themselves. In this social context of persistent poverty, they have come to devalue the conventional marital relationship, viewing women as a burden and children as even more of one. Moreover, a young man wants "to come as I want and go as I please," indulging important values of freedom and independence. Accordingly, from the perspective of the peer group, any such male-female relationship should be on the man's terms. Thus, in understanding the boy's relationship with the girl, his attitudes toward his limited financial ability and his need for personal freedom should not be underestimated.

Another important attitude of the male peer group is that most girls have multiple sexual partners: "If she was fucking you, then she was fucking everybody else." Whether or not there is truth to this in a particular case, a common working conception says it is true about young women in general. It is a view with which many young men approach females, assuming they are socially and morally deficient. The double standard is at work, and for any amount of sexual activity women are more easily discredited than men.

To be sure, there is a fair amount of promiscuity among the young men and women. In this atmosphere, doubt about paternity complicates many pregnancies. In self-defense, the young man often chooses to deny fatherhood; few are willing to "own up" to a pregnancy they can reasonably question. Among their peers, the young men gain ready support; a man who is "tagged" with fatherhood has been caught in the "trick bag." The boy's first desire, though he may know better, is often to attribute the pregnancy to someone else.

The boy may be genuinely confused and uncertain about his role in the pregnancy, feeling great ambivalence and apprehension over his impending fatherhood. If he admits paternity and "does right" by the girl, his peer group likely will label him a chump, a square, or a fool. If he does not, few social sanctions are applied, and he may even win points for his defiant stand, with his peers viewing him as fooling the mother and "getting over." But here there may also be ambivalence, for a certain regard is given to men who father children out of wedlock, as long as they are not "caught" and made financially responsible to support a family on something other than their own terms. Hence, the boy may give—and benefit from—mixed messages: one to the girl and perhaps the authorities, another to his peer group. To resolve his ambivalence and apprehension, the boy might at this point attempt to discontinue or cool his relationship with the expectant mother, particularly as she begins to show clear signs of pregnancy.

Upon giving birth, the young woman wants badly to identify the father of her child, at the insistence of her family and for her own peace of mind. When the baby is born she may, out of desperation, arbitrarily designate a likely young man as the father; at times it may be simply a lover who is employed. As I mentioned, there may be genuine doubt about paternity. In this atmosphere there are often charges and countercharges, with the appointed young man usually denying responsibility and easing himself out of the picture over time or accepting it and playing his new role of father part time.

There is sometimes an incentive for the young woman not to identify the father, even though she and the local community know "whose baby it is," for a check from the welfare office is much more dependable than the irregular support payments of a sporadically employed youth.

To be sure, many young men are determined to do right by the young woman, to try out the role of husband and father, often acceding to the woman's view of the matter and working to establish a family. Such young men often are only marginal members of their peer groups. They tend to emerge from nurturing families with positive outlooks, and religious observance is important in their lives. Locally, they are viewed as decent people. In addition, these men usually are employed, have a positive sense of the future, and tend to enjoy a deep and abiding relationship with the young woman that can withstand the trauma of youthful pregnancy.

Barring such resolution, a young man may rationalize his marriage as a "trap" the woman has tricked him into. This viewpoint may be seen as his attempt to make simultaneous claims on values of the peer group and on those of conventional society. As one young man said in an interview:

○ *My wife done that to me. Before we got married, when we had our first baby, she thought, well, hey, if she had the baby, then she got me, you know. And that's the way she done me. [She] thought that's gon' trap me. That I'm all hers after she done have this baby. So, a lot of women, they think like that. Now, I was the type of guy, if I know it was my baby, I'm taking care of my baby. My ol' lady*

[wife], *she knowed that. She knowed that anything that was mine, I'm taking care of mine. This is why she probably wouldn't mess around or nothing, 'cause she wanted to lock me up.* ◑

In general, however, persuading the youth to become "an honest man" is not simple. It is often a very complicated social affair involving cajoling, social pressure, and at times physical threats.

An important factor in determining whether the boy does right by the girl is the presence of the girl's father in the home (see Williams and Kornblum 1985). When a couple first begins to date, some fathers will "sit the boy down" and have a ritual talk; single mothers may play this role as well, sometimes more aggressively than fathers. Certain parents with domineering dispositions will "as a man," make unmistakable territorial claims on the dwelling, informing the boy that "this is my house, I pay the bills here," and that all activities occurring under its roof are his singular business. In such a household the home has a certain defense. At issue here essentially are male turf rights, a principle intuitively understood by the young suitor and the father of the girl. The boy may feel a certain frustration owing to the need to balance his desire to run his game against his fear of the girl's father.

Yet the boy often can identify respectfully with the father, thinking of how he might behave if the shoe were on the other foot. Both "know something"; that is, they know that each has a position to defend. The boy knows in advance that he will have to answer to the girl's father and the family unit more generally. If the girl becomes pregnant, he will be less likely to summarily leave her. Further, if the girl has brothers at home who are about her age or older, they too may influence his behavior. Such men, as well as uncles and male cousins, not only possess a degree of moral authority but may offer the believable threat of violence. As one boy said in an interview:

◑ *The boys kinda watch theyself more [when a father is present]. Yeah, there's a lot of that going on. The daddy, they'll clown [act out violence] about them young girls. They'll hurt somebody about they daughters. Other relatives too. They'll all get into it. The boy know they don't want him messing over they sister. That guy will probably take care of that girl better than the average one out there in the street.* ◑

In such circumstances, not only does the boy think twice about running his game, but the girl thinks twice about allowing him to do so.

A related important defense against youthful pregnancy is the conventional inner-city family unit. Two parents, together with the extended network of cousins, aunts, uncles, grandparents, nieces, and nephews, can form a durable team, a viable supportive group engaged to fight in a committed manner the problems confronting inner-city teenagers, including drugs, crime, pregnancy, and lack of social mobility (see Schulz 1969; Willie and Weinandy 1970; Perkins 1975). This unit, when it does endure, tends to be equipped with a survivor's mentality. It has weathered a good many storms, which have given it wisdom and strength. The parents are known in the community as "strict"; they impose curfews and tight supervision, demanding to know their children's whereabouts at all times. Determined that their offspring will not become casualties of the environment, they scrutinize their children's associates, rejecting those who seemed to be "no good" and encouraging others who seem on their way to "amount to something."

In contrast, in those domestic situations where there is only one adult—say, a woman with two or three teenage daughters, with no male presence—the dwelling may be viewed, superficially at least, as an unprotected nest. The local boys may be attracted to the home as a challenge, just to test it out, to see if they can "get over" by charming or seducing the women who live there. In such a setting no man, the figure the boys are prepared to respect, is there to keep them in line. Girls in this vulnerable situation may become pregnant earlier than those living in homes more closely resembling nuclear families. A young man made the following comments:

◑ *I done seen where four girls grow up under their mama. The mama turn around and she got a job between 3:00 P.M. and 11:00 P.M. These little kids, now they grow up like this. Mama working three to eleven o'clock at night. They kinda raise theyself. What they know? By the time they get thirteen or fourteen, they trying everything under the sun. And they ain't got nobody to stop 'em. Mama gone. Can't nobody else tell 'em what to do. Hey, all of 'em pregnant by age sixteen. And they do it 'cause they wanta get out on they own. They can get they own baby, they get they own [welfare] check, they get they own apartment. They wanta get away from mama.* ◑

The Baby Club

In the glaring absence of a strong family unit, a close-knit group of "street girls" often fills a social, moral, and family void in the young girl's life. With the help of her peers and sometimes older siblings and the usually very limited supervision of parents, after a certain age she primarily raises herself. On the street, she plays seemingly innocent games, but through play she becomes socialized into a peer group. Many of these neighborhood "street kids," with little parental supervision, are left to their own devices, staying out late at night, sometimes till 1:00 or 2:00 A.M. even on school nights. By the age of ten or twelve many are aware of their bodies and, according to some residents, are beginning to engage in sexual relations with very little knowledge about their bodies and even less about the long-term consequences of their behavior.

The street kids become increasingly committed to their peer groups, surviving by their wits, being "cool," and having fun. Some girls may begin to have babies by age fifteen or sixteen, and soon others follow. In the minds of many, at least in the short run, this behavior is rewarded.

As the girl becomes more deeply involved, the group helps shape her dreams, social agenda, values, and aspirations. The "hip" group operates as an "in crowd" in the neighborhood, although more conventional people refer to its members as "fast" and "slick" and believe they have "tried everything" at an early age. Girls raised by strict parents are considered by this hip crowd to be "lame" or "square" and may suffer social ostracism or at least ridicule, thus segmenting the neighborhood even further. The street peer group becomes a powerful social magnet, drawing in those only loosely connected to other sources of social and emotional support, particularly the weak and impoverished ghetto family headed by a single female.

When some of the girls get pregnant, it becomes important for others to have a baby, particularly as their dream of "the good life," usually with an "older man" of twenty-one or twenty-two, unravels. They may settle for babies as a consolation prize, enhancing and rationalizing motherhood as they attempt to infuse their state of value. Some people speak of these girls as "sprouting babies," and having a baby may become an expected occurrence.

As the babies arrive, the peer group takes on an even more provocative feature: the early play and social groups develop into "baby clubs." The girls give one another social support, praising each other's babies. But they also use their babies to compete, on the premise that the baby is an extension of the mother and reflects directly on her. This competition, carried on at social gatherings such as birthday parties, weddings, church services, and spontaneous encounters of two or more people, often takes the form of comparing one baby to another. First the baby's features are noted, usually along lines of "cuteness," "spoiledness," texture of hair, skin color, and grooming and dress. To enhance her chances at such competitions and status games, the young mother often feels the need to dress her baby in the latest and most expensive clothes "that fit" (rather than a size larger that the baby can grow into): a "$50 sweater" for a three-month-old or "$40 Reebok sneakers" for a six-month-old. This status-oriented behavior provokes criticism from more mature people, including some mothers and grandmothers. As one forty-five-year-old grand-mother said:

⬤ *Oh, they can't wait until check day [when welfare checks arrive] so they can go to the store. I listen at 'em, talking about what they gon' buy this time. [They say,] "Next time my check come, I'm gon' buy my baby this, I'm gon' buy my baby that." And that's exactly what they will do, expensive stores, too. The more expensive, the better. Some will buy a baby an expensive outfit that the baby only gon' wear for a few months. I seen a girl go . . . went out, and she paid, I think she paid $45 for a outfit. I think the baby was about six weeks old. Now, how long was that child gon' wear that outfit? For that kind of money? They do these silly, silly things.* ⬤

And as a twenty-three-year-old woman college graduate from Northton (who did not become pregnant) said:

⬤ *Once there was a sale at the church at Thirteenth and Buford. A friend of mine had some baby clothes for sale. They were some cute clothes, but they weren't new. They were sweat suits, older things. The young girls would just pass them by. Now the older women, the grandmothers, would come by and buy them for their grandchildren. But the girls, sixteen or seventeen, had to have a decked-out baby. No hand-me-downs. Some would pay up to $40 for a pair of Nike sneakers. They go to Carl's [an expensive downtown children's boutique]. And the babies sometimes are burning up in the clothes, but they dress them up anyway. The baby is like a doll in some ways. They [young mothers] sometimes do more to clothe the baby than to feed the baby.* ⬤

But the seeming irresponsibility of the young mother evolves in a logical way. For a young woman who fails to secure a strong commitment from a man, a baby becomes a partial fulfillment of the "good life." The baby club deflects criticism of the young mothers and gives them a certain status. "Looking good" negates the generalized notion that a teenage mother has "messed up" her life, and in this sea of destitution nothing is more important than to show others you are doing all right.

In public gathering places, the mothers lobby for compliments, smiles, and nods of approval and feel very good when they are forthcoming, since they signal affirmation and pride. On Sundays, the new little dresses and suits come out and the cutest babies are passed around, and this attention serves as a social measure of the person.

The young mothers who form such baby clubs develop an ideology counter to that of more conventional society, one that not only approves of but enhances their position. In effect, they work to create value and status by inverting that of the girls who do not become pregnant. The teenage mother derives status from her baby; hence her preoccupation with the impression that the baby makes and her willingness to spend inordinately large sums toward that end.

Having come to terms with the street culture, many of these young women have an overwhelming desire to grow up, a passage best expressed by the ability to "get out on her own." In terms of traditional inner-city experience, this means setting up one's own household, preferably with a "good man" through marriage and family. Sometimes a young woman attempts to accomplish this by purposely becoming pregnant, perhaps hoping the baby's father will marry her and help to realize her dream of domestic respectability. But there are an undetermined but some say growing number of young women, unimpressed with the lot of young single men, who want to establish households on their own, without the help or the burden of a man (see the discussion of the pool of marriageable males in Wilson 1987).

Sometimes a young woman, far from becoming victimized, will take charge of the situation, assertively using the man for her own ends, perhaps extracting money for his "spending her time." At parties and social gatherings, such women may initiate the sexual relationship, exerting some control of the situation from the start. Some men say that such "new" women are "just out to use you," to become pregnant "for the [welfare] check, then she through with you." Consistent with such reports, in the economically hard-pressed local community it is becoming socially acceptable for a young woman to have children out of wedlock—supported by a regular welfare check.

In this way, persistent poverty affects norms of the ghetto culture, such as the high value placed on children (see Lewis 1975; Tenhouten 1970; Dash 1989). Babies may become a sought-after symbol of status, of passage to adulthood, of being a "grown" woman. It may be less a question of whether the girl is going to have children than of when, for she may see herself as having little to lose and something to gain by becoming pregnant.

In their small, intimate groupings, the women discuss their afternoon soap operas, men, children, and social life, and they welcome new members to their generally affirmative and supportive gatherings. Although they may deride men for their actions, especially their lack of commitment, at the same time they accommodate such behavior, viewing it as characteristic of men in their environment. Yet in their conversations the women draw distinctions between "the nothin'" and the "good man." The nothin' is "a man who is out to use every woman he can for himself. He's somethin' like a pimp. Don't care 'bout nobody but himself." One older single mother, who now considers herself wiser, said:

◐ *I know the difference now between a nothin' and a good man. I can see. I can smell him. I can just tell a nothin' from the real thing. I can just look at a guy sometimes, you know, the way he dresses, you know. The way he carries himself. The way he acts, the way he talks. I can tell the bullshitter. Like, you know, "What's up, baby?" You know. "What's you want to do?" A nice guy wouldn't say, "What's you want to do?" A nice guy wouldn't say, "What's up, baby? What's goin' on?" Actin' all familiar, tryin' to give me that line. Saying, "You wan' a joint? You wan' some blow? You wan' some 'caine?" Hollerin' in the street, you know. I can tell 'em. I can just smell 'em.* ◐

The good man is one who is considerate of his mate and provides for her and her children, but at the same time he runs the risk of being seen as a pussy by the women as well as by his peer group. This inversion in the idea of the good man underscores the ambivalent position of girls squeezed between their middle-class dreams and the ghetto reality. As one woman said with a laugh, "There are so many sides to the bad man. We see that, especially in this community. We see more bad men than we do good. I see them [inner-city black girls] running over that man if he's a wimp, ha-ha."

Family support is often available for the young pregnant woman, though members of her family are likely to remind her from time to time that she is "messed up." She looks forward to the day when she is "straight" again—when she has given birth to the baby and has regained her figure. Her comments to girls who are not pregnant tend to center wistfully on better days. If her boyfriend stops seeing her regularly, she may attribute this to the family's negative comments about him, but also to her pregnancy, saying time and again, "When I get straight, he'll be sorry; he'll be jealous then." She knows that her pregnant state is devalued by her family as well as her single peers, who are free to date and otherwise consort with men, and she may long for the day when she can do so again.

When the baby arrives, however, the girl finds that her social activities continue to be significantly curtailed. She is often surprised by how much time and involvement being a mother takes. In realizing her new identity, she may very consciously assume the demeanor of a grown woman, emphasizing her freedom in social relations and her independence. During the period of adjustment to her new status, she has to set her mother straight about "telling me what to do." Other family members also go through a learning process, getting used to the young woman's new status, which she tries on with a variety of stops and starts. In fact, she is working at growing up.

Frustrated by the baby's continuing needs, especially as she becomes physically straight again, the girl may develop an intense desire to get back into the dating game. Accordingly, she may foist her child-care responsibilities onto her mother and sisters, who initially are eager to help. In time, however, they tire, and even extremely supportive relations can become strained. In an effort to see her daughter get back to normal, the grandmother, often in her midthirties or early forties, may simply informally adopt the baby as another one of her own, in some cases completely usurping the role of mother. In this way the young parent's mother may minimize the deviance the girl displayed by getting pregnant while taking genuine pride in her new grandchild.

Of Men and Women, Mothers and Sons

The relationship between the young man and woman undergoes a basic change during pregnancy; once the baby is born, it draws on other social forces, most notably their families. The role of the girl's family has been discussed. The boy's family is important in a different way. There is often a special bond between a mother and her grown son that competes with the claims of his girlfriend. The way this situation is resolved has important consequences for the family and its relationship to the social structure of the community.

In teenage pregnancy among the poor, the boy's mother often plays a significant role, while the role of the father, if he is present at all, is understated. Depending on the woman's personality, her practical experience in such matters, and the girl's family situation, the mother's role may be subtle or explicit. At times she becomes deeply involved with the young woman, forming a female bond that becomes truly motherly, involving guidance, protection, and control.

From the moment the boy's mother finds out a young woman is pregnant, it is important whether she knows the girl. If the young woman "means something" to her son, she is likely to know her or at least know about her; her son has talked about the girl. On hearing the news of the pregnancy, the mother's reaction might be anything from disbelief that her son could be responsible to certainty, even before seeing the child, that her son is the father. If she knows the girl's character, she is in a position to judge for herself. Here her relationship with the girl before "all this" happened comes into play, for if she likes her, there is a good chance the boy's mother will side with her. The mother may even go so far as to engage in playful collusion against her son, a man, to get him to do right by the girl. Here, we must remember that in this economically circumscribed social context, particularly from a woman's point of view, many men are known not to do right by their women and children. To visit certain streets of Northton is to see a proliferation of small children and women, with fathers and husbands largely absent or playing their roles part time. These considerations help explain the significance of the mother's role in determining how successful the girl will be in getting the boy to take some responsibility for her child.

The mother may be constrained, at least initially, because she is unsure her son actually fathered the child. She may be careful about showing her doubt, however, thinking that when the baby arrives she will be able to tell "in a minute" if her son is the father. Thus, during the pregnancy the young man's mother nervously waits, wondering whether her son will be blamed for a pregnancy not of his doing or whether she will really be a grandmother. In fact both the boy's and the girl's relatives often constitute an extended family-in-waiting, socially organized around the idea that the "truth" will be told when the baby arrives. Unless the parties are very sure, marriage—if agreed to at all—may be held off until after the birth.

When the baby arrives plans may be carried out, but often on condition that the child passes inspection. The presumed father generally lies low in the weeks after the baby's birth. He usually does not visit the baby's mother regularly in the hospital; he may come once, if at all. In an effort to make a paternal connection, some girls name the baby after the father, but by itself this strategy is seldom effective. In cases of doubtful paternity the boy's mother, sisters, aunts, or other female relatives or close family friends may form visiting committees to see the baby, though sometimes the child is brought to them. This inspection is often surreptitious, usually without the acknowledgment of the girl or her family. The visitors may go to the girl's house in shifts, with a sister dropping in now, the mother another time, and a friend still another. Social pleasantries notwithstanding, the object is always the same: to see if the baby "belongs" to the boy. Typically, after such visits these women will compare notes, commenting on the baby's features and on whom it favors. Some will blurt out, "Ain't no way that's John's baby." People may disagree, and a dispute may ensue. In the community, the identity of the father becomes a hot topic. The viewpoints have much to do with who the girl is, whether she is a "good girl" or "bad girl," and whether she has been accepted by the boy's family. If the girl is well integrated into the family, doubts about the paternity may be slowly put to rest, with nothing more said about it.

The word carrying the most weight in this situation is often that of the boy's mother, as shown in this account by a young man:

◐ *I had a lady telling me that she had to check out a baby that was supposed to be her grandbaby. She said she had a young girl that was trying to put a baby on her son, so she said she fixing to take the baby and see what blood type the baby is to match it with her son to see if he the daddy. 'Cause she said she know he wasn't the daddy. And she told the girl that, but the girl was steady trying to stick the baby on her son. She had checked out the baby's features and everything. She knowed that the blood type wasn't gon' match or nothing. So, the young girl just left 'em alone.* ◐

If the child clearly favors the alleged father physically, there may be strong pressure for the boy to claim the child and take on his responsibilities. This may take a year or more, since the resemblance may not initially be so apparent. But when others begin to make comments such as, "Lil' Tommy look like Maurice just spit him out [is his spitting image]," the boy's mother may informally adopt the child into her extended family and signal others to do the same. She may see the child regularly and develop a special relationship with the child's mother. Because of her social acknowledgment of her son's paternity, the boy himself is bound to accept the child. Even if he does not claim the child legally, in the face of the evidence he will often acknowledge "having something to do with him." As one informant said:

◐ *If the baby look just like him, he should admit to hisself that that's his. Some guys have to wait 'til the baby grow up a little to see if the baby gon' look like him 'fore they finally realize that was his'n. Because yours should look like you, you know, should have your features and image.* ◐

Here the young man informally acknowledging paternity may feel pressure to "take care of his own." But owing to his limited employment and general lack of money, he feels he "can only do what he can" for his child. Many young men enact the role of father part time. A self-conscious young man may be spied on the street carrying a box of Pampers, the name used generically for all disposable diapers, or cans of Similac—baby formula—on the way to see his child and its mother. As the child ages a bond may develop, and the young man may take a boy for a haircut or shopping for shoes or clothes. He may give the women token amounts of money. Such support symbolizes a father providing for his child. In fact, however, the support often comes only sporadically and—importantly—in exchange for the woman's favors, social or sexual. Such support may thus depend upon the largess of the man and may function as a means of controlling the woman.

If the woman "gets papers" on the man, or legalizes his relationship to the child, she may sue for regular support—what people call "going downtown on him." If her case is successful, the young man's personal involvement in making child support payments may be eliminated: they may simply be deducted from his salary, if he has one. Sometimes the woman's incentive for getting papers may emerge when the young man gets a "good job," particularly one with a major institution that includes family benefits. While sporadically employed the youth may have had no problem with papers, but when he finds a steady job he may be served with a summons. In some cases, particularly if they have two or three children out of wedlock by different women, young men lose the incentive to work, for much of their pay will go to someone else. After the mothers of his four children got papers on him and he began to see less and less of his money, one of my informants quit his job and returned to the street corner.

Under some conditions the male peer group will pressure a member to admit paternity. Most important is that there be no doubt in the group members' own minds as to the baby's father. When it is clear that the baby resembles the young man, the others may strongly urge him to claim it and help the mother financially. If he fails to acknowledge the baby, group members may do it themselves by publicly associating him with the child, at times teasing him about his failure "to take care of what's his." As one young man said:

○ *My partner's [friend's] girlfriend came up pregnant. And she say it's his, but he not sure. He waitin' on the baby, waitin' to see if the baby look like him. I tell him, "Man, if that baby look just like you, then it was yours! Ha-ha." He just kinda like just waitin'. He ain't claimin' naw, saying the baby ain't his. I keep tellin' him, "If that baby come out looking just like you, then it gon' be yours, partner." And there on the corner all of 'em will tell him, "Man, that's yo' baby." They'll tell him.* ○

Although the peer group may urge its members to take care of their babies, they stop short of urging them to marry the mothers. In general, young men are assumed not to care about raising a family or being part of one. Some of this lack of support for marriage is due to poor employment prospects, but it also may have to do with general distrust of women they are not related to. As my informant continued:

○ *They don't even trust her that they were the only one she was dealin' [having sex] with. That's a lot of it. But the boys just be gettin' away from it [the value of a family] a whole lot. They don't want to get tied down by talkin' about playin' house, ha-ha, what they call it nowadays, ha-ha. Yeah, ha-ha, they sayin' they ain't playin' house.* ○

In a great number of cases, peer group or no, the boy will send the girl on her way even if she is carrying a baby he knows is his. He often lacks a deep feeling for a woman and children as a family unit and does not want to put up with married life, which he sees as giving a woman something to say about how he spends his time. This emphasis on "freedom" is generated and supported in large part by the peer group itself. Even if a man agrees to marriage, it is usually considered to be only a trial. After a few months, many young husbands have had enough.

This desire for freedom, which the peer group so successfully nurtures, is deeply ingrained in the boys. It is, in fact, nothing less than the desire to perpetuate the situation they had in their mothers' homes. A son is generally well bonded to his mother, something she tends to encourage from birth. It may be that sons, particularly the eldest, are groomed to function as surrogate husbands because of the high rate of family dissolution among poor blacks (see Schulz 1969; Heiss 1975; Perkins 1975; Mangum and Seninger 1978).

Many young boys thus want what they consider an optimal situation. In the words of peer-group members, they want it all: they want a "main squeeze"—a steady and reliable female partner who mimics the role their mothers played, a woman who will cook, clean, and generally serve them, with few questions about the "ladies" they may be seeing and have even less to say about their male friends. The boy has grown accustomed to home-cooked meals and the secure company of his family, in which his father was largely absent and could not tell him what to do. He was his own boss, essentially raising himself with the help of his peer group and perhaps any adult [possibly an old head] who would listen but not interfere. For many, such a life is too much to give up in exchange for the "problems of being tied down to one lady, kids, bills, and all that." The young man's home situation with his mother thus competes effectively with the household he envisions with a woman his peer group is fully prepared to discredit.

Now that he is grown, the young man may want what he had while growing up plus a number of ladies on the side. At the same time he wants his male friends, whom he must impress in ways that may be inconsistent with being a good family man. Since the young men from the start have little faith in marriage, small things can inspire them to retreat to their mothers or whatever families they may have left behind. Some spend their time going back and forth between two families; if their marriages seem not to be working, they may ditch them and their wives, though perhaps keeping up with the children. At all times they must show others that they run the family, that they "wear the pants." This is the cause of many of the domestic fights in the ghetto. When there is a question of authority, the domestic situation may run into serious trouble, often leading the young man to abandon the idea of marriage or of "dealing" with only one woman. To "hook up" with a woman, to marry her, is to give her something to say about "what you're doing, or where you're going, or where you been." For many young men, such constraint is unacceptable.

In endeavoring to have it all, many men become part-time fathers and husbands, seeing the women and children on their own terms, when they have time, and making symbolic purchases for the children. In theory, the part-time father retains his freedom while having limited commitment to the woman and the little ones "calling me daddy." In many instances he does not mind putting up with the children, given his generally limited role in child rearing, but he does mind tolerating the woman, whom he sees as a significant threat to his freedom. As one man commented about marriage:

◐ *Naw, they [young men] getting away from that. They ain't going in for that 'cause they want to be free. Now, see, I ended up getting married. I got a whole lot of boys ducking that. Unless this is managed, it ain't no good. My wife cleans, takes care of the house. You got a lot of guys, they don't want to be cleanin' no house, and do the things you got to do in the house. You need a girl there to do it. If you get one, she'll slow you down. The guys don't want it.* ◐

Unless a man could handle his wife so that she would put few constraints on him, he may reason that he had better stay away from marriage. But with a growing sense of being independent from men, financially and otherwise, fewer women may allow themselves to be treated so.

As jobs become scarce for young black men, their success as breadwinners and traditional husbands declines. The notion is that with money comes control of the domestic situation. Without money or jobs, many men are unable to "play house" to their own satisfaction. It is much easier and more fun to stay home and "take care of Mama," some say, when taking care consists of "giving her some change for room and board," eating good food, and being able "to come as I want to and to go as I please." Given the present state of the economy, such an assessment of their domestic outlook appears in many respects adaptive.

Sex, Poverty, and Family Life

In conclusion, the basic factors at work here are youth, ignorance, the culture's receptiveness to babies, and the young man's resort to proving his manhood through sexual conquests that often result in pregnancy. These factors are exacerbated by persistent poverty. In the present hard times, a primary concern of many inner-city residents is to get along as best as they can. In the poorest communities, the primary financial sources are low-paying jobs, crime—including drugs —and public assistance. Some of the most desperate people devise a variety of confidence games to separate others from their money.

A number of men, married and single, incorporate their sexual lives into their more generalized efforts at economic survival. Many will seek to "pull" a woman with children on welfare, since she usually has a special need for male company, time on her hands, and a steady income. As they work to establish their relationships, they play a game not unlike the one young males use to "get over" sexually. There is simply a clearer economic motive in many of these cases. When the woman receives her check from the welfare department or money from other sources, she may find herself giving up part of it to ensure male company.

The economic noose restricting ghetto life encourages both men and women to try to extract maximum personal benefit from sexual relationships. The dreams of a middle-class life-style nurtured by young inner-city women are thwarted by the harsh socioeconomic realities of the ghetto. Young men without job prospects cling to the support offered by their peer groups and their mothers and shy away from lasting relationships with girlfriends. Thus girls and boys alike scramble to take what they can from each other, trusting only their own ability to trick the other into giving them something that will establish their version of the good life—the best life they can put together in their environment.

We should remember that the people we are talking about are very young—mainly from fifteen years old to their early twenties. Their bodies are grown, but they are emotionally immature. These girls and boys often have no very clear notion of the long-term consequences of their behavior, and they have few trustworthy role models to instruct them.

Although middle-class youths and poor youths may have much in common sexually, their level of practical education differs. The ignorance of inner-city girls about their bodies astonishes the middle-class observer. Many have only a vague notion of where babies come from, and they generally know nothing about birth control until after they have their first child—and sometimes not then. Parents in this culture are extremely reticent about discussing sex and birth control with their children. Many mothers are ashamed to "talk about it" or feel they are in no position to do so, since they behaved the same way as their daughters when they were young. Education thus becomes a community health problem, but most girls come in contact with community health services only when they become pregnant—sometimes many months into their pregnancies.

Many women in the black underclass emerge from a fundamentalist religious orientation and hold a "pro-life" philosophy. Abortion is therefore usually not an option (see Gibson 1980a, 1980b; Pope 1969). New life is sometimes characterized as a "heavenly gift," an infant is sacred to the young woman, and the extended family always seems to make do somehow with another baby. A birth is usually met with great praise, regardless of its circumstances, and the child is genuinely valued. Such ready social approval works against many efforts to avoid illegitimate births.

In fact, in cold economic terms, a baby can be an asset, which is without doubt an important factor behind exploitative sex and out-of-wedlock babies. Public assistance is one of the few reliable sources of money, and, for many, drugs are another. The most desperate people thus feed on one another. Babies and sex may be used for income; women receive money from welfare for having babies, and men sometimes act as prostitutes to pry the money from them.

The lack of gainful employment not only keeps the entire community in a pit of poverty, but also deprives young men of the traditional American way of proving their manhood—supporting a family. They must thus prove themselves in other ways. Casual sex with as many women as possible, impregnating one or more, and getting them to "have your baby" brings a boy the ultimate in esteem from his peers and makes him a man. "Casual" sex is therefore fraught with social significance for the boy who has little or no hope of achieving financial stability and hence cannot see himself taking care of a family.

The meshing of these forces can be clearly seen. Adolescents, trapped in poverty, ignorant of the long-term consequences of their behavior but aware of the immediate benefits, engage in a mating game. The girl has her dream of a family and a home, of a good man who will provide for her and her children. The boy, knowing he cannot be that family man because he has few job prospects, yet needing to have sex to achieve manhood in the eyes of his peer group, pretends to be the "good" man and so convinces her to give him sex and perhaps a baby. He may then abandon her, and she realizes he was not the good man after all, but a nothing out to exploit her. The boy has gotten what he wanted, but the girl learns that she has gotten something too. The baby may bring her a certain amount of praise, a steady welfare check, and a measure of independence. Her family often helps out as best they can. As she becomes older and wiser, she can use her income to turn the tables, attracting her original man or other men.

In this inner-city culture, people generally get married for "love" and "to have something." This mind-set presupposes a job, the work ethic, and perhaps most of all, a persistent sense of hope for an economic future. When these social factors are present, the more wretched elements of the portrait presented here begin to lose their force, slowly becoming neutralized. But for many of those who are caught up in the web of persistent urban poverty and become unwed mothers and fathers, there is little hope for a good job and even less for a future of conventional family life.

5

●

In the

Shadow

of the

Ghetto

*T*he Village can increasingly be described as a middle- to upper-
middle-class oasis. It is at present beset by the forces of gentrification, with developers, speculators, and more privileged classes
gradually buying up properties inhabited by less well-off people of
diverse backgrounds. Gambling on a steady rise in property values,
many old and new residents hope the area will become "hot," trendy,
and expensive. But they often do not count on the persistence of the
shadow cast by the nearby ghetto, which colors many aspects of life
in the Village.

For residents of the Village, proximity to the ghetto brings a variety of social complications and opportunities that may require new
learning and cultural adaptation. Perhaps the most important adjustment is sharing public institutions such as stores, schools, trolleys, and streets with black ghetto dwellers. This social situation
makes it possible that one's children will befriend poor children of
the ghetto, though in reality this seldom happens, since play groups
tend to be structured largely along class lines, ensuring that they are
often all white or all black. It means being exposed to occasional
crime and harassment on the streets and in other public places. And
though some residents ignore or deny it, living in this shadow encourages an often exaggerated concern for security, resulting in the
ultimate personal confusion of social class, color, and gender.

No group illustrates the myriad problems of adjusting to the
local environment better than those who are now buying and moving into the Village: the professionals. They tend to develop a cama-

raderie with other middle-class people, particularly whites who face the same problems, in contradistinction to the local black community and "the element" living within the Village. And in a peculiar manner, disparate elements of the community coalesce as they face the increasingly urgent question of survival within a middle-income community so close to an underclass ghetto.

These residents are young to middle-aged, primarily white professionals in search of elegant homes and promising real estate investments, or just a pleasant place to live. They choose the Village not only because it is near their jobs, the center of the city, major universities, and other institutions, but also because of its large yards and spacious homes and the promise, not always fulfilled, of an urban setting where they can raise children, plant gardens, and keep pets. The last features, of course, are important aspects of suburban life, and its call becomes insistent when such families first have children or suffer an act of incivility or crime on the street. They are not used to living in an environment that is so culturally heterogeneous. Indeed, the newcomers generally come from local or distant suburbs that are ethnically and racially less complex than the Village-Northton.

This new invasion profoundly affects the social definition of the area, not only for its residents, but also for local businesses and government officials. For instance, mortgages and home-improvement loans that would have been denied a few years earlier are now more readily available. Further, the new residents pressure government officials for municipal services, including better police protection. These demands are often met, and the whole neighborhood benefits. The once segregated schools gain some middle-class white students, whose parents become involved and require the schools to respond to their needs. Thus the schools improve. But with all these improvements, housing costs increase and so do taxes. Unable to afford to live in the neighborhood they have helped create, poorer people trickle out. The presence and anticipated presence of middle- and upper-income people have an important effect on real estate values and thus on the social organization of the Village. Over time, the neighborhood is gradually but surely transformed, becoming increasingly homogeneous in race and class.

Those Villagers who were part of the counterculture of the 1960s sometimes draw sharp distinctions between themselves and the "young urban professionals" now moving in. The presence of outsiders "with money" and a perceived concern with "material" things disturbs many of them. The professional groups get together at block meetings and other informal gatherings; generally the working-class residents have little interest in attending these events or are simply not invited. When working-class people do attend block meetings, it is usually because the topic personally concerns them, whereas others come to socialize. One black man, for instance, was not keeping his house up to standards, so he became a topic of the regular block meetings. When he heard about this, he began attending every meeting because he felt he had something at stake.

Many of the former counterculturalists, who sometimes view themselves as the vessels of the "hip" Village identity, consider theft and harassment "facts of life" in the city, and they display little interest in stories of who did what to whom until it affects them personally. As one such resident commented: "Those [block] meetings are pretty much alike—boring." One thirty-nine-year-old former draft counselor commented on a block meeting entitled "Violence in the Village." "A lot of 'who got mugged where and when,' and all that old shit," she said. She did not plan to attend. But given that such old-timers must negotiate the sometimes tricky public spaces, they are vulnerable to many of the same stresses newcomers face. Many have become streetwise and have developed a rather sophisticated way of handling themselves. Such comments and the attitudes they represent say much about their unhappiness with the presence of newcomers, whom they are prepared to see as very different from themselves. But as we will see, these people find that they have much in common with the newcomers, particularly as they come to feel themselves under siege.

At times the young blacks and the young counterculturalists come together to deplore the recent influx of "yuppies," whom they see as partly responsible for rent increases and stricter standards of porch and yard maintenance. Some ridicule the newcomers, calling them "squares" or "uptight" and believing their complaints about theft and violence are not always to be taken seriously, but they express these attitudes with growing ambivalence. In time, the lines of difference blur.

To some counterculturalists who are highly resistant to change, the "decline" of the community becomes objectified by the newcomers, who become a focal point of intolerance, providing the old-timers with striking examples of what they are not. The former hippies are concerned that the area will become superficial, shallow, homogeneous, and intolerant of diversity. The traditional residents thus close ranks, finding the newcomers deviant from their own "superior" social rules and values.

As the newcomers wittingly or unwittingly establish a cultural outpost of the larger society, they tend to discount this significant proportion of the host community and are fairly criticized for not following in the cultural footsteps of their predecessors—the liberal Quakers. For instance, in the early 1960s such progressive people worked very hard in their campaign for a new public school in the Village, which they hoped would persist as a model of "integrated education," benefiting not only themselves but also their poorer black neighbors of the Village and Northton. Thus many of the old-time residents are tolerant of a local home for delinquent youths, many of them black, on a main Village street. They pride themselves on their progressive values.

In contrast to the early Quakers, who felt a strong need to make social peace with their diverse, lower-income neighbors and others with whom they shared public space, the current newcomers seek distance in their encounters with strangers or else simply tolerate what they see as a difficult situation. Fortunately for them, the peace has largely been made because of the beachhead established by their predecessors, who promoted local norms of racial and social tolerance.

The primary goal of many of these traditional white and black residents has been an integrated community where "all different kinds of people can live." Many feel strongly that to live in a homogeneous white neighborhood is to cheat oneself and one's family of an important social and moral education. In this fundamental respect the traditional Quakers and their followers are staunchly against bigotry in their self-presentation, and they judge others by their tolerance. To be racially and ethnically tolerant is to be a progressive person, goes this local ethos, and they believe they can make a significant difference by living here and spreading their values. At the same time, they tend to be highly sensitive to any behavior, in themselves or in others, that reveals intolerance or racist attitudes. Thus they work to preserve the interracial character of their community, but encroaching development and the growing presence of professionals make this increasingly difficult.

The newcomers threaten to overwhelm the longtime black and white residents, many of whom see themselves as part of a unique urban experiment. White veterans hark back to the 1950s and 1960s and invoke their civil rights, antiwar, or countercultural credentials. The few blacks among them tend to be middle-class and have long since left the ghetto. There is a bond among such people, and together they reminisce with pride about their days as community organizers, civil rights activists, or sympathizers with the counterculture. Some have a self-righteous sense of having worked hard to defend society's underdogs, and many feel deeply committed to the "continuing struggle for justice and equality" in American life.

Having developed a tradition of civic pride and responsibility by dedicating themselves to the "betterment" of the community, many of the old residents find little redeeming social value in the supposed character of the new yuppie residents. At social gatherings, the old-timers may shudder when they arise as a topic of conversation and attempt to ridicule them. As one old-timer said:

◑ *You know John Frazier? He's definitely one of those new wave entrepreneurial types. And at meetings of the Civic Association, he talks about "fiduciary responsibility," and things like that, ha-ha. It sends shivers up our [traditional Villagers'] spines. He walks his children around in designer strollers, ha-ha, and knapsacks.* ◐

Stereotypically viewed as ostentatious and materialistic, the newcomers incur further resentment because of the general belief that they are of a higher economic class or at least have more money than most of their neighbors. Some support for this belief comes from the quasi-public knowledge of the selling prices of homes, which a good many residents keep tabs on. They are thought to have support from their parents or income from both spouses. Coming into the community "with money" makes them obnoxious to some, though certainly not all, residents.

Further, a story told and retold by traditional residents says that the newcomers look forward impatiently to the day when their houses will be worth considerably more, and that "the first thing they want to know is, 'Is it safe?' You'd think they'd appreciate what a unique place this is."

It is probably true that many of the new homeowners would be reluctant to invest in the area if they believed it would remain the same. They bargain on change, from low income to well-to-do. In this respect, current and prospective neighbors become commodities of a sort. As older and poorer residents move, room is made for those of a higher socioeconomic class, who will pay well, sometimes "outrageously," for homes.

On the whole, though they may be seen as preoccupied with status, the yuppies, muppies, or whatever older residents choose to call them appear indifferent to the ethnicity of those next door. What matters is class, signaled by place of work, occupation, and position. Such attributes define a person when there may be little else to go on.

Whereas the earlier residents might celebrate racial tolerance by inviting a "Negro friend" home to lunch or dinner, the newcomers like to think they view race as irrelevant. Many try to deemphasize color and ethnicity in their social relations. In a word, they pretend to be color-blind, conveniently forgetting, ignoring, or downplaying the long history of discrimination toward blacks. In sociable conversation with other whites, however, such people as well as their supposedly more liberal counterparts may find themselves referring to a black friend as "this black guy" or "this black gal," immediately making race prominent in their personal relations, their defenses to the contrary notwithstanding. And many of their black friends may also deemphasize race, which can be a source of tension. In the interest of harmony, color is sometimes politely but conspicuously ignored.

In public places, though, this pretense of indifference fades. There newcomers gravitate toward others they feel most comfortable with, people who are superficially similar to them in both social class and color. This public behavior is an area of convergence between old and new white residents.

After living in the Village for a year or so, some newcomers do give up and leave for the surburbs. By this time they have encountered urban life firsthand. For instance, they have usually had their cars broken into, their batteries stolen, or worse. The following field note illustrates this:

○ *Susan and Ted and their young daughter Ellen had been living in the Village for approximately a year when Ted decided to buy an expensive German automobile. The car was his pride and joy, with its elaborate sound system and other exclusive extras. A few months after buying the car, he parked it on the street in front of his house. The next morning he was shocked to find the window smashed, the door open, and the dashboard virtually destroyed. Taking the very expensive sound system was the thief's main object, but during the theft he vandalized the interior. Ted was very upset, feeling that his very self had been violated. The family is now planning to sell out and move to a suburb of Eastern City.* ◑

When newcomers begin to partake of community life, they meet the public culture of their neighbors, including people with dark skin, loud radios, peculiar accents, exotic dress, and other presentational emblems they often cannot appreciate or understand. Sometimes they are met by unsettling verbal and even physical assaults.

Some residents have had their homes robbed, even while they were there. Others have been mugged on the streets and have learned to fear strangers, especially young black males. When they report such crimes, the local police sometimes act as though the crime were their own fault for living in a "black neighborhood." Some tolerate the situation, treating minor abuses as a novelty or as an interesting experience to share with friends. But others simply withdraw, retreating inside their homes and automobiles to wait for better days. All this suggests that the "invasion" of the well-to-do outsiders is an ongoing social process, if not a full-blown struggle for dominance of the community.

Thus the presence of yuppies raises many tensions in the local social atmosphere, mainly because their values are perceived to differ so profoundly from those of their black and white predecessors. The old-timers, with their history of liberal, progressive civic action, have tried to be empathic, wise, and benevolent in their relations with local blacks. The former counterculturalists and others copy the old-timers in this regard. The newcomers, to be sure, try to get along, but they simply are not actively engaged in this endeavor, as were the Quakers of many years ago or even the counterculturalists of today. But those wishing to draw invidious distinctions between themselves and others use the border of race to accomplish this goal.

The yuppies are seen by most others within the community as having very little interest in getting along with their black and lower-income neighbors. People are inclined to view the young professionals as bent on profiting from their investments over the short run. From this perspective, hastening the exodus of undesirables would improve the value of their homes as well as their own comfort on the streets. Further, instead of welcoming color differences as old residents did, the newcomers are believed to feel fear, hostility, or at best indifference toward blacks. Their agenda is not cultural diversity but class homogeneity. Because they are an expression of an upwardly

mobile group (unlike the more stable middle-class or upper-class former residents), they feel tremendous tension around anyone they
think is from the underclass. Consistent with this working conception of the local community, in confronting the daily challenges and
difficulties of urban street life, veteran residents have often gone beyond a superficial public etiquette to street wisdom. Because of their
egalitarian values, they have searched for a broader understanding of
types and subtypes of minority people. The gentrifying newcomers,
in general, do not share this drive. In response to difficulties and fears
on the street, they do not extend themselves. Instead they pull in,
and if the feeling of being under siege overwhelms them, they cash in
their investment and leave. There are many who cannot adjust to
the tensions of this area. Others, though, are slowly won over by its
special quality.

Some young newcomers move into the area without children
and, considering the city a poor place to raise a family, tend to appreciate only a small part of the social life of the Village. But, parents
come to know the neighborhood from a different perspective. As one
parent commented:

◐ *I didn't care so much about my neighborhood until I had children. I wasn't aware of the various facets of the community. Then
came a lot of other things that I began to do as the parent of a child
in this neighborhood. We became committed to the area.* ◐

When newcomers do have children, they display serious concern
for their safety and welfare, becoming highly sensitive to the potential dangers of the public environment where their children play. In
line with this concern, they take care to find them suitable playmates, working with other middle-class parents, some of whom they
may not know well. They become involved in activities such as
school, car pools, and parent-teacher meetings.

Children often become the focus of social life within the community. Typically, the parents cater to the children's needs, driving
them around, walking them here and there, scrutinizing their potential friends and their families. When parents find an appropriate
playmate, they may cultivate the relationship, sometimes inviting
the whole family over for dinner. In these circumstances "Tommy's
dad" and "Sarah's mom" take on their real names and identities and
have the rare chance to be known for themselves, providing a spark
for the couples to see each other socially. In this way, children can
become important agents for knitting the community together so-

cially. Political and social ideologies are often deemphasized, people are more often taken as individuals or as just families, and distinctions between old and new residents blur. Thus the social lives of children are indirectly responsible for a certain amount of neighborhood solidarity and friendly involvement. As one person told me:

◑ *Since our children have grown up, we don't have any friends. When they were growing up, there was always something going on. What with the car pools and stuff, our friends were almost ready-made. Now that they're gone, we have to work harder.* ◑

Although old-timers lament the slow but certain alteration of their "laid-back," tolerant community, there seems to be a certain cultural convergence between the youthful old-timers and some incoming young professionals. In earlier days, members of the traditional group saw themselves as vessels of the youthful counterculture, expressing their disdain for behaviors and values attributed to the wider "straight" society, including an overconcern with money, material possessions, and "unhealthy" diets. Many such proudly unconventional veterans of the late sixties and seventies are now homeowners with young families. They attempt to hold on to their old political and social values, but in the present context they are not as insistent as they once were. As one pointed out:

◑ *It took me a long while to come to like the Village. When I first moved in, the people I associated with tended to be young people of the counterculture. I mean, we'd go to parties where there would be ten different versions of lentils, natural fruit juices, and other health foods, ha-ha. Today, it's very different. The emphasis is different. You go to a party, and it's simply a middle-class party.* ◑

Such a comment indicates not only the maturation of members of the youthful counterculture, which has largely disappeared from the Village, but also the emerging influence of the "professional" culture, replete with its own eating styles and etiquette.

In addition to the yuppies, the community continues to draw socially liberal residents who appreciate its relaxed social atmosphere. Impressed by the area's reputation and ambiance, not to mention its promise of rising property values, they gravitate to the Village. Many have values that are resonant with the area's reputation. In fact, some were at one time deeply involved with the counterculture, which makes it difficult to adjust to the suburbs where they were raised.

Among such new people are former hippies who have grown up to be merchants, house squatters who have become homeowners, and 1960s antiwar protestors who have gone into law or business. By now they have acquired families, a certain maturity, and an important strain of conventionality. For the most part they play down "conspicuous consumption." Clothing is not stressed for its expense and flash value, but rather is plain and appropriate for the season. Homes tend to be simply decorated. Cars are usually the "no frills" variety, particularly if new. Extra money may be spent on expensive nonmaterial or intrinsic satisfactions, such as private schooling for children or long vacations to far-off places. Moreover, their sixties experience leaves them open to at least superficial associations with fellow residents from a variety of backgrounds, often encouraged by occasional racial and class tension related to the nearby ghetto of Northton.

The old residents' prejudices notwithstanding, these newcomers may actually be more like them than they generally recognize or acknowledge, because class compounded by color is an organizing principle of community and local social life. Compared with the nearby black ghetto, the whites of the traditional community have much in common with those now moving in, particularly on issues of crime and the safety of the streets; in these respects color and social class intrude loudly on the public consciousness. The following narrative of a middle-aged white man who has been living in the Village for ten years illustrates these concerns:

⊙ *My son Jonathan has a young black friend named Marvin. They have an on again/off again relationship; he likes Marvin, then he doesn't. He's from Northton.*

The other morning . . . I had met Marvin a few times because I had been involved in the school. He's a bright, energetic kid, you know, a very good student.

He popped up at the door the other morning at about 8:00. At first I didn't recognize him—out of context, you know. I was wondering, What's a little boy here for? We exchanged hellos. We sort of went back and forth.

Oh, it's Marvin, it's Marvin. I feel bad that I didn't recognize him. I mean I've been speaking to his class, but I didn't recognize Marvin.

A lot of things went through my mind at first. It's 8:00 in the morning. Why is he here? He probably wants to come in. I said to myself. Should I let Marvin in? And I feel this fear. And I say, Why am I afraid of letting a six- or seven-year-old black child come in?

I thought about this for a bit. Am I afraid of him being a friend of Jonathan's? So I'm distressed by this feeling. And I start to think about why am I distressed about this. Because these feelings go against what I've been saying I want for my child, you know, to be in an integrated school, and his friends should be black and of all different nationalities, but here I am a little bit nervous about it. I think, well, is Marvin going to be connected up with drugs when he gets older? Is Jonathan going to be a friend of a child who is going to be connected up with drugs? Marvin looks as though he is well taken care of. But along the same line, I say, well, why is he out at this time of the morning, going to school so early? And I say, well, maybe he's just going over to play ball in the school yard early. I know his mother works, and once my wife brought him to our house. His older brother brings him out. He's safe enough, you know. Well, I say it's a justifiable worry. If he has black friends coming from Northton, then he's going to run into drugs. And I have to say that is one way Marvin will run into drugs more often. But what does that mean for me?

So Marvin comes in, and I get this sort of straightened out in my mind. So I say, "Come on in, Marvin. Jonathan's upstairs taking a bath. Would you like some orange juice?" He says, "Yeah." I pour him some orange juice. I say, "Or would you like grapefruit juice?" He says, "Grapefruit juice!" Then I start saying to myself, Is he this indecisive because he's never had a choice before? So I say, "Marvin, would you like to have some breakfast? Would you like some cereal? I bring out four or five boxes of cereal. I'm not sure whether it's that he's never had cereal before, whether he's never had a choice before, or whether he's never been in a white person's home before or what. I'm feeling uncomfortable. I'm feeling like I'm the rich folk, and he's the poor folk. And I'm wondering if he's going to come every morning for breakfast. I'm not thinking these things consciously. I'm just thinking about them. Then he says, "How many people live in this house?" I say, "Well, there's four of us." I'm thinking, should I feel bad about this or what? Should I be introducing Marvin to this? Do I have a choice? Or is this the way it is? Especially when he gets to be seventeen. Is he gonna become a druggy, and is he gonna rip us off? I was thinking, I'm telling Eli about these great things, right? I felt well, when you're living in a community like the Village, you are confronted with these kinds of issues. Sometimes it's more direct than others. Every day, you've got to reassess your values. You've got to say, What am I gonna choose to worry about? Am I going to

choose ten years from now to worry about or five years from now?
Am I gonna take it day by day? Is it affecting my child? Would I feel
the same about Eli's son, or about Abdul [black son of local middle-
class black parent]? It's problematic, but it's also reinforcing. Marvin
came back about three or four days later, and two days ago I saw
him come back again. We'll make a choice as it goes on and on. ❍

This tension extends to the public environment. Comity between neighbors exists when people "know" one another. There is a
good deal of suspicion and distrust, particularly when one of the parties is black and male and displays the emblems of the underclass.
When black and white residents meet spontaneously, there is often a
somewhat strained civility between them, particularly for white
newcomers who have little familiarity with street life and with encountering unknown blacks in public. In such encounters, the civility is mixed with tolerance.

A significant factor has been the emergence of a large black
underclass that to many city people represents the local "criminal
element." Old residents have become as concerned as newcomers
about the crime and violence potential of local black youths. But
they worry because this is reminiscent of oldtime racism, which they
have spent much of their lives combating. They wonder whether social conditions in the Village have made them into racists of a sort.
But the resulting isolation may not be so much a matter of direct racial feeling as an outgrowth of the play of economic factors involving
housing, color, and social class.

The impending changes in this community seem beyond the control of the residents because of the structural component involving
the social economics of gentrification. As housing values increase, as
long-vacant and boarded-up buildings are renovated, as service institutions on the periphery emerge and expand, and as investors and
speculators take advantage of these developments, the area promises
to become increasingly middle to upper income and predominantly
white, despite being bounded on two sides by the crime-ridden and
economically depressed black ghetto of Northton. Some traditional
residents view the impending changes with alarm, but many are
mollified by the promise of a precipitous rise in property values and
rents. Some homes have already doubled or tripled their value in the
past few years.

The signs of change are everywhere. Walking through the area, one sees that building after building has been refurbished or is being renovated. Workers seem all around as cement trucks block the street here, a lumber truck is parked there, and young Irish and Italian men move around with tools hanging from their canvas aprons, an occasional black man among them. They hammer boards, fit new windows, or stand around smoking cigarettes. The rare silence is spiced with their voices and the motors of their tools. At times a radio blares rock music. Facades are being sandblasted, reinforced, and painted. Ladders lean precariously against buildings, and the air smells of hot tar.

More and more houses are being reconverted from multiple-unit to single-family dwellings, giving the Village a more solid residential definition. Many of the developers and upper-income residents are concerned not simply with reclaiming the neighborhood, but also with restoring the housing to something approaching their conception of its former beauty.

The construction disrupts the physical record of the past decade of social life in the Village—buildings that used to house people with few resources, including ordinary working people, black and white, as well as students, hippies, and squatters.

Today renovations are made more carefully, particularly to the exteriors. The area has recently been historically certified, though many residents fail to understand the meaning and implications of that status. Many of the poorer and black homeowners are suspicious of this designation and see it as simply more red tape that will make maintaining their homes more difficult. Some comment that the new rules make it hard for them to make proper repairs without consulting an expert in renovating Victorian buildings. True or not, the view is meaningful because the residents interpret the new rules as influencing their living situation.

The accelerated renovation of dwellings testifies both to the financial strength of the community and to the confidence new and prospective residents have in the area's potential. Developers and yuppie homeowners bet on the likelihood that the area will undergo significant positive change, making buying real estate and settling here for a while a good investment. Thus many purchase homes hoping it will become a "good" neighborhood, with outsiders bidding for a chance to get in on the latest trendy residential area. But this road to economic salvation is fraught, at least at the local level, with starts and setbacks, victories and pitfalls, as issue after issue emerges and dissipates concerning the future of the Village, illustrating how the winds of development are blowing.

In general, the yuppies and the developers would like to see the Village become trendy and are interested in helping this vision become a reality. Developers are hard at work buying up and renovating properties and requesting zoning changes so certain streets can more adequately service new traffic patterns and prospective "upscale" residents. Other areas in Eastern City have undergone such changes, bringing a quick rise in property values, and cultural and social heterogeneity have often been sacrificed to progress. For as property values have risen, poorer residents, who tend to be white ethnics, blacks, and the elderly, find the cost of living there too high, and rising taxes have become a special problem. Such areas thus grow more homogeneous in social class, race, and age.

The prospective changes include a dream of less crime, better police protection, and a cleaner environment. Homes and buildings are to be painted in designer colors and fitted with shiny brass doorknobs and antique wooden doors. Streets will be lined with late-model automobiles; shops will provide amenities and conveniences close at hand; neighbors will be wealthy, or at least solidly upper middle class.

This dream is coming to be shared by many old-time Villagers, erstwhile counterculturalists, local blacks, and others. Given a choice of "progress" or "regress," most would opt for the former. Gentrification is more easily seen as progress and the reappearance of blight and poor people as regression. However, though many Villagers share some version of the dream of gentrification, they would like to have it on their own moral terms, insisting on tolerance, inclusiveness, diversity, and kindness to those less fortunate. They really want to live in a "decent, middle-class community," since many, especially the homeowners, have an investment in staying in the general area.

La Casa, a new Mexican restaurant on a busy thoroughfare, and Mr. Hu's, a convenience store/deli near the corner of one of the Village's "most beautiful" streets, exemplify the way the social and economic winds are blowing. The Mexican restaurant, about two blocks from Eastern Technical University, caters to middle-class residents. It is often full of local college students, former counterculture members, newcomers, and an occasional old-time Villager. Many of the local residents, weary of having to leave the area to eat out, view a "real" restaurant as "just what the Village needs."

The restaurant's recent application for a liquor license caused controversy. Community hearings were called, and the pros and cons were stated. Although there was opposition, the liquor license was overwhelmingly approved. As one resident said:

◑ Apparently, La Casa's liquor license was opposed by only four or five people. The story I hear is that Cindy Murphy and three or four others opposed it because she thought there'd be a parking problem, and she wouldn't be able to park near her house so easily. Most people are frustrated by her and say they don't know what Cindy wants or why she's complaining about this seemingly innocuous bar. ◑

The restaurant's liquor license was opposed by a local black leader because the bar "would be too close" to the local segregated high school. Others opposed it because they feared that if the establishment failed, the license might be passed on to new owners who could do what they wanted with the bar, including making it a hangout for university students. Still others were against the liquor license because of misgivings about gentrification and its implications for life in the Village as they know it and wish it to be. The new restaurant is highly symbolic of the furthering of the gentrifiers' dream, described above, like other nearby establishments that provide new services to the Village community. Such developments send a clear signal that the vision of progress is alive and well, which most residents can tacitly support.

On the other side of the Village, near the boundary of Bellwether Street, sits Mr. Hu's, a convenience store and deli "owned by a Korean man." The establishment appears to be efficiently run, with attentive workers and shelves neatly stocked with cakes, bread, and candy. Against one wall are new coolers containing a variety of soft drinks, eggs, and dairy products. Behind the glass counter are trays of breaded cut-up chicken ready for deep frying, cole slaw, potato salad, and other deli products. A Korean man and two women wait on customers and prepare foods.

This establishment caters to lower-income blacks from Northton and is boycotted by many Villagers who disapprove of its presence. Residents generally complain that "the food is bad and the milk is old," but with probing it becomes clear that they particularly resent what the establishment represents for the present and future life of the Village: regression rather than progression.

The store is in an abandoned service station that the Korean man purchased and renovated. After a few months the store was not doing well financially, so the owner installed video games and a pool table, attracting a young black clientele from nearby Northton, who have come to use the place as a hangout. The Village residents who live nearby complain bitterly about the noise of the boom boxes, the loud talk, and the fights that occasionally break out after the place closes at midnight.

To make matters worse from the point of view of most Villagers, the owner recently applied for a liquor license, which was almost unanimously opposed by local residents, including middle-class blacks who empathize with those who live nearby. The yuppies do not want the store. The old-time Village people resist it. The counter-culture people don't want it. And the local students, though generally indifferent, have no great need for it. It appears that few people other than the blacks from Northton appreciate the place.

Because of the noise, the presence of "street blacks," and the possibility of drugs and crime, to most residents the establishment represents a definite setback for the neighborhood. This is an issue that brings the various groups of the Village together, pointing up the interests they have in common by what they are bound to oppose. Many feel the establishment "brings the ghetto into the Village," meaning drugs, crime, violence, and poverty. Yet such a statement makes many tolerant people wonder about the racial implications of their actions. The issues become particularly incisive in light of the recent controversy over La Casa, which gained overwhelming support from the local community.

Those opposed to the convenience store invoke the evil of drugs and crime, not to mention the noise and late-night activities. They are also concerned about the image such a place gives their own property, particularly if they live close by. These are practical considerations. As one forty-five-year-old middle-class resident so aptly put it:

○ *La Casa, personally. . . . I'm not really keen about wanting to have it in the neighborhood one way or the other. I know I'll go there two or three times a year; it'll be the same old thing. It's not going to become a hangout for me. So I know it's gonna be so much yuppie stuff. But I'll go there. I'll enjoy it. I can definitely live without it. But it does fit within my image of the Village. Oh, it's more positive than it is negative. It certainly has no negative thing in my mind about it. Whereas Mr. Hu's has negative connotations. It is not what I consider to be beautiful. It doesn't look nice. It has implications that it might have some practical problems with it. Could be-*

come a drug hangout. It could have people fighting, especially if they got a liquor license. ◐

Significantly, for most the convenience store symbolizes a dream deferred, a threat to gentrification. But also important, it is a provocative preview of what lies on the other side of Bellwether Street.

The Edge

Many middle-class whites and blacks around the city see an area with a large visible black presence as "bad" or marginal, even if blacks constitute a minority. Black presence thus operates as a symbol that prejudicially gauges a neighborhood's quality. By such superficial standards the Village itself qualifies as marginal in the minds of many, and the side near Northton is considered much worse.

The area that is the social and geographical boundary separating the Village and Northton is referred to by many Village residents, particularly middle-class ones, as the "edge," and even those who have never heard the term readily understand its referent. It is the place where the two communities meet, where the lower-income black residents come into contact with the middle- and upper-income white ones. In this local area, which is inhabited primarily by the poor, housing often is crumbling. Front porches may literally be falling down; the bricks of foundations are broken or disintegrating. And small black children, street kids, play loudly and run wild, raising the assumption that only poor black people inhabit the area. On close inspection, however, it becomes clear that the street is a mixture of middle- to upper-income whites and working-class to poor blacks.

Because the edge is primarily black, with only a scattering of whites, in the minds of many Eastern City residents it is a "bad" area. By contrast, the white areas of the Village that have a peppering of blacks are viewed as "good."

The whites who live in this vicinity may be referred to as urban pioneers, evoking the image of genteel whites surviving in the wilderness. In this case the white middle-class people inhabit the margin between the two communities to take advantage of the relatively low rents or house prices. The new homeowners hope that their present situation will be only temporary, that conditions will change for the better. Their friends and family frequently caution them, questioning their choice of a home location. At social gatherings or at work, particularly outside the immediate area, they are bombarded with questions about their neighborhood. The newcomers may respond awkwardly because they themselves are unsure of the wisdom of their decision, especially if they have small children.

But living here, they find, is an education. Some become familiar with the lives of poor black people, whom they have always seen from a distance. Their children sometimes have lower-income black children for playmates. Some become friends with neighbors, or at least they come to know who they are on a more intimate level. White students from Eastern Tech may be found in this area or even deeper into Northton; some live communally, making friends with their black neighbors, surprised by how kind and sociable they are. They play with the black children, serving as an important positive influence. But a mugging, a rape, a killing, or simple racial harassment of someone they closely identify with can cause them to reconsider their choice of residence, if not to leave for another part of the city or the suburbs. Sometimes it only takes a close call.

◐ *On Saturday evening at about 7:30 David, a white, thirty-seven-year-old architect who is an old-time Village resident, and his eight-year-old son Chucky walked the one block to the convenience store to buy some milk. They bought the milk and some candy for Chucky and began the walk home. The store is on a corner at the boundary separating the Village and Northton. As they left, a young black man walked up behind them and said to David, "Alright, give me your money or I'll kill you!" Instinctively David turned around and began yelling at him. Startled by David's barrage, the man turned and fled. A shaken David and Chucky resumed what was supposed to have been an uneventful walk home. Chucky was upset and began to cry. After reaching home he calmed down, but since the encounter he has become fearful. It has been a year now since the attempted robbery, but Chucky does not yet feel secure outside the house. His parents say, "Chucky doesn't like to go outside." They are understanding and have considered moving, but they feel too attached to the Village to leave for the suburbs or some other part of the city.* ◐

Residents, both black and white, come to respect the informal boundary separating Northton and the Village. Young black men of Northton informally patrol their side; they look for "trouble" and may materialize when they believe their turf has been violated or when they spot strangers who are "up to no good." This is illustrated in the following interview with a thirty-two-year-old black professional:

◐ *I live right on the boundary, right on Bellwether Street. The thing that messes my street up about being the boundary is that it looks so peaceful—because of a Catholic school. It's a special school with a fenced-in yard. The only people who go across that fence to play on the grass are the football team. They let the football team use the yard; but you never see people jumping the fence. The fence says this is a separation point. It's identified by all the community; blacks and whites respect that identification. In the summertime the nicest grass and shade are right there, but you never see anyone violating that. Right on the boundary of the Village and Northton you have about fifty by fifty yards of grass, trees, and shade that nobody violates.* ◐

Formal agencies have also helped set neighborhood boundaries. The Eastern City school district divides Bellwether Street down the middle, allowing students on one side to attend the Village elementary school, while others attend all-black schools in Northton.

Equally important for a sense of community boundaries are the stark differences in the life-styles of the people of the Village and those of Northton. To an important extent these differences may be attributed to social class, but to many who approach the matter perfunctorily, including many whites and some blacks, the differences appear to be racial. There is a profound confusion of race and class concerning the local culture. For instance:

◐ *At approximately 11:30 [on a Thursday night in mid-September] I walked down Bellwether Street, the boundary separating the Village and Northton. I was startled by the sound of breaking glass. A six-year-old had just thrown a liquor bottle into the street. Four or five children played in the street, on the sidewalk, and in a nearby yard. They were shouting and laughing loudly. A woman, presumably the mother of one of the children, yelled from an upstairs window, "Y'all quiet down out there." The children all but ignored her, as they simply looked up and directly returned to their games. I sat down on the stoop of a nearby building to gain a long view and stayed there over an hour. During this time six-year-olds, four-year-olds, and one three-year-old played in the center of the intersection. I walked over and asked one youngster if his mother knew where he was. He answered, "Yeah." I wondered how long the children would stay outside, so I waited. It was 1:00 A.M. when the last child went in, not because someone had called him, but because he was exhausted.*

After much reflection I concluded that, far from being unsupervised, these children had been supervising themselves, not in a manner appreciated by middle-class people, but in a way that ensures some protection for the youngest. What appeared to be a hierarchy of supervision revealed itself whenever danger approached. For instance, it was up to an older child to watch out for a younger one when a car pulled up to the stop sign.

When a strange dog approached, an older child instinctively stepped between the dog and his "baby sister." The older children would mimic their parents, shouting harsh orders to the smaller ones. And the little children "listened up." It appeared they had been well trained for these roles. ◑

Another feature of the edge is that it is a place of "trouble." On many nights police are called to the scene of a domestic fight, a stickup, or a dispute among neighbors or friends. There is also much more street crime here than further into the Village. Moreover, there are numerous social gatherings and parties, often spontaneous, where adults have plenty to drink. In the course of having fun, some become loud and boisterous, irritating neighbors, who may call the police.

These observations may seem to imply that one community is black, poor, and bad, and the other is white (in fact, racially mixed) and good. Ironically, this distinction protects the properties of Northton from the invasion of the well-to-do. The generalized notion that Northton is a bad neighborhood, and that the edge is a preview of what to expect as one goes deeper into the black community, causes many would-be gentrifiers to hesitate. The characteristics of the edge help to depress property values nearby. Yet as the area becomes established as desirable to middle-class people, even the edge is unlikely to escape the tide of development and gentrification.

One thirty-unit apartment building stands on the dividing line between Northton and the Village. A few years ago it housed working poor families, indigent black women with small children, narcotics users, hoodlums, and prostitutes, a motley group of people having only skin color in common. Two years ago, all the residents were given notice to leave because the building was "unfit for human habitation." After the blacks had moved out and the building had been vacant about six months, Southeast Asians began to occupy it, eventually filling it. Nearby black residents resented the incursion of the Asians, charging that they had in effect displaced the black tenants.

Approximately a year after the Asians moved in, they too were told to move. Today the building is undergoing extensive renovation and remodeling. It is a safe bet that the people who ultimately occupy it will not be Asian, black, or poor. The new residents are more likely to be Tech students or middle- to upper-income whites, part of an emerging housing market that will pay relatively high rent. Although the new landlord is unlikely to be very concerned about color, he will prefer to rent to whites. At first he may be able to attract only low to middle-income blacks because the building is so close to the ghetto. A block one way or the other in relation to the informal line dividing the black community from the Village can determine the immediate racial makeup of a rental building.

At present some of the dilapidated buildings of Northton near the boundary of the Village are boarded up, apparently abandoned. But once some of the buildings are renovated, adjacent ones become candidates for renewal by developers, speculators, or new homeowners.

As real estate properties turn over, and as new shops and stores follow, confidence in the area's investment potential grows. With this confidence comes further real estate speculation. As development is consolidated by a growing number of middle-class and professional residents and a corresponding decrease in poorer residents, developers and individual homeowners benefit from their investments, which stimulates even more buying and selling and contributes to the general rise of land and housing prices.

With each renovation the community becomes more economically viable as a place likely to sustain future investment. As the pioneers literally change the complexion and raise the perceived value of the area, others are encouraged to follow their lead. The overflow of pioneers may reach the black community of Northton, influencing real estate values and thus extending by accretion the edges of the relatively prestigious Village. The more the community becomes consolidated both physically and socially, the more the edge will be extended—probably in time renaming parts of Northton "the Village."

Urban gentrification like that occurring in the Village-Northton area may be a significant social and cultural force for years to come. Though its ultimate consequences have yet to be seen, the more immediate implications are clear. As young, primarily white middle- to upper-middle-income professionals invade areas inhabited by the poor and the marginally employed, the phrase "inner city" takes on new meaning.

Before the onset of gentrification, the Village was probably the most socially diverse and tolerant area of Eastern City. As the newcomers move in, their presence threatens to undermine the heterogeneous character of the neighborhood, though many of them were attracted by just this aspect. To live close to the center of the city, they must tolerate an urban environment where security is uncertain at best, which many of them are utterly unprepared for.

Continued development contributes to the influx of upper-income people, who tend to be white. While this process is occurring, a perfunctory look around the area suggests it is racially integrated. One sees whites and blacks sharing the streets and public spaces, and occasionally biracial groups are in evidence. Public comity between the races seems to prevail, giving the appearance of integration.

In reality, very little fraternizing occurs between blacks and whites except when they are of the same social class. To be sure, there are some who assume the role of culture brokers, including biracial couples, those involved in serious black-white friendships, and others who locate themselves on the margins of either group. They may help to bridge the social gap between blacks and whites, many of whom are satisfied with limited social contact with those not of their own color and class background. Since the blacks of the area tend to be poor to working class while whites are mainly middle or upper-middle class, class distinctions are compounded by color differences. Comity and civility generally prevail, but true racial integration and social equality are often illusory. Only where class is constant does there exist a real opportunity for primary relations between blacks and whites.

Middle- and upper-income residents adopt a special public etiquette (see chap. 8), based on a practical gender- and color-coded prejudice used to get up and down the streets safely. This sort of prejudice is a source of tension for middle-class blacks of the area, though many of them take similar precautions and make similar adaptations.

Although some middle-class blacks live within the shadow of the ghetto, the area tends not to be highly attractive to them, particularly if they are professionals. Members of this class appear to have great difficulty living close to the black lower classes. One of the most important problems is social status. Many are highly concerned about being confused with members of the underclass; they complain that whites and others take them for "people of Northton." One young black "professional" who sometimes wears dark jackets and sunglasses said this:

◑ *I take my son up to the little playground on occasion, and I'll push him on the swings. When I go there, I feel like a stranger, sometimes even to the whites I know. My wife is involved in neighborhood affairs, and I've come to know certain ones, and some of them are really strange, though I have to say there are a lot of nice ones. I mean people I know, now. And I can just be walking up to the park, and that'll be an* experience, *depending on who I meet, of course. John Edwards [a new white Village resident], now he won't give me the time of day on the street. He'll look at me funny, like I'm gon' rob him, or something. It's a trip. He put me right in a bag. [Facetiously] Because I'm black, he just knew I was from Northton, ha-ha. I got his number, ha-ha.* ◑

Members of the black middle class also are concerned about their treatment by the local police, who often are not willing or able to make distinctions between blacks in the public spaces of the Village. These problems, which are obvious to many blacks, contribute to the assessment of the area's social marginality, and thus of its undesirability. Imbued with the conviction that they have struggled hard for their newly won class position, middle-class blacks are impatient with what they consider "bad" treatment. Part of this impatience has to do with status anxiety, because many view themselves as hanging on to their general position in society by a thread. Beset with their perceived vulnerability to political changes, they sense the uncertainty, if not the precariousness, of their social position.

In dealing with status anxiety, many middle-class blacks carefully scrutinize other blacks for evidence of class orientation, and they gravitate toward those who exhibit a connection with their own position. Hence for some there is an almost ritualistic concern with propriety and decorum—the attributes they find lacking in their encounters with "street blacks" or "people from Northton." Members of the black middle class often criticize the blacks of Northton as "loud," "boisterous," and "ignorant." In measuring "street blacks" against their own conceptions of "decency," middle-class blacks cite the welfare of their children. They are inclined to label strange black children who appear unruly as street kids and thus bad, and they are concerned that their own children not "turn out that way." These concerns have important implications for how middle-class black life in the Village relates to lower-class black life in Northton, and they define middle-class blacks as strikingly different from their white counterparts in the Village. As one young woman said, "The liberal white person can rest assured that his kid is not going to become a street black by living in this area. I have to worry about mine."

In general, middle-class black families see their children as highly vulnerable to the influence of the ghetto. They fear that they will associate too closely with ghetto children, thereby gaining "bad habits" that might impede their upward mobility or keep them from assimilating dominant values and achieving social rewards. Among their chief fears are teenage pregnancy, drugs, gangs, and general street crime, causing them to be especially observant of behaviors that place social distance between themselves and those they see as being from Northton. These fears surface as the children approach grade school. One white woman describes her middle-class black friend's problem in the area:

◗ *You know Darlene's little girl who's just the same age as our son, George. She just started at the Village elementary school. They're both eight. They wanted her in public school, out of the social context she was getting into with the private school she was attending. They like the school very much, but Darlene tells me things about the Village School that I never knew. Because immediately, Marla has hooked up with the black kids in a way. . . . With the little girls, for one thing. Our son's only eight, and all of his black friends are very middle class. Darlene says that Marla has been coming home, boys have been calling her up, and asking her to be their girlfriend, and giving her presents, activities that I didn't even know were going on at that age. And then, she says, the jump-rope rhymes the girls chant are just absolutely obscene. All of this has completely escaped me, in my cozy, insulated little* [world]. *Our kids don't even hook up with that.* ◗

Middle-class black people are often especially sensitive to the behavior of members of the ghetto community. On the streets and in their homes, they feel impelled to advertise that they are not from Northton. Engaging in this campaign, they may display expensive possessions inside their homes. Their speech, particularly around whites, is self-consciously middle class. Their walk and demeanor have an air of propriety. Black males are "extra nice" in their speech and dress. And some tell whites outright that they have never "lived in the ghetto."

Because of this constant shadow over their lives, members of the black middle class are not eager to live in neighborhoods like the Village. Many seek to be as far as possible from the black underclass, believing that the closer to the ghetto they live, the more likely they are to receive the same treatment as their poorer counterparts. Perhaps only when the surrounding area becomes "white enough," affluent enough, and thus "safe enough" will it become acceptable to black middle-class and professional people.

The trail of gentrification appears self-sustaining, destined to continue as long as there is a supply of housing. The past successes of the developers, recent activity, and the prospects of high profits from the renovation of still more homes will help fuel future development. Once the process begins in earnest, its continuation appears inevitable. But the change initiated by developers and young urban professionals will not come quickly or easily. It will be a slow and arduous struggle, at times almost imperceptible and at other times very evident.

For centuries blacks and whites have lived in separate communities; this separation was institutionalized and supported by law until only recently. Generally the development of the groups has been separate and unequal. Today those blacks and whites who live together in the inner city do so almost by historical accident. Their communities may be referred to as integrated, but this label is deceptive. Rather, such areas, including the Village, are in transition, changing from "racially mixed" to white and from lower income to upper income. The rare black professionals who live there seem even more likely to succumb to the strong attraction of the suburbs and other areas. In time these dynamics leave the community predominantly white, a consequence of class as well as race.

6

o

The

Black Male

in

Public

*A*n overwhelming number of young black males in the Village are committed to civility and law-abiding behavior. They often have a hard time convincing others of this, however, because of the stigma attached to their skin color, age, gender, appearance, and general style of self-presentation. Moreover, most residents ascribe criminality, incivility, toughness, and street smartness to the anonymous black male, who must work hard to make others trust his common decency.

This state of affairs is worth exploring at some length for at least two reasons. First, the situation of young black men as a group encapsulates the stigmatizing effect of "negative" status-determining characteristics, in this case gender and race. Because public encounters between strangers on the streets of urban America are by nature brief, the participants must draw conclusions about each other quickly, and they generally rely on a small number of cues. This process is universal, and it unavoidably involves some prejudging—prejudice—but its working out is especially prominent in the public spaces of the Village-Northton.

Second, in the Village itself, as we saw in chapter 5, the presence and behavior of anonymous young black men is the single dominating concern of many who use its public spaces. The central theme in maintaining safety on the streets is avoiding strange black males. The consequences of this situation for the overall street etiquette of the Village are a major focus of chapter 8; the consequences for the black males themselves are my concern here.

Anonymous black males occupy a peculiar position in the social fabric of the Village. The fear and circumspection surrounding people's reactions to their presence constitute one of the hinges that public race relations turn on. Although the black male is a provocative figure to most others he encounters, his role is far from simple. It involves a complex set of relationships to be negotiated and renegotiated with all those sharing the streets. Where the Village meets Northton, black males exercise a peculiar hegemony over the public spaces, particularly at night or when two or more are together. This influence often is checked by the presence of the local police, which in turn has consequences for other public relationships in the Village.

The residents of the area, including black men themselves, are likely to defer to unknown black males, who move convincingly through the area as though they "run it," exuding a sense of ownership. They are easily perceived as symbolically inserting themselves into any available social space, pressing against those who might challenge them. The young black males, the "big winners" of these little competitions, seem to feel very comfortable as they swagger confidently along. Their looks, their easy smiles, and their spontaneous laughter, singing, cursing, and talk about the intimate details of their lives, which can be followed from across the street, all convey the impression of little concern for other pedestrians. The other pedestrians, however, are very concerned about them.

When young black men appear, women (especially white women) sometimes clutch their pocketbooks. They may edge up against their companions or begin to walk stiffly and deliberately. On spotting black males from a distance, other pedestrians often cross the street or give them a wide berth as they pass. When black males deign to pay attention to passersby, they tend to do so directly, giving them a deliberate once-over; their eyes may linger longer than the others consider appropriate to the etiquette of "strangers in the streets." Thus the black males take in all the others and dismiss them as a lion might dismiss a mouse. Fellow pedestrians in turn avert their eyes from the black males, deferring to figures who are seen as unpredictable, menacing, and not to be provoked—predators.

People, black or white, who are more familiar with the black street culture are less troubled by sharing the streets with young black males. Older black men, for instance, frequently adopt a refined set of criteria. In negotiating the streets, they watch out particularly for a certain *kind* of young black male; "jitterbugs" or those who might belong to "wolf packs," small bands of black teenage boys believed to travel about the urban areas accosting and robbing people.

Many members of the Village community, however, both black and white, lack these more sophisticated insights. Incapable of making distinctions between law-abiding black males and others, they rely for protection on broad stereotypes based on color and gender, if not outright racism. They are likely to misread many of the signs displayed by law-abiding black men, thus becoming apprehensive of almost any black male they spot in public. The kind of situation that results is illustrated by the interview with the black professional quoted in chapter 5, where the image of "young father" taking his child to the playground was not strong enough to offset his maleness, blackness, and dress in the eyes of strangers and even of acquaintances.

Two general sociological factors underlie the situation in which the black man in the Village finds himself. The first, the "master status-determining characteristic" of race (Hughes 1944), is at work in the most casual street encounter. Becker's application of Hughes's conception of the contradictions and dilemmas of status has special relevance:

> Some statuses, in our society as in others, override all other statuses and have a certain priority. Race is one of these. Membership in the Negro race, as socially defined, will override most other status considerations in most situations; the fact that one is a physician or middle class or female will not protect one from being treated as a Negro first and any of these other things second. The status of deviant (depending on the kind of deviance) is this kind of master status. One receives the status as a result of breaking a rule, and the identification proves to be more important than most others. One will be identified as a deviant first, before other identifications are made. The question raised: "What kind of person would break such an important rule?" And the answer given: "One who is different from the rest of us, who cannot or will not act as a moral human being and therefore might break other important rules." The deviant identification becomes the controlling one.
>
> Treating a person as though he were generally rather than

specifically deviant produces a self-fulfilling prophecy. It sets in motion several mechanisms which conspire to shape the person in the image people have of him. (Becker 1963, 33, 34)

In the minds of many Village residents, black and white, the master status of the young black male is determined by his youth, his blackness, his maleness, and what these attributes have come to stand for in the shadow of the ghetto. In the context of racism, he is easily labeled "deviant" in Becker's sense. In public, fellow pedestrians are thus uncertain about his purpose and have a strong desire to make sense of him quickly, so that they can get on with their own business. Many simply conclude that he is dangerous and act accordingly. Thus in social encounters in the public spaces of the Village, before he can be taken for anything as an individual (that is, "specifically" in Becker's terms), he is perceived first and foremost as a young black man from the ghetto (that is, "generally").

Here the second element comes into play. An assessment like this is really a *social definition*, normally something to be negotiated between labeler and labeled. Goffman's description of the process is classic:

> When an individual enters the presence of others, they commonly seek to acquire information about him or to bring into play information already possessed. They will be interested in his general conception of self, his attitude toward them, his competence, his trustworthiness, etc. Although some of this information seems to be sought almost as an end in itself, there are usually quite practical reasons for acquiring it. Information about the individual helps to define the situation, enabling others to know in advance what he will expect of them and what they may expect of him. Informed in these ways, the others will know how best to act in order to call forth a desired response from him. (Goffman 1959, 1)

In a city one has many encounters with anonymous figures who are initially viewed as strangers, about whom little is known or understood. As Goffman suggests, there are ways strangers can rapidly become known or seen as less strange. In negotiating public spaces, people receive and display a wide range of behavioral cues and signs that make up the vocabulary of public interaction. Skin color, gender, age, companions, clothing, jewelry, and the objects people carry help identify them, so that assumptions are formed and communication can occur. Movements (quick or slow, false or sincere, comprehensible or incomprehensible) further refine this public communication. Factors like time of day or an activity that "explains" a person's presence can also affect in what way and how quickly the image of "stranger" is neutralized (See Simmel 1971; Wirth 1928; Schutz 1969; Goffman 1971).

If a stranger cannot pass inspection and be assessed as "safe" (either by identity or by purpose), the image of predator may arise, and fellow pedestrians may try to maintain a distance consistent with that image. In the more worrisome situations—for example, encountering a number of strangers on a dark street—the image may persist and trigger some form of defensive action.

In the street environment, it seems, children readily pass inspection, white women and white men do so more slowly, black women, black men, and black male teenagers most slowly of all. The master status assigned to black males undermines their ability to be taken for granted as law-abiding and civil participants in public places: young black males, particularly those who don the urban uniform (sneakers, athletic suits, gold chains, "gangster caps," sunglasses, and large portable radios or "boom boxes"), may be taken as the embodiment of the predator. In this uniform, which suggests to many the "dangerous underclass," these young men are presumed to be troublemakers or criminals. Thus, in the local milieu, the identity of predator is usually "given" to the young black male and made to stick until he demonstrates otherwise, something not easy to do in circumstances that work to cut off communication (see Becker 1963; Goffman 1963).

In the Village a third, concrete factor comes into play. The immediate source of much of the distrust the black male faces is the nearness of Northton. White newcomers in particular continue to view the ghetto as a mysterious and unfathomable place that breeds drugs, crime, prostitution, unwed mothers, ignorance, and mental illness. It symbolizes persistent poverty and imminent danger, personified in the young black men who walk the Village streets (see Katz 1988, 195–273). The following narrative of a young black indicates one response of Villagers to the stereotype they fear so much:

⊙ *A white lady walkin' down the street with a pocketbook. She start walkin' fast. She get so paranoid she break into a little stride.*

Me and my friends comin' from a party about 12:00. She stops and goes up on the porch of a house, but you could tell she didn't live there. I stop and say, "Miss, you didn't have to do that. I thought you might think we're some wolf pack. I'm twenty-eight, he's twenty-six, he's twenty-nine. You ain't gotta run from us." She said, "Well, I'm sorry." I said, "You can come down. I know you don't live there. We just comin' from a party." We just walked down the street and she came back down, walked across the street where she really wanted to go. So she tried to act as though she lived there. And she didn't. After we said, "You ain't gotta run from us," she said, "No, I was really in a hurry." My boy said, "No you wasn't. You thought we was gon' snatch yo' pocketbook." We pulled money out. "See this, we work." I said, "We grown men, now. You gotta worry about them fifteen-, sixteen-, seventeen-year-old boys. That's what you worry about. But we're grown men." I told her all this. "They the ones ain't got no jobs; they're too young to really work. They're the ones you worry about, not us." She understood that. You could tell she was relieved and she gave a sigh. She came back down the steps, even went across the street.

We stopped in the middle of the street. "You all right, now?" And she smiled. We just laughed and went on to a neighborhood bar. ◑

Experiences like this may help modify the way individual white residents view black males in public by establishing conditions under which blacks pass inspection by disavowing the image of predator, but they do little to change the prevailing public relationship between blacks and whites in the community. Common racist stereotypes persist, and black men who successfully make such disavowals are often seen not as the norm but as the exception—as "different from the rest"—thereby confirming the status of the "rest."

In the interest of security and defense, residents adopt the facile but practical perspective that informs and supports the prevailing view of public community relations: whites are law-abiding and trustworthy; anonymous young black males are crime-prone and dangerous. Ironically, this perceived dangerousness has become important to the public self-identity of many local black men.

Greetings

Among blacks, the act of greeting is of great cultural importance. Children are often chastised at home if they fail to "speak" to their elders when they enter a room. The caretaking adult may become indignant when a charge fails in his duty to "be polite." A visitor will then comment, "Young man, can't you speak?" This places the blame squarely on the child, who then may sheepishly say, "Hi, Mr. Jones."

To some degree this practice may derive from "southern" or rural norms, but it has been brought to northern urban areas and survived. In the days of strict racial segregation, the black community was a haven to blacks, who tended to see every other black person as an ally in the fight against oppression (see Cox 1948; Doyle 1937). Furthermore, blacks were ready to see one another as special—as a "friend," a "brother," or someone with whom they had much in common. In this social context, even unacquainted blacks were inclined to greet each other easily and comfortably. Blacks in the Village still spontaneously greet other blacks they are sure they do not know. In fact Northton blacks, many of whom have southern roots, seem to be more forthcoming with such greetings to fellow blacks on the streets of the Village than they are on their home turf, reflecting a need to express color-caste solidarity. In contrast, middle-income blacks of the Village are more likely to greet their white counterparts, while remaining somewhat reserved in their overall behavior.

To many blacks, greetings carry an obligation to respond in kind. Not to return a greeting is uncommon, and the person is considered "strange." Blacks are more likely to speak to those they do not know, including whites, than whites are to speak to unfamiliar whites or to blacks in public places. When with a black person, a white person may be amazed that so many "unknown" blacks will speak. In this way, unacquainted blacks can give the appearance of a unified public community on the streets of the Village. Such greeting behavior is not simply an ingrained ritual; it may be viewed as instrumental, as a way for Northton blacks in the Village to come to terms with an environment they see as not always welcoming or safe.

Codified forms of greeting, or lack of greeting, clearly provide a means for negotiating encounters with strangers, so it is hardly surprising that many black males use such behavior as a device, even a ploy, of getting safely past the next black male of uncertain purpose. These greetings become tools for gauging intent and for assessing the safety of a public situation. Black youths are well aware of how "dangerous" they are seen to be, and they may help place each other in that category, which can be advantageous. When one black youth encounters another on the street, he may be circumspect and some-what cautious, and he will try to read his counterpart. As one young black man said:

◐ You know by the way they respond to you that you get a cer-tain ease in the relationship. If they respond a certain way, I know a lot of times when I'm not sure about someone, and see, they'll be the same age as me. I know we doing this for each other. If I see a young black male that I'm not sure about, well, you know, he doesn't ex-actly put me at ease right away. I might say, "What's up?" or "How ya feel?" You then can kinda know, by the way he responds to you, like if he don't answer you, or if one of your own people [a black per-son] don't say something to you, then kinda automatically you kinda put a shield around you. You just makin' sure. You act differently than you woulda acted if he hada responded to you in some compat-ible way. You have to establish something, especially if you never saw the person before.

I can automatically pick up on when somebody's going at me. I mean like a lot of times, I can tell if a brother I see on the street comes from my old neighborhood; I can feel at ease a bit. But if a brother is coming from some other neighborhood, I don't consciously try to predict their acts. But the way I react to them is just saying to them that I'm not sure. I don't perceive them to be necessarily about the same things that I'm about. I don't know whether he's about snatching a pocketbook or holding somebody up. See, I have to won-der when I see a strange black male. I have to watch my back. ◐

When the stranger responds in kind to a greeting on the street, the situation is over: the other youth leaves, and the young black can relax. Typical passing rituals between strange young black males include: "Hey, now," "Hey, hometown," "Hey, home," "Alright," "Hey," "What's up?" "How ya feel," or even an audible grunt. In the streets there is a profound need to acknowledge the presence of the other, to communicate awareness of the other's awareness, but this communication is intended to be superficial and not to go further. Typically, as the two continue on their ways, neither looks back; they have thus said much by not saying more. The hidden tension among black males is elaborated by a young black man from Northton:

◐ When I go down the street, I go straight to my friends. I watch out for certain people I don't know from the neighborhood. I go straight to my friends; they be on the corner. I watch my back. I observe everything, look in the bushes. I know which way to go *home. I never walk in the middle of the street, unless there's a dog on the side. I don't trust no dogs. And I never cross the street when I see dudes [other black males] coming, because I feel as though they see you doin' that, they feel as though, "What's up with him?" When you cross the street, that means you're scared or you can't fight.*

But you walk on the same side, first thing they think—he might got a knife, he might be into martial arts, or he might be a boxer. Shit, that means you intimidatin' them. I can come right to 'em; I don't give a shit how many are there. I'm too dumb to run. When people cross the street rather than meet me, I know they scared to death. When I pass some dude, I just say, "How ya doin'?" They say, "What's up?" If he starts to say somethin' to you, you keep walking. At times, I have an expression on my face that I'm not to be messed with. I stare at the person. Intimidate a person. Eye to eye. See who back off first, things like that. I don't pay 'em no mind. If someone bump into me on purpose, I keep on rollin'. ◖

The greeting used in this manner is intended to evade or defuse interaction rather than to move toward personal involvement. An important, if subtle, rule is that participants remain within the negotiated confines of the simple initiation. An attempt to go beyond the superficial greeting might, in the words of Erving Goffman (1959), "flood out" the situation. Further advances may undermine the delicate relationship between passersby, particularly those of different colors and genders.

The greeting becomes particularly important at night, when it is a kind of peace offering, a means of communication designed to advise the next person of one's civil intentions, or even of one's ability to deal with trouble. A variety of signs may be given to help the individual feel more at ease on the streets, even if they are not understood or taken seriously by his counterpart. The following field note illustrates this:

◖ *On successive summer nights I walked or drove around the Village streets. Weather permitting, people sit on their porches in lawn chairs and swings, sometimes completely hidden from passersby. The streets are often quiet except for the faint chirps of crickets or the sound of cars. Occasionally the silence is broken by the clamor of a passing youth's radio, but then it grows quiet again. One weeknight, at about 9:00, I saw a young black woman walking. As we met, she said "Hi." I returned her greeting and continued. Then I saw an elderly black man on the other side of the street, and though the streets are not wide, he did not acknowledge me. Next I saw a young black woman pushing a stroller, with her three- or four-year-old child walking eight to ten feet behind her. Acknowledging me, she said "Hi," and I said "Hey," politely returning her greeting. Farther down the street I encountered four black youths. As we approached I said, "How y'all feelin'?" a greeting common among blacks of the city. One youth returned, "Alright." They continued, and I went on my way. ◐*

Such greetings run the social gamut from relatively simple to highly complex: they may signal superficial acceptance of the next person on the street or exhibit varying degrees of personal closeness between sender and recipient. Because most local blacks, regardless of where they reside, are not culturally far removed from the ghetto and are at least conversant with its rules and symbols, they are often better able to read such public situations than are whites or blacks with very limited urban experience. Blacks tend to think of themselves as streetwise in a way whites are not—to feel that they have a special empathy and connection with those blacks who might be dangerous in public. With such attitudes in mind, they have developed a number of strategies for dealing with the anonymous black male, including sometimes aggressive greeting behavior. The "street" repertoire of such individuals includes the strategy of "getting ignorant," which they invoke in conversations with others and enact in public to deal with supposed adversaries. Getting ignorant is taken to mean getting down to the level of a street-oriented person and capably adopting the supposed behavior of underclass blacks who would engage in loud talk and profanity and if necessary violence to deal with a public dispute. For instance:

◐ *In an adjacent community that shares some social and cultural patterns with the Village, Thomas Waters, a well-educated middle-class black man, became involved in a dispute with his underclass neighbor. The exchange on the street went something like this: Robert Johnson, the less well-off man, complained, "I don't like you parking in front of my house with your big car [Lincoln Town Car], because you break up my curb. Look at that, see. Now, don't do it again, and ruin my curb, or you gon' pay for it." "What? What are you talking about, man? You want me to pay for your curb? Well, you can just hold your breath on that one. You'll sip ice water in hell before I'll pay for your curb! Do you hear me? That's what you can do!" This exchange grew louder and verged on violence. It never got* to that point, but those looking on were worried, not knowing whether to call the police. ❍

In the words of middle-class blacks, the posture and behavior Thomas Waters assumed is "getting ignorant," and because of caste experience, particularly familiarity with an underclass code of behavior, such individuals can sometimes act out the script rather convincingly. It is just this familiarity, and the ability to switch codes situationally, going back and forth between middle-class propriety and an assumed "street" orientation, that allows many middle-income blacks to feel less nervous and constricted in public than their white counterparts. The following field note illustrates this:

❍ *On a Saturday night in November at about 11:00, I was at a self-service gas station on the edge of the Village. Because it was cold, I pumped my gas with one hand on the nozzle and the other in my pocket. Suddenly a young black man appeared. He walked over and asked if I had the time. Instinctively I looked him in the eye and said, "What's up, buddy?" as though I expected an answer. There was silence. Then I said, "I ain't got no watch, man." Experience on the streets had taught me that one ruse muggers use is to ask the intended victim a question that distracts him, getting him to drop his guard and setting him up for the mugging. By saying "What's up, buddy?" I gave him pause and made him rethink his intentions. In a stickup or a mugging, timing is crucial. My body language, my tone of voice, and my words, all taken together in that instant, may have thrown him off, possibly averting an attempted stickup. Context was important here. The rules of the streets say that a strange black male does not approach another black male around midnight on a Saturday and ask for the time. Such a person, goes the rule, deserves what he gets in the way of an answer. I understood that, and I presume the possible mugger did too. I was able to switch codes from that of the middle class to that of the street—to "get ignorant." ❍*

Claiming Turf Rights

Yet both blacks and whites are cautious with strangers and take special care in dealing with anonymous young blacks. This caution is encouraged by a certain style of self-presentation that is common on the street. Many black youths, law-abiding or otherwise, exude an offensive/defensive aura because they themselves regard the streets as a jungle. A young black man said:

❍ *A friend of mine got rolled. He was visiting this girl up near*

Mercer Street. He come out of this house, and somebody smacked him in the head with a baseball bat. He had all these gold chains on. Had a brand new $200 thick leather jacket, $100 pair of Michael Jordon sneaks, and they were brand new, first time he had them on his feet. He had leather pants on too. And I'm surprised they didn't take his leather pants. I mean, he had a gold chain this thick [shows quarter-inch with his fingers]. I mean pure gold—$800 worth of gold. He came out this girl's house, after visiting his baby. Cats hit him in the head with a baseball bat, and they took everything. Took his sneaks, his coat, everything. When the paramedics got there he had no coat, no sneaks on. They took his belt, took his Gucci belt, the junkies did. I went to visit him in the hospital, and I'm sorry I went in there. I seen him. The boy had stitches . . . they shaved his head, stitches from here to all the way back of his head. Beat him in the head with a baseball bat. They say it was two guys. They was young boys, typical stupid young boys. Now my boy's life is messed up. He home now, but poor guy has seizures and everything. It's a jungle out here, man. But he sold drugs; the cops found cocaine in his underwear. They [the muggers] got what they wanted. ⦿

The young black males' pose is generally intended for people they perceive as potentially aggressive toward them. But at the same time it may engender circumspection and anxiety in law-abiding residents, both black and white, whose primary concern is safe passage on the streets.

In this public environment, pedestrians readily defer to young black males, who accept their public position. They walk confidently, heads up and gazes straight. Spontaneous and boisterous, they play their radios as loud as they please, telling everyone within earshot that this is their turf, like it or not. It may be that this is one of the few arenas where they can assert themselves and be taken seriously, and perhaps this is why they are so insistent.

Other pedestrians withdraw, perhaps with a defensive scowl, but nothing more. For the Village is not defended in the way many working-class neighborhoods are. As the black youths walk through late at night with their radios turned up, they meet little or no resistance. This lack of challenge shows how "tame," weak, or undefended the neighborhood is, except in certain areas where white college students predominate and fraternity boys succeed in harassing apparently defenseless blacks such as women with children, lone women, and an occasional single black man. Black youths tend to avoid such areas of the Village unless they are in groups.

The same black youths might hesitate before playing a radio loud in the well-defended territories of Northton, however. There they would likely be met by two or three "interceptors" who would promptly question their business, possibly taking the radio and punching one of the boys, or worse, in the process. No such defending force exists within the Village.

❍ *At about 5:30 on a Tuesday evening in September, three black youths appeared on quiet Linden Avenue. One carried a large box radio, with the volume turned high. The sound was distinctively "rap" [music], and the boys were "jamming" to the beat. They seemed to be in their own world, oblivious to others on the sidewalk and on the porches they passed. Halfway down the block, they stopped at an inviting stoop. They sat on the steps, legs sprawled, as though they were used to the spot. While the music played, the youths spoke loudly, in competition with the radio. One boy sang along with the tape, bobbing his head to the beat. No one complained. The three boys sat there on the stoop, enjoying themselves and filling the air with their music for fifteen to twenty minutes. Then they left as suddenly as they had appeared, transporting their "rap" music down the street, the sounds becoming fainter as they moved on.* ❍

Another aspect of claiming turf rights is public talk—its idiom, duration, intensity, and volume. At times the language of young black males, even those who are completely law-abiding, is harsh and profane. This language is used in many public spaces, but especially at trolley stops and on trolleys and buses. Like the rap music played loudly on boom boxes, it puts others on the defensive. The "others" tend not to say much to the offenders; rather, they complain to one another (though some residents have in fact come to appreciate the young males and enjoy the music).

On public transportation young blacks, including some girls, may display raucous behavior, including cursing and loud talk and play. Because most people encounter the youths as strangers, they understand them through the available stereotypes. Law-abiding black youths often don the special urban uniform and emulate this self-presentation, a practice known as "going for bad" and used to intimidate others. As one young black man said:

◐ *You see the guys sometimes on the bus having this air about them. They know that the grown people on the bus hope that these guys are not problems. The boys play on that. I'm talking about with women old enough to be their mothers. Now, they wouldn't be doing this at home. But they'll do it on that bus. They'll carry on to such an extent. . . . Now, I know, especially the young boys. I know they [older people] be scared. They really wondering, 'cause all they know is the headlines, "Juvenile Crime. . . ," "Problems of Youth Kids," or "Chain Snatchers." This is what they know. And these people are much more uncertain than I am, 'cause I know.* ◐

In some cases black males capitalize on the fear they know they can evoke. They may "put on a swagger" and intimidate those who must momentarily share a small space on the sidewalk. When passing such a "loud" dark-skinned person, whites usually anticipate danger, though they hope for a peaceful pass. Whites and middle-income blacks are often more than ready to cross the street to avoid passing a "strange" black person at close range. Young blacks understand this behavior and sometimes exploit the fear, as illustrated in the following narrative by a young white woman:

◐ *I went out for something at the store at about 9:00, after it was already dark. When I came back, there was no place to park in front of my house anymore. So I had to park around the corner, which I generally don't do because there's a greater chance of getting your car broken into or stolen over there, since a lot of foot traffic goes by at night. So I parked the car, turned out the lights, and got out. I began walking across the street, but I got into a situation I don't like to get into—of having there be some ominous-looking stranger between me and my house. So I have to go around or something. And he was a black fellow between twenty and thirty, on the youngish side. He certainly wasn't anybody I knew. So I decided not really to run, just sort of double-time, so I wouldn't meet him at close distance at the corner. I kind of ran diagonally, keeping the maximum distance between him and me. And it must have been obvious to him that I was running out of fear, being alone at night out in the street. He started chuckling, not trying to hide it. He just laughed at what I was doing. He could tell what he meant to me, the two of us being the only people out there.* ◐

At times even civil and law-abiding youths enjoy this confusion. They have an interest in going for bad, for it is a way to keep other youths at bay. The right look, moves, and general behavior ensure safe passage. However, this image is also a source of subtle but enduring racial and class distinctions, if not overt hostility, within the community.

Some black youths confront others with behavior they refer to as "gritting," "looking mean," "looking hard," and "bumping." Youths have a saying, "His jaws got tight." Such actions could easily be compared to threatening animal behavior, particularly dogs warning other dogs away from their territory or food. Gritting is a way of warning peers against "messing with me." To grit is to be ready to defend one's interests, in this case one's physical self. It conveys alertness to the prospect of harmful intent, communicating and defining personal boundaries. As one young black man said concerning strategies for negotiating the Northton streets near the Village:

○ When I walk the streets, I put this expression on my face that tells the next person I'm not to be messed with. That "You messing with the wrong fellow. You just try it, try it." And I know when cats are behind me. I be just lookin' in the air, letting them know I'm checkin' them out. Then I'll put my hand in my pocket, even if I ain't got no gun. Nobody wants to get shot, that shit burns, man. That shit hurt. Some guys go to singing. They try to let people know they crazy. 'Cause if you crazy [capable of anything], they'll leave you alone. And I have looked right in they face [muggers] and said, "Yo, I'm not the one." Give 'em that crazy look, then walk away. 'Cause I know what they into. They catch your drift quick. ○

Another young black man described his use of body language this way:

○ It's certain ways you can give him body language that you're not to be messed with. Some people ball their fists up or just walk, or they're built a certain way. You move the hand. Walk with his hand like this, means he's a fighter. I handle myself. I can handle three guys. See, if you're fightin' three guys, if you swing at the same time they swing, you get tired first, you fightin' three guys. But you use your head. One swing, you snatch him, knock the shit out of him. Another one comes, bam! Throw him off balance. You don't go swinging as much as they do. Use your head. ○

The youth is caught up here in a cultural catch-22: to appear harmless to others might make him seem weak or square to those he feels a need to impress. If he does not dress the part of a young black man on the streets, it is difficult for him to "act right." If he is unable to "act right," then he may be victimized by strangers in his general

peer group. The uniform—radio, sneakers, gold chain, athletic suit—
and the selective use of the "grit," the quasi-military swagger to the
beat of "rap" songs in public places, are all part of the young man's
pose. Law-abiding and crime-prone youths alike adopt such poses, in
effect camouflaging themselves and making it difficult for more conventional people to know how to behave around them, since those
for whom they may not be performing directly may see them as
threatening. By connecting culturally with the ghetto, a young black
may avoid compromising his public presentation of self, but at the
cost of further alienating law-abiding whites and blacks.

In general, the black male is assumed to be streetwise. He also
comes to think of himself as such, and this helps him negotiate public spaces. In this sense others collectively assist him in being who he
is. With a simple move one way or the other, he can be taken as a
"dangerous dude." He is then left alone, whereas whites may have
more trouble.

Civility and law-abidingness are stereotypically ascribed to the
white male, particularly in the public context of so many "dangerous" and "predatory" young blacks. (In fact, white men must campaign to achieve the status of being seen as dangerous in public
places.) The white male is not taken seriously on the streets, particularly by black men, who resist seeing him as a significant threat.
They think that most white men view conflict in terms of "limited
warfare," amounting to little more than scowls and harsh words. It is
generally understood that blacks from Northton do not assume this
but are open to unlimited warfare, including the use of sticks, stones,
knives, and guns, perhaps even a fight to the death.

Most conventional people learn to fear black youths from reading about crimes in the local papers and seeing reports of violence on
television, but also by living so near and having the chance to observe them. Every time there is a violent crime, this image of young
blacks gains credibility. Such public relations attribute to blacks control over the means and use of violence in public encounters, thus
contributing to dominant stereotypes and fear. As is clear from the
following interview, black men pick up on that fear:

◑ *They [white men] look at you strange, they be paranoid. Especially if you walkin' behind 'em. They slow down and let you walk
in front or they walk on the other side. You know they got their eye
on you. I walk past one one time. My mother live on Fortieth and
Calvary and I did that. I said, "You ain't gotta slow down, brother. I*

ain't gonna do nothin' to you, I ain't like that." He looked at me and laughed. He knew what I meant, and I knew what he was thinkin'. He had a little smile. It was late at night, about 1:00 A.M. He let me get in front of him. He was comin' from a bar, and he had a six-pack. I'm a fast walker anyway; you can hear my shoes clickin'. I see him slowing down. I said, "I ain't gonna do nothin' to you, I ain't like that." He just laughed; I kept on walking and I laughed. That's the way it went. ◐

Whereas street interactions between black strangers tend to be highly refined, greetings of whites toward blacks are usually ambiguous or have limited effectiveness. This general communication gap between blacks and whites is exacerbated by the influx of white newcomers. In contrast to the longtime residents, the newcomers are unaccustomed to and frequently intolerant of neighboring blacks and have not learned a viable street etiquette. The run-ins such new people have with blacks contribute to a general black view of "the whites" of the Village as prejudiced, thus undermining the positive race relations promoted over many years by egalitarian-minded residents.

The result is that the white and black communities become collapsed into social monoliths. For instance, although blacks tend to relate cautiously to unknown black youths, they are inclined to look at them longer, inspecting them and noting their business to see whether they deserve to be trusted. Whites, on the other hand, look at blacks, see their skin color, and dismiss them quickly as potential acquaintances; then they furtively avert their gaze, hoping not to send the wrong message, for they desire distance and very limited involvement. Any follow-up by black youths is considered highly suspect unless there are strong mitigating factors, such as an emergency where help is needed.

A common testimonial from young blacks reflects the way whites encounter them. They speak about the defensiveness of whites in general. White women are said to plant broad grins on their faces in hopes of not being accosted. The smile may appear to be a sign of trust, but it is more likely a show of deference, especially when the woman looks back as soon as she is at a safe distance. When the black stranger and the perceived danger have passed, the putative social ties suggested by the smile are no longer binding and the woman may attempt to keep the "dangerous" person in view, for a sudden move could signal an "attempted robbery" or "rape."

A young black man who often walks through the Village reports this reaction from white women:

○ *They give the eye. You can see 'em lookin' right at you. They look at you and turn back this way, and keep on walkin'. Like you don't exist, but they be paranoid as hell. Won't say hello. But some of 'em do. Some of 'em say hi. Some of 'em smile. But they always scared.* ○

One young white woman confirmed this: "I must admit, I look at a black [male] on the street just for a few seconds. Just long enough to let him know I know of his presence, and then I look away." The black man just quoted gave an observant report of the general behavior of white Village women on the streets:

○ *Most of the white women will wear pants. You don't see a white woman with a dress on unless she with her boyfriend. She by herself, she'll go right on a porch when she see some [black] guys comin' this way. Most girls walk with a pack of girls. They feel safe they got at least two girls with 'em. Two don't feel too safe. You get a group of three or four, they feel they have a better chance. They have a dog with 'em, a man, or a pack of four or five. And they dress in jeans. You can tell they paranoid. They don't know what to do. They say: "Are they good blacks or bad blacks?" Most of 'em will take a chance. Chance is good; nobody do that no more, they know they got the cops. In the Village, cops sit on the porch, park between cars; they lookin' at every move you makin' and you don't even see 'em. But they see you and waitin'! The women'll stay home. And they have a car. Don't come out at certain times. Especially after eleven or twelve at night. They don't go in bars. They go to clubs downtown.*

The young black men are the ones they [women] got to worry about. The young ones walk around lookin' mean and tough. They don't care about the white guys. No, they goin' to catch the trolley to the movies. You gotta go through the Village to catch the trolley, bus, el [subway]. ○

Out of a sense of frustration, many young blacks mock or otherwise insult the whites they see in public spaces, trying to "get even" with them for being part of the "monolithic" group of whites. When they encounter whites who display fear, they may laugh at them or harass them. They think, "What do I have to lose?" and may purposely create discomfort in those they see as "ignorant" enough to be afraid of them. Of course the whites of the Village are anything but a monolithic group. But it is convenient for certain blacks to see things this way, placing all whites, whom they see as the source of their troubles, into an easily manageable bag. In this way blacks as well as whites become victims of simplistic thinking.

Black men's resentment, coupled with peer-group pressure to act tough, may cause them to shift unpredictably from being courteous to whites to "fulfilling the prophecy" of those who are afraid and uncomfortable around blacks. When confronting a white woman on the streets some youths may make lewd or suggestive comments, reminding her that she is vulnerable and under surveillance. The following account describes such an encounter:

○ *On a Wednesday afternoon in June at about 2:00, Sandra Norris pushed her nine-month-old daughter down Cherry Street. The gray stone facades of the Victorian buildings sparkled in the sun. The streets seemed deserted, as the Village usually is at this time. Suddenly three black youths appeared. They looked in their late teens. As they approached her, one of the young men yelled to the others, "Let's get her! Get her!" Making sexual gestures, two of the youths reached for her menacingly. She cringed and pulled the stroller toward her. At that the boys laughed loudly. They were playing with her, but the feigned attack was no fun for Mrs. Norris. It left her shaking.* **○**

As indicated above, an aggressive presentation—though certainly not usually so extreme—is often accepted as necessary for black youths to maintain regard with their peers. They must "act right" by the toughest ghetto standards or risk being ridiculed or even victimized by their own peers. Feeling a certain power in numbers, some groups will readily engage in such games, noisily swooping down on their supposed "prey" or fanning out in a menacing formation. Children, white and black, sometimes are intimidated and form fearful and negative feelings about teenage "black boys."

Such demeanor may be a way of identifying with the ghetto streets, but it is also a way of exhibiting "toughness" toward figures who represent the "overclass," which many view as deeply implicated in the misfortunes of their communities. Such conduct is easily confused with and incorporated into ordinary male adolescent behavior, but the result is complicated by race and gender and the generalized powerlessness of the black community. Understandably, middle-class residents, black and white, become even more likely to place social distance between themselves and such youths, conceptually lumping anonymous black males together for self-defense.

Of course not everyone is victimized by crime, but many people take incivility as an indication of what could happen if they did not keep up their guard. When representatives of Northton walking through the Village intimidate residents either verbally or physically, many middle-class people—whites in particular—become afraid of black males in general. They may have second thoughts about "open" and to some degree friendly displays they may previously have made toward blacks in public. Blacks and whites thus become increasingly estranged. In fact there is a vicious circle of suspicion and distrust between the two groups and an overwhelming tendency for public relations between them to remain superficial and guarded.

Public Disavowal

It is not surprising that the law-abiding black man often feels at a disadvantage in his interactions with whites. Most whites, except possibly those who are streetwise (see chap. 8) and empathic about the plight of inner-city blacks, are conditioned to consider all black male strangers potential muggers. The average black, because of his own socialization on the streets and his understanding of the psychology of whites, understands this position very well and knows what whites are thinking.

Many blacks and whites seem alarmed when a black youth approaches them for any reason, even to ask the time. Such overtures may simply be the youth's attempt to disavow criminal intent or to neutralize the social distance generally displayed on the streets. But these attempts are easily interpreted as a setup for a mugging, causing the other person to flee or to cut off the interaction. The public stigma is so powerful that black strangers are seldom allowed to be civil or even helpful without some suspicion of their motives (see Becker 1963; Goffman 1963; Hughes 1944; Simmel 1971).

Even law-abiding black men who befriend whites and belong to biracial primary groups face "outsider" status. For example, when a black visits a white friend's house, knocks on the door or rings the bell and waits, he risks being taken by the neighbors as someone whose business on the stoop is questionable. Some people will keep an eye on him, watching every move until their neighbor comes to the door. It may not matter how well the visitor is dressed. His skin color indicates his "stranger" status, which persists until he passes inspection when the white person answers the door. A white man with the same self-presentation would pass much sooner.

Although they do not usually articulate the problem in just this manner, many black middle-income Villagers feel somewhat bitter about the prejudice of their white neighbors, who are caught up in a kind of symbolic racism. Dark skin has a special meaning, which Village residents have come to associate with crime. Though white Villagers may not have contempt for blacks in general, they do experience anxiety over the prospect of being victimized. So, since blacks are believed to make up a large proportion of the criminals, pedestrians tend to be defensive and short with strange black males. The same people may have intimate black friends and may pride themselves on their racial tolerance. Yet, concerned with safety, they regard blacks as an anonymous mass through which they must negotiate their way to their destination. They may pass right by black "friends" and simply fail to see them because they are concentrating not on the friend but on the social context. Such reactions frustrate many black-white friendships before they have a chance to begin. Blacks generally complain more than whites about such shortcomings of friendly relations. But as blacks make their way around the streets, they too may miss a "friend" of the other color. Such events may have more to do with the ambiguous nature of public race relations than with racial feeling itself. But whatever the cause, these problems are an impediment to spontaneous and biracial interactions.

Although blacks and whites may harbor similar cognitive views of the dangers of life in the Village, their perceptions of real situations commonly vary. Blacks generally feel less threatened than whites by anonymous blacks, because they are better able to read the signs indicating another person's intentions and to determine whether a situation is safe or dangerous. But there are times for them too when a "mock attack" signals real alarm. The following instance of harassment was witnessed by a forty-year-old black man living near the Village:

◐ *On Sunday night at about 11:30 I was walking home when I saw these eight young brothers [black men] messing with this older white man. He was riding an old three-speed down the street when he met the young black men. They assaulted him. One shouted, "Hey! Gimme that bicycle." Another said, "Hey old man, where you going?" With that, they surrounded him. It must have scared the shit*

*out of him. It seemed like that was just what they wanted to do.
They didn't really want his bicycle. It wasn't like the bicycle was a
new ten-speed. They just wanted to mess with him. One guy grabbed
the handlebars and shook the whole bicycle. I thought about saying
something, but I was worried about my own safety. You know how
these wolf packs can be. After a while one of the guys slapped him
upside his helmet, and then they all left the man, laughing as they
walked. The old man was very frightened, I know. And down the
street a ways he flagged down a police car. The cop was a sister [black woman]. Some other cars soon came, and they put his bicycle in the trunk of one of the cars, and they went looking for the
brothers.* ◐

In this situation the black man empathized with the victim, but
he was concerned for his own safety during the assault. Also, he felt
that any attempt to help might be taken by the victim or the police
as further harassment, or even that he might be mistaken for one of
the perpetrators.

An impressive number of blacks deplore such antagonism and
feel somewhat responsible to change it. They may view themselves
as among the few members of their race who can help bridge the gap.
To play this role, not only must they be outstanding (to set an example of what a black person is capable of for those powerful whites
who are in a position to judge), but they must also set an example
for other blacks. Thus a number of black men try very hard to dis-
abuse whites of their misjudgments. Often they go to great lengths to
behave contrary to the assumed expectations of whites, and they encourage other blacks to do so. They respond to prejudice by putting
on a performance of civility.

A young black man in street uniform may extend obvious cour-
tesies such as moving over to allow a white person extra space to
pass, making friendly eye contact, or offering a greeting. He may try
to confront and allay the stranger's fear. For example, when walking
down a dark street behind a white person, he might say, "Hey, you
don't have to be afraid, I'm not that man. I'm not out to rob you. You
don't have to worry." Unfortunately, the person is likely to be startled
and often does not know how to respond. The actions are in such
contrast to the common black male dress and self-presentation that
only an unusual person would immediately trust the verbal message
over the visual image. Furthermore, the words go beyond the expected superficiality in greetings and threaten *some* personal involve-

ment. Thus the plea to look beyond the black's self-presentation is rarely successful, and the stereotype of the dangerous black persists.

The black man who is determined to fight his bad image may handle what is often an uncomfortable situation for the white person by being too nice:

◐ *On Saturday afternoon at Lee's grocery store, on the edge of the Village, a young white woman was standing in line. She had bought many items and had two large bags full. As she picked them up off the counter and started for the front door, one bag slipped out of her hands and spilled on the floor. Three black men aged nineteen to twenty-two quickly came to her aid. Within seconds they were on their knees retrieving the groceries. They worked silently, while other customers watched them. They picked up every item and helped rebag the groceries. After this one young man asked, "Want me to take these out for you, Miss?" Clearly grateful but surprised, she sheepishly declined the offer and quickly left the store.* ◐

Such shows can be witnessed repeatedly around the Village and may be considered public demonstrations for whites who know little about the black community. They try to say, "We're not all like that [bad]," and at times they are a direct attack on the presumed prejudiced thinking of whites and an attempt to discredit such views— a public disavowal of incivility and criminality.

In public interactions between anonymous blacks and whites, there seems to be a strong concern with the immediate situation. The black person wants to get out with his self-esteem intact, which requires that the white person do the same. Because the black has the upper hand, he can in principle define the situation in a positive manner, such as by being gracious. In practice this is very difficult, as the last few examples illustrate. He hopes that, by his behavior, whites who are inclined to be suspicious of all black males will change their opinions.

The result of this informal public relations campaign is that whites may receive better treatment than blacks do from such people. Fellow blacks are not the primary object of this campaign; presumably they "understand" the existence of integrity and civility in the average black. A young black man made these comments:

◐ *I find myself being extra nice to whites. A lot of times I be walking down the streets, you know. And I see somebody white. Going back to my street smarts, I know they are afraid of me. They don't know me, but they intimidated. I pick that intimidation up, so*

I might smile, just to reassure them. And I know I'm doing that con-
sciously. I know it. At other times I find myself opening doors, you
know. Holding the elevator. Putting myself in a certain light, you
know, to change whatever doubts they may have. Look, I do this in
my neighborhood, when I go downtown to work, because I know
how uptight white people are in their relationship with young blacks
in town. In the building I work in, I see them. They look at me all
funny, so I'll go in the men's room and use the key. I say to a com-
plete stranger, "Hey, how you doing?" I speak [offer a greeting]. I
don't have to speak. But it's because I want them to feel comfortable
with me in the bathroom. I find myself doing this all the time. ◐

It might be tempting to attribute such behavior to the "race
man" ethic described in chapter 2, but such an evaluation would be
one-dimensional: there may be some of this ideology motivating the
black man who acts as a paragon of civility in the presence of whites,
but there is an instrumental element as well. Dealing with others in
public requires an enormous amount of effort from the black male
and produces unwanted distraction. Such a young man must put
strangers at ease so he can go about his own business. He can sense
when his presence makes whites nervous and unsettled. Blacks who
must repeatedly endure this reaction feel emotional stress and want
to relieve themselves of the burden.

In adapting to this reality, blacks assume the general principle of
public order that trustworthiness is an ascribed characteristic for
whites but that blacks, particularly young males, must work to
achieve it. One consequence is the development of public communities based on color. Usually the relationships between anonymous
whites and blacks in public are truncated and perfunctory, since most
people are concerned with "just getting by" and reaching their destination and do not want relations to go further. The intimate biracial
friendships that do occur tend to be sponsored through third parties
or fostered by an institutional framework. The release of tension
when a black male turns out to be "known" is evident in the following incident recounted by a middle-aged white Village resident,
which occurred one Halloween:

◐ *I know this kid named Tommy Hatfield; he was in Sarah Tay-*
lor's class, third or fourth grade, I forget now which one it was. But
anyway, Tommy was having some problems with his family. He was
a very angry boy. He wasn't a bad kid, but he was very angry. Sarah
was very patient with him, and he liked her a whole lot. And I knew

him for these eight weeks. Once a week I'd meet him in the class of about thirty or forty kids for an hour and a half to two hours. We got along fairly well. Anyway, he graduated, and he began going to another school. I hadn't seen him for a while, but then one time just at Halloween, my kids and I were sitting out on the steps.

A group of young black boys were coming to our stoop, we live on Spencer Street. And we could see that they were sidling up next to one another, and they were thinking, "How are we going to get candy off of this guy, now?" They didn't have any masks on or anything. Was he going to give them a hard time? Now maybe I was reading a lot into this. You could see that they were sort of moping around. They were not going to do anything bad, but you could see they were trying to figure out how to handle this situation. Well, Tommy looked up and saw that it was me and said, "Oh, it's Mr. Regis," and he poked his other friend with his elbow, and said, "It's Mr. Regis. He's taught us architecture."

And I looked up at him, and I said, "Oh, it's Tommy." And you could see there was just a whole difference in feeling. You could see that his facial expression changed, and mine probably did. And I said, "Tommy, you'll have to have some candy, here. What would you like?" He probably got more than he would have before. It was resolved in a good way. It was a good feeling. And it could have been a tension-filled situation [had the boys been strangers]. Not dangerous, but a tension-filled situation. ◐

In what circumstances can the anonymous black male become known as something other than a predator? Older black men earn greater trust through their appearance and demeanor, which suggest maturity and even a caretaking role toward others on the street. They often go so far as to become guardians of the public peace, concerned for the safe passage of others. They inform strangers about certain corners, warning them where not to go. Most often they offer advice only to whites who, they presume, are ignorant of the ways of the streets. There is an element of patronage in such interactions.

In determining the degree to which a man is seen as predator, the main question is What's his business? The extent to which he seems to be preoccupied, engaged in doing something, determines whether he is taken as being "up to no good." Daytime generally makes a black man in the Village seem less suspicious, mainly because others can see what he is doing, with the implication that because he can be watched he is also controlled and is less likely to commit a crime. A black man pushing a baby stroller at 3:00 in the afternoon would probably be taken as safe, whereas the same man alone at 11:30 at night would not. Eating an ice-cream cone can lessen a fearsome image, since watchers might reason that such an image is inconsistent with this "human" action. The time of day, the season of the year, the neighborhood's social history—events of the past thirty years or of the past few days—all affect the meaning this black man has for the residents who watch and informally guard the streets and public spaces.

Another important consideration here is what Goffman (1971) has described as the "with" and how its nature defines the individuals involved. Seeing a black man walk down the street with a conservatively dressed white man or woman mitigates what may otherwise be taken as a "tough" image or an unknown quantity and introduces elements of "weakness" or law-abidingness into the social equation.

In trying to take precautions, people look for signs that will indicate the nature of the black male. Whether he wears the uniform of the streets makes a difference in how he will be regarded. Also, the way he walks, whether he makes "false" or suspicious moves, is important. Blacks who desire the public trust feel a great need to distance themselves publicly from the black males who seem most untrustworthy, those wearing street attire or displaying the emblems of the underclass that increase their estrangement from conventional society. Black men who want to be seen as "safe" often display cultural emblems that suggest a connection with this conventional society and, by implication, public civility. Probably the most evocative emblem is the business suit and tie, which suggests that its wearer is committed to civility and thus is unlikely to engage in street fighting, to rob others, or to curse at passersby. Carrying books is another emblem, and black university students might display their books and briefcases to gain trust. Moreover, these are emblems known to be controlled by members of the "overclass"—people who can take for granted the full rights, duties, and civil obligations of ordinary citizens.

Yet even a black man in a suit and tie or carrying books is not necessarily by himself a "full person" in the minds of prejudiced whites concerned about their safety. Rather, he must be considered relative to his "ghetto" counterparts; in contrast to them, he can be seen as trustworthy and possibly law-abiding. That the person may be seen as symbolically negotiating his way suggests that his public identity is precarious and that he is thus discreditable (see Goffman 1963), particularly compared with those who start with the "master status-determining characteristic" of white skin. The anonymous black male is a person apart until he proves he has a connection, and therefore he is more persistently a stranger on the streets.

On the streets and in public places, young blacks are repeatedly sent the message that they are crime-prone and that their neighbors have little faith in their willingness to be law-abiding. And certainly, as the crime statistics and reports of victims illustrate, there are many of whom this is true. But for others this state of affairs creates a gnawing dilemma, for they are victimized from two sides. They must simultaneously prove that they are worthy of respect for their common decency, and they must protect themselves from predatory youths by looking tough and capable of "handling the streets."

This situation further polarizes racial attitudes in the special circumstances of the Village. By encouraging both whites and blacks to see those of the other color not as individuals but as representatives of their "untrustworthy" race, it is eroding the biracial harmony the previous generation of Village residents worked so hard to achieve.

One might wonder what all the second-guessing and fear on the part of middle-income people—black and white—does to the young black men who must live and operate in the Village. Certainly it gives them the sense that they are, if not losers, then at least not "born winners" in the local community or in life in general.

In their campaign for respectability, some young black men have become crusaders, particularly in those city areas that whites and blacks share. In their quest for positive judgment, they have become some of the most generous, helpful, kind, and courteous people around, contributing, to an often unacknowledged degree, to public safety. Nonetheless, it is impossible for them to overcome the pervasive stereotype. In the Village, no young black male has an easy time on the streets. The residents fear him. The police generally consider him out to rob people or insult passersby. Perceiving him as a threat, they view him as someone they must contain. This is one of the reasons many middle-class blacks are deflected from moving into the area or may leave soon after they arrive: they do not want such easy confusion of themselves and their children with the black underclass, particularly as it becomes caught up with the working conceptions and stereotypes of others in the neighborhood.

7

०

The Police

and the

Black Male

*T*he police, in the Village-Northton as elsewhere, represent society's formal, legitimate means of social control.[1] Their role
includes protecting law-abiding citizens from those who are not law-
abiding, by preventing crime and by apprehending likely criminals.
Precisely how the police fulfill the public's expectations is strongly
related to how they view the neighborhood and the people who live
there. On the streets, color-coding often works to confuse race, age,
class, gender, incivility, and criminality, and it expresses itself most
concretely in the person of the anonymous black male. In doing their
job, the police often become willing parties to this general color-
coding of the public environment, and related distinctions, particularly those of skin color and gender, come to convey definite
meanings. Although such coding may make the work of the police
more manageable, it may also fit well with their own presupposi-
tions regarding race and class relations, thus shaping officers' perceptions of crime "in the city." Moreover, the anonymous black male is
usually an ambiguous figure who arouses the utmost caution and is
generally considered dangerous until he proves he is not.

In July 1988, in the area just south of the Village, my own automobile was taken from its parking place on a main thoroughfare.
Convinced that a thief had stolen the car, I quickly summoned the
police. Within ten minutes of my calling 911 a police car arrived,
driven by a middle-aged white officer. He motioned for me to get in.
Because the front seat was cluttered with notebooks and papers, I
opened the back door and got in on the right-hand side. I intro-

1. See Rubinstein (1973); Wilson (1978); Fogelson (1977); Reiss (1971);
Bittner (1967); Banton (1964).

duced myself to Officer John Riley, mentioning that I was a professor, mainly to help establish myself with him. He was courteous, commiserated with me, then asked for the basic information. What time did I park the car? Could a friend or relative have taken it? During our exchanges I said that my family and I were planning a trip to the Midwest the next day to attend a family reunion, and I could feel his empathy. He said he would call in the report right away, and since the case was "hot," meaning the theft had just occurred, there might be a good chance of getting the car back soon, if not that very night. He then reported the theft and put out a bulletin. Into his radio he said, "Be on the lookout for a maroon 1982 Oldsmobile four-door sedan, heading northwest on Warrington Avenue." Every police car in the city, particularly those in the same district, was thus given a description of my car and would presumably be on the lookout for it. I was pleased with his attention to my misfortune.

As we sat in the patrol car, the officer interviewed me; and I took the opportunity to interview him as well. We spoke about policing the local area, about car thefts, and about the general crime rate. We discussed the characteristics of car thieves, robbers, muggers, and other antisocial persons in the area. I did not tell him I was a sociologist. I think he thought of himself as simply doing his job, treating me as just another victim of local crime—which I was indeed.

During this conversation the police officer seemed to be feeling me out, attempting to get a fix on me as a person, perhaps wondering where I stood politically. At one point we discussed jobs and crime and their relation to one another. Then the officer mentioned the way "he" had messed up this city and how the "big boys" had already gotten to "him." I took this as implicit criticism of the city's black mayor, so I deferred and listened intently, thinking I could learn something about his attitude concerning local city politics. But I also did not want to alienate this person who was trying to find my car. Hence I played along, pointing out that the mayor's stock had declined in the black community, that even many blacks were not satisfied with his performance.

After this conversational give and take, the officer seemed favorably impressed. He appeared genuinely sympathetic with my fear of missing my family reunion. More than once he suggested that I try to forget the theft for now, rent a Lincoln Town Car like his own, and drive to the reunion. I demurred, insisting that I wanted my own car back as soon as possible.

Through our conversation, he seemed to open up and trust me. Then he offered, "Listen, why don't we drive around and see if we can spot your car. Maybe some kids just took it for a joyride and ditched it." I was appreciative and encouraged him, but I stayed in the backseat, wondering where he would take me to look for my car. We headed north through the Village, across Bellwether, and into Northton. After driving up and down a number of the familiar streets of Northton, we headed for "the projects," about a mile northwest of the Village. When I asked why he had chosen to come here, he replied, "This is where they usually take them [cars]." It seemed he had a definite idea who he was talking about. *They* were the thieves, the robbers, the muggers, and generally the people who cause trouble. And they lived in Northton. As we proceeded, we passed numerous street corner groups of young black men, with some young women among them. Many were simply loitering. He knew some of them and greeted them in a familiar way as we slowly drove past. He would wave and say, "How y'all doin'" in what sounded like affected Black English. By showing this level of familiarity, he let me know he knew the community: it was to some degree his turf.

As we drove through the projects and the neighborhoods of Northton, ostensibly looking for my car, I felt strange—as though I was somehow identified with "the enemy"—though I was safe in the backseat. Also, when a young black man is sitting in a police car, most people perceive him to be in custody, in some kind of trouble, regardless of the real circumstances. This seems to go with the general definition of affairs in the neighborhood—that to be black and male, particularly when young, is to be suspect; that the young man must prove he is law-abiding. Even though I was sitting in the backseat, so that many onlookers might know the officer considered me "safe" or a victim to be aided, this reality goes strongly against the common sense of the community: a young black male is a suspect until he proves he is not. The burden of proof is not easily lifted.

After riding around Northton for about twenty minutes, we met another police car. The driver, who was white, middle-aged, and alone, had stopped at the corner, preparing to make a right-hand turn. My driver turned left onto the same street, and both stopped with the two cars facing in opposite directions. As they exchanged pleasantries, the second policeman kept looking at me with puzzlement. Black male alone in rear seat. Officer Riley felt the need to explain me and said, "Oh, somebody stole his car, and we're out looking for it. It's a maroon '82 Delta 88. The other policeman nodded. The two continued to make small talk, but the second officer could not keep his eyes off me. I felt that if I made a false move he would come after me. In essence the policeman played his role, and I played mine; notwithstanding that I was a victim of crime, my color and gender seemed to outweigh other claims.

Such roles are expected by the young black men of the neighborhood, who have a clear sense of who they are and what they mean to the police. It is from this knowledge that they infer how to act, and how the police will act, believing both must behave according to an elaborate script of the streets. Much of this may be viewed as symbolic display, but it works to maintain a certain ordering of affairs in the public arena.

In the presence of police officers, who clearly have the upper hand, black youths check themselves. They defer to the police or try to avoid them. And some black men, because of their profound distrust of the criminal justice system, say they would never allow a white policeman to arrest them. A young black male told me, "A white policeman would never go out of his way for a black man."

After about fifteen minutes the policemen finished their talk and said their good-byes. Meanwhile I was simply a nonperson, not their equal, and my time and business were clearly secondary in their minds. As we drove slowly up and down the streets, Officer Riley continued to nod, speak, and wave to people. Finally he gave up, saying he was "sorry, but maybe we'll have some luck tonight or tomorrow. I'll stay on it, and hopefully we'll get your car back." He then offered me a ride home, which I gladly accepted. On the way Officer Riley talked about his own misfortunes with theft, attempting to commiserate with me. I saw one of my white colleagues on a street corner near my house, reading a newspaper while waiting for a bus. As the patrol car pulled up to the light, he casually looked over at me, looked away, then looked again with astonishment. "Eli! Is that you? Are you okay? What's the trouble?" I quickly assured him that everything was all right, that I was with the policeman because my car had been stolen. But my colleague looked unconvinced. The light changed, and Officer Riley drove toward my house. He again expressed his regret for my predicament but said he was hopeful. We parted company, and I never saw him again. But the next morning at 9:00 I got a call that my car had been found and I could come and retrieve it.

There are some who charge—and as this account indicates, perhaps with good reason—that the police are primarily agents of the middle class who are working to make the area more hospitable to middle-class people at the expense of the lower classes. It is obvious that the police assume whites in the community are at least middle class and are trustworthy on the streets. Hence the police may be seen primarily as protecting "law-abiding" middle-class whites against anonymous "criminal" black males.

To be white is to be seen by the police—at least superficially—as an ally, eligible for consideration and for much more deferential treatment than that accorded blacks in general. This attitude may be grounded in the backgrounds of the police themselves. Many have grown up in Eastern City's "ethnic" neighborhoods.[2] They may serve what they perceive as their own class and neighborhood interests, which often translates as keeping blacks "in their place"—away from neighborhoods that are socially defined as "white." In trying to do their job, the police appear to engage in an informal policy of monitoring young black men as a means of controlling crime, and often they seem to go beyond the bounds of duty. The following field note shows what pressures and racism young black men in the Village may endure at the hands of the police:

◑ *At 8:30 on a Thursday evening in June I saw a police car stopped on a side street near the Village. Beside the car stood a policeman with a young black man. I pulled up behind the police car and waited to see what would happen. When the policeman released the young man, I got out of my car and asked the youth for an interview.*

"So what did he say to you when they stopped you? What was the problem?" I asked. "I was just coming around the corner, and he stopped me, asked me what was my name, and all that. And what I had in my bag. And where I was coming from. Where I lived, you know, all the basic stuff, I guess. Then he searched me down and, you know, asked me who were the supposedly tough guys around here? That's about it. I couldn't tell him who they are. How do I know? Other gang members could, but I'm not from a gang, you know. But he tried to put me in a gang bag, though." "How old are you?" I asked. "I'm seventeen, I'll be eighteen next month." "Did he

---

2. For an illuminating typology of police work that draws a distinction between "fraternal" and "professional" codes of behavior, see Wilson (1968).

give any reason for stopping you?" "No, he didn't. He just wanted my
address, where I lived, where I was coming from, that kind of thing.
I don't have no police record or nothin'. I guess he stopped me on
principle, 'cause I'm black." "How does that make you feel?" I asked.
"Well, it doesn't bother me too much, you know, as long as I know
that I hadn't done nothin', but I guess it just happens around here.
They just stop young black guys and ask 'em questions, you know.
What can you do?" ◑

On the streets late at night, the average young black man is suspicious of others he encounters, and he is particularly wary of the
police. If he is dressed in the uniform of the "gangster," such as a
black leather jacket, sneakers, and a "gangster cap," if he is carrying
a radio or a suspicious bag (which may be confiscated), or if he is
moving too fast or too slow, the police may stop him. As part of the
routine, they search him and make him sit in the police car while
they run a check to see whether there is a "detainer" on him. If there
is nothing, he is allowed to go on his way. After this ordeal the youth
is often left afraid, sometimes shaking, and uncertain about the area
he had previously taken for granted. He is upset in part because he is
painfully aware of how close he has come to being in "big trouble."
He knows of other youths who have gotten into a "world of trouble"
simply by being on the streets at the wrong time or when the police
were pursuing a criminal. In these circumstances, particularly at
night, it is relatively easy for one black man to be mistaken for another. Over the years, while walking through the neighborhood I
have on occasion been stopped and questioned by police chasing a
mugger, but after explaining myself I was released.

Many youths, however, have reason to fear such mistaken identity or harassment, since they might be jailed, if only for a short
time, and would have to post bail money and pay legal fees to extri-
cate themselves from the mess (Anderson 1986). When law-abiding
blacks are ensnared by the criminal justice system, the scenario may
proceed as follows. A young man is arbitrarily stopped by the police
and questioned. If he cannot effectively negotiate with the officer(s),
he may be accused of a crime and arrested. To resolve this situation
he needs financial resources, which for him are in short supply. If he
does not have money for an attorney, which often happens, he is left
to a public defender who may be more interested in going along with
the court system than in fighting for a poor black person. Without
legal support, he may well wind up "doing time" even if he is inno-

cent of the charges brought against him. The next time he is stopped for questioning he will have a record, which will make detention all the more likely.

Because the young black man is aware of many cases when an "innocent" black person was wrongly accused and detained, he develops an "attitude" toward the police .The street word for police is "the man," signifying a certain machismo, power, and authority. He becomes concerned when he notices "the man" in the community or when the police focus on him because he is outside his own neighborhood. The youth knows, or soon finds out, that he exists in a legally precarious state. Hence he is motivated to avoid the police, and his public life becomes severely circumscribed.

To obtain fair treatment when confronted by the police, the young man may wage a campaign for social regard so intense that at times it borders on obsequiousness. As one streetwise black youth said: "If you show a cop that you nice and not a smartass, they be nice to you. They talk to you like the man you are. You gonna get ignorant like a little kid, they gonna get ignorant with you." Young black males often are particularly deferential toward the police even when they are completely within their rights and have done nothing wrong. Most often this is not out of blind acceptance or respect for the "law," but because they know the police can cause them hardship. When confronted or arrested, they adopt a particular style of behavior to get on the policeman's good side. Some simply "go limp" or politely ask, "What seems to be the trouble, officer?" This pose requires a deference that is in sharp contrast with the youths' more usual image, but many seem to take it in stride or not even to realize it. Because they are concerned primarily with staying out of trouble, and because they perceive the police as arbitrary in their use of power, many defer in an equally arbitrary way. Because of these pressures, however, black youths tend to be especially mindful of the police and, when they are around, to watch their own behavior in public. Many have come to expect harassment and are inured to it; they simply tolerate it as part of living in the Village-Northton.

After a certain age, say twenty-three or twenty-four, a black man may no longer be stopped so often, but he continues to be the object of police scrutiny. As one twenty-seven-year-old black college graduate speculated:

◐ *I think they see me with my little bag with papers in it. They see me with penny loafers on. I have a tie on, some days. They don't*

stop me so much now. See, it depends on the circumstances. If some-
thing goes down, and they hear that the guy had on a big black
coat, I may be the one. But when I was younger, they could just stop
me, carte blanche, any old time. Name taken, searched, and this
went on endlessly. From the time I was about twelve until I was
sixteen or seventeen, endlessly, endlessly. And I come from a lower-
middle-class black neighborhood, OK, that borders a white neigh-
borhood. One neighborhood is all black, and one is all white. OK,
just because we were so close to that neighborhood, we were stopped
endlessly. And it happened even more when we went up into a sub-
urban community. When we would ride up and out to the suburbs,
we were stopped every time we did it.

If it happened today, now that I'm older, I would really be upset.
In the old days when I was younger, I didn't know any better. You
just expected it, you knew it was gonna happen. Cops would come
up, "What you doing, where you coming from?" Say things to you.
They might even call you nigger. ◐

Such scrutiny and harassment by local police makes black youths
see them as a problem to get beyond, to deal with, and their attempts
affect their overall behavior. To avoid encounters with the man,
some streetwise young men camouflage themselves, giving up the urban uniform and emblems that identify them as "legitimate" objects
of police attention. They may adopt a more conventional presentation of self, wearing chinos, sweat suits, and generally more conservative dress. Some youths have been known to "ditch" a favorite
jacket if they see others wearing one like it, because wearing it increases their chances of being mistaken for someone else who may
have committed a crime.

But such strategies do not always work over the long run and
must be constantly modified. For instance, because so many young
ghetto blacks have begun to wear Fila and Adidas sweat suits as
status symbols, such dress has become incorporated into the public
image generally associated with young black males. These athletic
suits, particularly the more expensive and colorful ones, along with
high-priced sneakers, have become the leisure dress of successful
drug dealers, and other youths will often mimic their wardrobe to
"go for bad" in the quest for local esteem. Hence what was once a
"square" mark of distinction approximating the conventions the
wider culture has been adopted by a neighborhood group devalued
by that same culture. As we saw earlier, the young black male enjoys

a certain power over fashion: whatever the collective peer group embraces can become "hip" in a manner the wider society may not desire (see Goffman 1963). These same styles then attract the attention of the agents of social control.

The Identification Card

Law-abiding black people, particularly those of the middle class, set out to approximate middle-class whites in styles of self-presentation in public, including dress and bearing. Such middle class emblems, often viewed as "square," are not usually embraced by young working-class blacks. Instead, their connections with and claims on the institutions of the wider society seem to be symbolized by the identification card. The common identification card associates its holder with a firm, a corporation, a school, a union, or some other institution of substance and influence. Such a card, particularly from a prominent establishment, puts the police and others on notice that the youth is "somebody," thus creating an important distinction between a black man who can claim a connection with the wider society and one who is summarily judged as "deviant." Although blacks who are established in the middle class might take such cards for granted, many lower-class blacks, who continue to find it necessary to campaign for civil rights denied them because of skin color, believe that carrying an identification card brings them better treatment than is meted out to their less fortunate brothers and sisters. For them this link to the wider society, though often tenuous, is psychically and socially important. The young college graduate continues:

◑ I know [how] I used to feel when I was enrolled in college last year, when I had an ID card. I used to hear stories about the blacks getting stopped over by the dental school, people having trouble sometimes. I would see that all the time. Young black male being stopped by the police. Young black male in handcuffs. But I knew that because I had that ID card I would not be mistaken for just somebody snatching a pocketbook, or just somebody being where maybe I wasn't expected be. See, even though I was intimidated by the campus police—I mean, the first time I walked into the security office to get my ID they all gave me the double take to see if I was somebody they were looking for. See, after I got the card, I was like, well, they can think that now, but I have this [ID card]. Like, see, late at night when I be walking around, and the cops be checking me out, giving me the looks, you know. I mean, I know guys, stu-

dents, who were getting stopped all the time, sometimes by the same officer, even though they had the ID. And even they would say, "Hey, I got the ID, so why was I stopped?" ◐

The cardholder may believe he can no longer be treated summarily by the police, that he is no longer likely to be taken as a "no count," to be prejudicially confused with that class of blacks "who are always causing trouble on the trolley." Furthermore, there is a firm belief that if the police stop a person who has a card, they cannot "do away with him without somebody coming to his defense." This concern should not be underestimated. Young black men trade stories about mistreatment at the hands of the police; a common one involves policemen who transport youths into rival gang territories and release them, telling them to get home the best way they can. From the youth's perspective, the card signifies a certain status in circumstances where little recognition was formerly available.

"Downtown" Police and Local Police

In attempting to manage the police—and by implication to manage themselves—some black youths have developed a working conception of the police in certain public areas of the Village-Northton. Those who spend a good amount of their time on these corners, and thus observing the police, have come to distinguish between the "downtown" police and the "regular" local police.

The local police are the ones who spend time in the area; normally they drive around in patrol cars, often one officer to a car. These officers usually make a kind of working peace with the young men on the streets; for example, they know the names of some of them and may even befriend a young boy. Thus they offer an image of the police department different from that displayed by the "downtown" police. The downtown police are distant, impersonal, and often actively looking for "trouble." They are known to swoop down arbitrarily on gatherings of black youths standing on a street corner; they might punch them around, call them names, and administer other kinds of abuse, apparently for sport. A young Northton man gave the following narrative about his experiences with the police.

◐ *And I happen to live in a violent part. There's a real difference between the violence level in the Village and the violence level in Northton. In the nighttime it's more dangerous over there.*

It's so bad now, they got downtown cops over there now. They doin' a good job bringin' the highway patrol over there. Regular cops don't like that. You can tell that. They even try to emphasize to us the certain category. Highway patrol come up, he leave, they say somethin' about it. "We can do our job over here." We call [downtown police] Nazis. They about six feet eight, seven feet. We walkin', they jump out. "You run, and we'll blow your nigger brains out." I hate bein' called a nigger. I want to say somethin' but get myself in trouble.

When a cop do somethin', nothing happen to 'em. They come from downtown. From what I heard some of 'em don't even wear their real badge numbers. So you have to put up with that. Just keep your mouth shut when they stop you, that's all. Forget about questions, get against the wall, just obey 'em. "Put all that out right there"—might get rough with you now. They snatch you by the shirt, throw you against the wall, pat you hard, and grab you by the arms, and say, "Get outta here." They call you nigger this and little black this, and things like that. I take that. Some of the fellas get mad. It's a whole different world.

Yeah, they lookin' for trouble. They gotta look for trouble when you got five, eight police cars together and they laughin' and talkin', start teasin' people. One night we were at a bar, we read in the paper that the downtown cops comin' to straighten things out. Same night, three police cars, downtown cops with their boots on, they pull the sticks out, beatin' around the corner, chase into bars. My friend Todd, one of 'em grabbed him and knocked the shit out of him. He punched 'im, a little short white guy. They start a riot. Cops started that shit. Everybody start seein' how wrong the cops was—they start throwin' bricks and bottles, cussin' 'em out. They lock my boy up; they had to let him go. He was just standin' on the corner, they snatch him like that.

One time one of 'em took a gun and began hittin' people. My boy had a little hickie from that. He didn't know who the cop was, because there was no such thing as a badge number. They have phony badge numbers. You can tell they're tougher, the way they dress, plus they're bigger. They have boots, trooper pants, blond hair, blue eyes, even black [eyes]. And they seven feet tall, and six foot six inches and six foot eight inches. Big! They the rough cops. You don't get smart with them or they beat the shit out of you in front of everybody, they don't care.

We call 'em Nazis. Even the blacks among them. They ride along with 'em. They stand there and watch a white cop beat your brains out. What takes me out is the next day you don't see 'em. Never see 'em again, go down there, come back, and they ride right back downtown, come back, do their little dirty work, go back downtown, and put their real badges on. You see 'em with a forty-five or fifty-five number: "Ain't no such number here, I'm sorry, son." Plus, they got unmarked cars. No sense takin' 'em to court. But when that happened at that bar, another black cop from the sixteenth [local] district, ridin' a real car, came back and said, "Why don't y'all go on over to the sixteenth district and file a complaint? Them musclin' cops was wrong. Beatin' people." So about ten people went over there; sixteenth district knew nothin' about it. They come in unmarked cars, they must have been downtown cops. Some of 'em do it. Some of 'em are off duty, on their way home. District commander told us they do that. They have a patrol over there, but them cops from downtown have control of them cops. Have bigger ranks and bigger guns. They carry .357s and regular cops carry little .38s. Downtown cops are all around. They carry magnums.

Two cars the other night. We sittin' on the steps playing cards. Somebody called the cops. We turn around and see four regular police cars and two highway police cars. We drinkin' beer and playin' cards. Police get out and say you're gamblin'. We say we got nothin' but cards here, we got no money. They said all right, got back in their cars, and drove away. Downtown cops dressed up like troopers. That's intimidation. Damn!

You call a cop, they don't come. My boy got shot, we had to take him to the hospital ourselves. A cop said, "You know who did it?" We said no. He said, "Well, I hope he dies if y'all don't say nothin'." What he say that for? My boy said, "I hope your mother die," he told the cop right to his face. And I was grabbin' another cop, and he made a complaint about that. There were a lot of witnesses. Even the nurse behind the counter said the cop had no business saying nothin' like that. He said it loud, "I hope he dies." Nothin' like that should be comin' from a cop. ◐

Such behavior by formal agents of social control may reduce the crime rate, but it raises questions about social justice and civil rights. Many of the old-time liberal white residents of the Village view the police with some ambivalence. They want their streets and homes defended, but many are convinced that the police manhandle "kids" and mete out an arbitrary form of "justice." These feelings make many of them reluctant to call the police when they are needed, and they may even be less than completely cooperative after a crime has been committed. They know that far too often the police simply "go out and pick up some poor black kid." Yet they do cooperate, if ambivalently, with these agents of social control.

In an effort to gain some balance in the emerging picture of the police in the Village-Northton, I interviewed local officers. The following edited conversation with Officer George Dickens (white) helps place in context the fears and concerns of local residents, including black males:

○ *I'm sympathetic with the people who live in this neighborhood [the Village-Northton], who I feel are victims of drugs. There are a tremendous number of decent, hardworking people who are just trying to live their life in peace and quiet, not cause any problems for their neighbors, not cause any problems for themselves. They just go about their own business and don't bother anyone. The drug situation as it exists in Northton today causes them untold problems. And some of the young kids are involved in one way or another with this drug culture. As a result, they're gonna come into conflict even with the police they respect and have some rapport with.*

We just went out last week on Thursday and locked up ten young men on Cherry Street, because over a period of about a week, we had undercover police officers making drug buys from those young men. This was very well documented and detailed. They were videotaped selling the drugs. And as a result, right now, if you walk down Cherry Street, it's pretty much a ghost town; there's nobody out. [Before, Cherry Street was notorious for drug traffic.] Not only were people buying drugs there, but it was a very active street. There's been some shock value as a result of all those arrests at one time.

Now, there's two reactions to that. The [television] reporters went out and interviewed some people who said, "Aw, the police overreacted, they locked up innocent people. It was terrible, it was harassment." One of the neighbors from Cherry Street called me on Thursday, and she was outraged. Because she said, "Officer, it's not fair. We've been working with the district for well over a year trying to solve some of the problems on Cherry Street." But most of the neighbors were thrilled that the police came and locked all those kids up. So you're getting two conflicting reactions here. One from the people that live there that just wanta be left alone, alright? Who are really being harassed by the drug trade and everything that's in-

volved in it. And then you have a reaction from the people that are in one way or another either indirectly connected or directed connected, where they say, "You know, if a young man is selling drugs, to him that's a job." And if he gets arrested, he's out of a job. The family's lost their income. So they're not gonna pretty much want anybody to come in there to make arrests. So you've got contradicting elements of the community there. My philosophy is that we're going to try to make Northton livable. If that means we have to arrest some of the residents of Northton, that's what we have to do.

You talk to Tyrone Pitts, you know the group that they formed was formed because of a reaction to complaints against one of the officers of how the teenagers were being harassed. And it turned out that basically what he [the officer] was doing was harassing drug dealers. When Northton against Drugs actually formed and seemed to jell, they developed a close working relationship with the police here. For that reason, they felt the officer was doing his job.

I've been here eighteen months. I've seen this neighborhood go from . . . Let me say, this is the only place I've ever worked where I've seen a rapport between the police department and the general community like the one we have right now. I've never seen it anyplace else before coming here. And I'm not gonna claim credit because this happened while I happened to be here. I think a lot of different factors were involved. I think the community was ready to work with the police because of the terrible situation in reference to crack. My favorite expression when talking about crack is "crack changed everything." Crack changed the rules of how the police and the community have to interact with each other. Crack changed the rules about how the criminal justice system is gonna work, whether it works well or poorly. Crack is causing the prisons to be overcrowded. Crack is gonna cause the people that do drug rehabilitation to be overworked. It's gonna cause a wide variety of things. And I think the reason the rapport between the police and the community in Northton developed at the time it did is very simply that drugs to a certain extent made many areas in this city unlivable.

In effect the officer is saying that the residents, regardless of former attitudes, are now inclined to be more sympathetic with the police and to work with them. And at the same time, the police are more inclined to work with the residents. Thus, not only are the police and the black residents of Northton working together, but different groups in the Village and Northton are working with each other against drugs. In effect, law-abiding citizens are coming together, regardless of race, ethnicity, and class. He continues:

Both of us [police and the community] are willing to say, "Look, let's try to help each other." The nice thing about what was started here is that it's spreading to the rest of the city. If we don't work together, this problem is gonna devour us. It's gonna eat us alive. It's a state of emergency, more or less.

In the past there was significant negative feeling among young black men about the "downtown" cops coming into the community and harassing them. In large part these feelings continue to run strong, though many young men appear to "know the score" and to be resigned to their situation, accommodating and attempting to live with it. But as the general community feels under attack, some residents are willing to forgo certain legal and civil rights and undergo personal inconvenience in hopes of obtaining a sense of law and order. The officer continues:

Today we don't have too many complaints about police harassment in the community. Historically there were these complaints, and in almost any minority neighborhood in Eastern City where I ever worked there was more or less a feeling of that [harassment]. It wasn't just Northton; it was a feeling that the police were the enemy. I can honestly say that for the first time in my career I don't feel that people look at me like I'm the enemy. And it feels nice; it feels real good not to be the enemy, ha-ha. I think we [the police] realize that a lot of the problems here [in the Village-Northton] are related to drugs. I think the neighborhood realizes that too. And it's a matter of "Who are we gonna be angry with? Are we gonna be angry with the police because we feel like they're this army of occupation, or are we gonna argue with these people who are selling drugs to our kids and shooting up our neighborhoods and generally causing havoc in the area? Who deserves the anger more?" And I think, to a large extent, people of the Village-Northton decided it was the drug dealers and not the police.

I would say there are probably isolated incidents where the police would stop a male in an area where there is a lot of drugs, and this guy may be perfectly innocent, not guilty of doing anything at all. And yet he's stopped by the police because he's specifically in that area, on that street corner where we know drugs are going hog wild. So there may be isolated incidents of that. At the same time, I'd

*say I know for a fact that our complaints against police in this divi-
sion, the whole division, were down about 45 percent. If there are
complaints, if there are instances of abuse by the police, I would expect that our complaints would be going up. But they're not; they're
dropping.* ◐

Such is the dilemma many Villagers face when they must report
a crime or deal in some direct way with the police. Stories about police prejudice against blacks are often traded at Village get-togethers.
Cynicism about the effectiveness of the police mixed with community suspicion of their behavior toward blacks keeps middle-class Villagers from embracing the notion that they must rely heavily on the
formal means of social control to maintain even the minimum freedom of movement they enjoy on the streets.

Many residents of the Village, especially those who see themselves as the "old guard" or "old-timers," who were around during
the good old days when antiwar and antiracist protest was a major
concern, sigh and turn their heads when they see the criminal justice
system operating in the ways described here. They express hope that
"things will work out," that tensions will ease, that crime will decrease and police behavior will improve. Yet as incivility and crime
become increasing problems in the neighborhood, whites become
less tolerant of anonymous blacks and more inclined to embrace the
police as their heroes.

Such criminal and social justice issues, crystallized on the streets,
strain relations between the newcomers and many of the old guard,
but in the present context of drug-related crime and violence in the
Village-Northton, many of the old-timers are adopting a "law and
order" approach to crime and public safety, laying blame more directly on those they see as responsible for such crimes, though they
retain some ambivalence. Newcomers can share such feelings with
an increasing number of old-time "liberal" residents. As one middle-
aged white woman who has lived in the Village for fifteen years said:

◐ *When I call the police, they respond. I've got no complaints.
They are fine for me. I know they sometimes mistreat black males.
But let's face it, most of the crime is committed by them, and so they
can simply tolerate more scrutiny. But that's them.* ◐

Gentrifiers and the local old-timers who join them, and some traditional residents continue to fear, care more for their own safety
and well-being than for the rights of young blacks accused of wrongdoing. Yet reliance on the police, even by an increasing number of

former liberals, may be traced to a general feeling of oppression at the hands of street criminals, whom many believe are most often black. As these feelings intensify and as more yuppies and students inhabit the area and press the local government for services, especially police protection, the police may be required to "ride herd" more stringently on the youthful black population. Thus young black males are often singled out as the "bad" element in an otherwise healthy diversity, and the tensions between the lower-class black ghetto and the middle and upper-class white community increase rather than diminish.

8

○

Street

Etiquette

and

Street

Wisdom

*T*he streets have a peculiar definition in the Village community. Usually pedestrians can walk there undisturbed. Often they seem peaceful. Always they have an elegant air, with mature trees, wrought-iron fences, and solid architecture reminiscent of pre-war comfort and ease. But in the minds of current residents the streets are dangerous and volatile. Lives may be lost there. Muggings occur with some regularity. Cars are broken into for tape decks and other valuables. Occasionally people suffer seemingly meaningless verbal or even physical assaults. For these reasons residents develop a certain ambivalence toward their neighborhood. On the one hand, they know they should distrust it, and they do. But on the other hand, distrusting the area and the people who use it requires tremendous energy. To resolve this problem, they tentatively come to terms with the public areas through trial and error, using them cautiously at first and only slowly developing a measure of trust.

How dangerous an area seems depends on how familiar one is with the neighborhood and what one can take for granted. Villagers often use the euphemism "tricky." Depending on how long they have lived here and how "urban" they are, the streets may seem manageable or unmanageable.

Most people in the Village, because of their social class as well as the cultural history of the community (which includes a legacy of nonviolence), shy away from arming themselves with guns, knives, and other weapons. A more common "defense" is simply avoiding the streets. Many whites and middle-income blacks use them as infrequently as they can, particularly at night.

Because public interactions generally matter for only a few crucial seconds, people are conditioned to rapid scrutiny of the looks, speech, public behavior, gender, and color of those sharing the environment. As discussed in detail in chapter 6, the central strategy in maintaining safety on the streets is to avoid strange black males. The public awareness is color-coded: white skin denotes civility, law-abidingness, and trustworthiness, while black skin is strongly associated with poverty, crime, incivility, and distrust. Thus an unknown young black male is readily deferred to. If he asks for anything, he must be handled quickly and summarily. If he is persistent, help must be summoned.

This simplistic racial interpretation of crime creates a "we/they" dichotomy between whites and blacks. Yet here again the underlying issue is class. One may argue that the average mugger is primarily concerned with the trouble or ease of taking his victim's property and only secondarily with race or with the distant consequences of his actions. It is significant, then, that the dominant working conception in the black community at large is that the area is being overrun by well-to-do whites. Not only do the perpetrators of crime often view anonymous whites as invaders but, perhaps more important, they see them as "people who got something" and who are inexperienced in the "ways of the streets."

Middle-income blacks in the Village, who also are among the "haves," often share a victim mentality with middle-income whites and appear just as distrustful of black strangers. Believing they are immune to the charge of racism, Village blacks make some of the same remarks as whites do, sometimes voicing even more incisive observations concerning "street blacks" and black criminality.

That middle-class whites and blacks have similar concerns suggests a social commonality and shared moral community, allowing people the limited sense that all residents of the neighborhood have comparable problems with street navigation. But this assumption ultimately breaks down, affecting neighborhood trust and the social integrity of the community. For in fact the experiences and problems on the streets of a person with dark skin are very different from those of a white person, for several reasons.

First, whereas the law-abiding black possesses a kind of protective coloration, the white man or woman has none. This defense allows the black person to claim street wisdom, which the white person generally does not find it easy to do.

Second, there is a felt deterrent to black-on-black crime because the victim may recognize his assailant later. This possibility may cause the potential mugger, for a crucial instant, to think twice before robbing another black person. Not only may the victim "bump into" his assailant again, but there is a chance he will try to "take care of him" personally. Many a mugger would not like to carry such a burden, especially when there are so many "inexperienced" whites around who may be assumed, however erroneously, to be easier to rob, unlikely to recognize their assailant, and certainly less likely to retaliate.

Finally, the white male does not represent the same threat in the public arena, making him, and by implication whites generally, feel especially vulnerable and undermining respect for his defensive capabilities. Perhaps in response to this cultural truth, some white men take a generalized, exaggerated, protective posture toward white women in the presence of "threatening" black males. One young black man described this scene:

◐ *One evening I was walking down the street and this older white lady was at the middle of the block, and I was walking toward her. It was just me and her. Then all of a sudden this young white man runs across the street and just stands between me and this lady. He just kept watching me, and I stared him down. When I passed him, I turned and kept on looking at him. I know he thought I was gon' mess with that woman or something.* ◐

This deliberate confrontation is rare on Village streets. Rather, whites and middle-class blacks are skilled in the art of avoidance, using their eyes, ears, and bodies to navigate safely. Although this seems to work for the residents, however, it vitiates comity between the races. One class of people is conditioned to see itself as law-abiding and culturally superior while viewing the other as a socially bruised underclass inclined to criminality. This perspective creates social distance and racial stereotyping, to which middle-income blacks are especially sensitive. Further, it makes even liberal whites vulnerable to the charge of racism.

Although such prejudice is at work in the Village community, there is a deceptive appearance of an effortlessly ordered and racially tolerant public space. All individuals walking the streets, whether white or black, must negotiate their passage with others they encounter. There are essentially two ways of doing this. One is to formulate a set of rules and apply them in every situation, employing what I call "street etiquette." This requires only a generalized perception of the people one encounters, based on the most superficial characteristics. Because it represents a crude set of guidelines, street etiquette makes the streets feel somewhat comfortable to the user, but it may be a security blanket rather than a real practical help. For many it becomes a learning tool.

Pedestrians who go beyond the simplistic rules of street etiquette develop a kind of "street wisdom," a more sophisticated approach. Those who acquire this sophistication realize that the public environment does not always respond to a formal set of rules rigidly applied to all problems. So they develop coping strategies for different situations, tailoring their responses to each unique event. By doing so they develop a "conception of self" in public that in itself provides some safety; in effect, they learn how to behave on the streets.

Street Etiquette

A set of informal rules has emerged among residents and other users of the public spaces of the Village. These rules allow members of diverse groups orderly passage with the promise of security, or at least a minimum of trouble and conflict. The rules are applied in specific circumstances, particularly when people feel threatened. Public etiquette is initiated where the jurisdiction of formal agents of social control ends and personal responsibility is sensed to begin. Because crime is a central issue to most residents, their concern for safety leads them to expend great effort in getting to know their immediate area. Potential and actual street crime inspires the social process of mental note taking, which lays a foundation for trust among strangers, dictated by the situation and proceeding by repeated face-to-face encounters. It works to form the basis of public community within the immediate neighborhood.

The process begins something like this. One person sees another walking down the street alone, with another person, or perhaps with a few others. Those seen might be getting out of an unusual car, riding a ten-speed bicycle, walking a dog, strolling on the grounds of a dwelling in the neighborhood, or simply crossing the street at the light or leaving a store carrying groceries. The sight of people engaging in such everyday activities helps to convey what may be interpreted as the usual picture of public life—what residents take for granted.

Skin color, gender, age, dress, and comportment are important markers that characterize and define the area. Depending on the observer's biases, such specific markers can become the most important characteristics determining the status of those being watched, superseding other meaningful attributes. However, the most important aspect of the situation is simply that the observer takes mental note of the other person: a significant social contact, though usually not a reciprocal one, is made. The person seen, and the category he or she is believed to represent, comes to be considered an ordinary part of the environment.

Although the initial observation is important, it is not the crucial element in "knowing about" others and feeling comfortable. Rather, it helps determine the social context for any other meaningful interactions, whether unilateral or bilateral. It gives users of the streets a sense of whom to expect where and when, and it allows them to adjust their plans accordingly.

The significance of the initial encounter is contingent upon subsequent meetings and interactions. If the person is never seen again, the encounter gradually loses significance. But if the observer sees the person again or meets others who are similar, the initial impression may become stronger and might develop into a theory about that category of people, a working conception of a social type. The strength of such impressions—nurtured and supported through repeated encounters, observations, and talk with other residents—gradually builds.

Background information and knowledge may provide a basis for social connection. A stranger may be seen in one context, then in another, then in a third. In time the observer might say to himself, "I know that person." Certainly he does know the person, if only by sight. He has noticed him many times in various neighborhood contexts, and with each successive encounter he has become increasingly familiar with him and the class he has come to represent. Probably the two are not yet speaking, though they may have exchanged looks that establish the minimal basis for trust. If asked directly, the observer might say, "Yeah, I've seen him around." In this way strangers may know each other and obtain a degree of territorial communion without ever speaking a word. It is quite possible that they will never reach speaking terms.

But there are circumstances where the social gap between visual and verbal interaction in public is pressed and the relationship between incomplete strangers is required to go further. People sometimes feel silly continually passing others they know well by sight without speaking to them. They may resolve their discomfort by greeting to them or by contrived avoidance. If they choose to speak, they may commit themselves to a series of obligatory greetings.

Introductions may also occur when two people who have seen each other in the neighborhood for some time happen to meet in a different part of town; there, despite some awkwardness, they may feel constrained to greet each other like long-lost friends. Perhaps they had not yet reached the point of speaking but had only warily acknowledged one another with knowing looks, or even with the customary offensive/defensive scowl used on the street for keeping strangers at a distance. After this meeting, previously distant Villagers may begin to speak regularly on the neighborhood streets. In this way trust can be established between strangers, who may then come to know each other in limited ways or very well.

Just the fact of their regular presence offers a sense of security, or at least continuity, to their neighbors. Thus, many people walk the streets with a confidence that belies their serious concerns. They use those they "know" as buffers against danger. Although they may still be strangers, they feel they can call on each other as allies when neighborhood crises emerge, when they would otherwise be seriously short of help, or when they must protect themselves or their loved ones. For example, during emergencies such as house fires, street crimes in which someone clearly needs help, or some other event where partial strangers have an opportunity to gather and compare notes with neighbors who seemed out of reach before, they may first provide help and only then reach out a hand and introduce themselves, saying, "Hello, my name is . . ."

This invisible but assumed network of reserve relationships binds together the residents and regular users of the public spaces of the Village. However, the person-specific designations that Villagers make every day are not always conducive to the flourishing of "ideal-typical gemeinschaft" relations. On the contrary, mental note taking like that described above also allows neighbors *not* to become involved in indiscriminate social exchange. For example, lower-income black people are often observed closely by whites who use the streets, perhaps primarily because they remain exotic and sometimes dangerous to many Villagers. Many whites may wish to get closer to the blacks, but for complicated reasons having to do with local history, class etiquette, and lingering racism, they normally maintain their established social distance. Most residents want social contact only with others of their own social class. In public they note the speech patterns of lower-class blacks. They pay attention to how "they" walk and how "they" treat their children, absorbing everything and shaping and reshaping their notions. It is not unusual to see whites, particularly women, observing the ways lower-income black women handle their children in public. The following field note illustrates this:

◐ *On a Saturday morning in May at approximately 11:00, a young black woman was managing a little girl of three, a boy of about five, and a small baby in a stroller. They were standing at Linden Avenue and Cherry Street in the Village, waiting for the bus. Two young white women and a middle-aged black man, apparently from the Village, were waiting for the bus too.*

The two small children began to fight over a toy. The older child won, and the smaller one began to have a temper tantrum. She wailed and stamped. Her face contorted, the mother cursed at the children, yelling obscenities at them and trying to get them to behave themselves. The white women paid "civil inattention," their actions and words belying their interest. As the woman spanked the three-year-old, one of the white women visibly cringed, as if to say to her friend and anyone else caring to pay attention, "Oh! What a way to treat your child!" Meanwhile, the other white woman didn't say a word. The black man, in silence, simply observed the performance. The woman continued to berate the children. She clearly had her hands full. Finally the bus arrived. ◐

Such critiques are not for the black woman's benefit, nor are they always made openly. Whereas in the gemeinschaft type of community people may become quite openly involved with the lives of their neighbors, trading favors and various kinds of help without keeping an account of who owes what to whom, Villagers generally avoid the responsibilities and social obligations that emerge from deeper forms of interpersonal involvement. Instead of intervening in either a helpful or a critical way, the two white women chose to strengthen the bond between them—their shared values—and to distance themselves from this other "element" of the public community.

Talk

In the Village, as in various neighborhoods of the city, young black males are carefully observed. They are often blamed for crimes when no contrary evidence is available. However, neighborly talk about crime becomes a problem when the age, ethnicity, or other defining attributes of the assailant and victim are introduced. In the Village, the all-too-easy dichotomizing by race into criminal and victim categories is complicated by the friendly, even intimate, relations between some blacks and whites. Neighbors bound by the dominant Village ideology of racial harmony and tolerance risk offending some members of their audience when they make broad racial remarks. Hence neighbors tread lightly, except when they forget themselves or presume they are in "safe" company and can speak freely.

There are many times when whites educate other whites who believe their prejudices are generally shared. A thirty-year-old white man who grew up in an Irish working-class section of the city had this to say:

◐ *I had a small gathering at my house just the other night. Tommy Jones, Charlie, Dave, and some women. Well, Dave started in talking about crime in the streets. And he started to talk about "niggers." And I just said to him, "Whoa, whoa, man. I don't allow that kind of talk in my house. If you want to talk like that, you gotta go outside, or go somewhere else." And I meant it. Yeah, I meant it. You should have seen the look on his face. Well, he didn't use that word no more.* ◐

Patterns of information exchange develop where neighbors talk to each other with different degrees of frankness about the alleged or actual attributes of assailants and victims. For instance, a white person might tell his black neighbor a story in which the assailant was believed to be black, but he might politely omit race if he thinks the black neighbor will be offended.

As neighbors come to know one another, fewer offenses are likely to occur; identifications with certain social circles become known, and information exchanges can proceed by neighborhood-specific code words in which race need not be overtly stated but is subtly expressed. For instance, a young couple moving in from the suburbs learns from an upstairs neighbor that the reason Mrs. Legget (white) walks with a cane is not just that she is eighty-five years old. Until a few years ago, she took her regular afternoon walks unaided by the thick wooden stick she now relies on. One afternoon she was knocked to the pavement by a "couple of kids" outside Mr. Chow's, the neighborhood market where black high-school students stop for candy and soda and congregate on their way home from school. In the scuffle, Mrs. Legget's purse was taken. The police took her to the hospital, and it was discovered that she had a broken hip.

Since her injury, Mrs. Legget's gait is less steady. She still takes her walks, but now she goes out earlier and avoids Mr. Chow's at the time school lets out. When the new couple ask her about the mugging, she is unwilling to describe the "kids" who knocked her down. She only smiles and gestures toward the small, low-slung cloth bag in which she now carries her valuables. "This one is mug-proof, they tell me," she says, a playful glimmer in her eye. It is a poignant lesson for the young couple. Purse straps should be worn across the chest bandolier style, not carelessly hooked over the arm, and perhaps Mr. Chow's is worth avoiding at 3:00 in the afternoon. As time goes by the young couple will come to understand the special meaning of the term "kids," which Villagers, particularly whites, often use in stories about street muggings to mean "black kids."

Through neighborly talk, inhabitants of the Village provide new arrivals, as well as established residents, with rules concerning the use of sidewalks at different times of day. Newcomers learn the schedule of the nearby black high school, enabling them to avoid the well-traveled north-south streets when the high-school students are there in force. They slowly learn how the racial and age composition of the clientele at Mr. Chow's varies with time of day, so they can choose safer hours, "working around" those they view as threatening. In addition, they come to recognize other Villagers and frequent visitors from Northton, though they may not always be conscious of the process. The more general color-coding that people in racially segregated areas apply goes through a refinement process because of the heterogeneous makeup of the Village.

When neighbors tell horror stories from the next block over, the shape of the tale and the characteristics of the actors depend on the values that the storyteller and his audience share. In this sense a general moral community is forged each time neighbors get together and talk about crime. A we/they dichotomy often becomes explicit, and a community perspective of "decent" people is articulated:

◐ *While casually sitting in their backyard, Adam and Lisa (a newly arrived white professional couple; he is an architect, she is a schoolteacher) and I were discussing their upcoming vacation to California. They were concerned about their house and wanted me to keep an eye on things. They lamented having to be so worried about break-ins but conceded that the Village was "not the suburbs." "If we have a break-in, they wouldn't know what to take; they wouldn't know the value of our things. I just worry about my Sony," Adam said with a laugh. From his tone of voice, his glance, and his nod toward Northton, it was clear that the would-be intruders, at least in his mind, were poor, ignorant, and black.* ◐

Coded or not, the collective definitions of "safe," "harmless," "trustworthy," "bad," "dangerous," and "hostile" become part of the Village perspective. Reports of personal experiences, including "close calls" and "horror stories," initiate and affirm neighborhood communion. At social gatherings, dinner parties, and the like, middle-class white Villagers mingle with other city dwellers and exchange stories about urban living. Conversation invariably turns to life in their neighborhoods—particularly its more forbidding aspects. Middle-class people commiserate, casting themselves and others they identify with in the role of victim. Recent stickups, rapes, burglaries, and harassment are subjects that get their attention, and they take note of where certain kinds of trouble are likely to occur and in what circumstances.

This type of communication enables residents to learn more about the streets, adding to what they have gleaned from experience. Though initially superficial, this information and the mental maps it helps form let strangers and residents of various life-styles and backgrounds navigate the Village streets with a reserve of social knowledge and a "working conception," a coherent picture, of local street life.

Neighborhood talk also affirms the belief that "city people" are somehow special, deserving commendation for tolerating the problems of being middle class in an environment that must be shared with the working class and the poor. "I'm convinced," one middle-class woman said while out on her porch fertilizing the geraniums, "that city people are just so much more ingenious." (She was discussing a friend who had moved out to one of the city's posh suburbs.) "We *have* to be," she concluded matter-of-factly.

Passing Behavior

Even the deceptively simple decision to pass a stranger on the street involves a set of mental calculations. Is it day or night? Are there other people around? Is the stranger a child, a woman, a white man, a teenager, or a black man? And each participant's actions must be matched to the actions and cues of the other. The following field note illustrates how well tuned strangers can be to each other and how capable of subtle gestural communication:

◐ *It is about 11:00 on a cold December morning after a snow-fall. Outside, the only sound is the scrape of an elderly white woman's snow shovel on the oil-soaked ice of her front walk. Her house is on a corner in the residential heart of the Village, at an intersection that stands deserted between morning and afternoon rush hours. A truck pulls up directly across from the old lady's house. Before long the silence is split by the buzz of two tree surgeons' gasoline-powered saws. She leans on her shovel, watches for a while, then turns and goes inside. A middle-aged white man in a beige overcoat approaches the site. His collar is turned up against the cold, his chin buried within, and he wears a Russian-style fur-trimmed hat. His hands are sunk in his coat pockets. In his hard-soled shoes he hurries along this east-west street approaching the intersection, slipping a bit, having to watch each step on the icy sidewalk. He crosses the north-south street and continues westward.*

A young black male, dressed in a way many Villagers call "street-ish" (white high-top sneakers with loose laces, tongues flopping out from under creased gabardine slacks, which drag and soak up oily water; navy blue "air force" parka trimmed with matted fake fur, hood up, arms dangling at the sides) is walking up ahead on the same side of the street. He turns around briefly to check who is coming up behind him. The white man keeps his eye on the treacherous sidewalk, brow furrowed, displaying a look of concern and determination. The young black man moves with a certain aplomb, walking rather slowly.

From the two men's different paces it is obvious to both that either the young black man must speed up, the older white man must slow down, or they must pass on the otherwise deserted sidewalk.

The young black man slows up ever so slightly and shifts to the outside edge of the sidewalk. The white man takes the cue and drifts to the right while continuing his forward motion. Thus in five or six steps (and with no obvious lateral motion that might be construed as avoidance), he maximizes the lateral distance between himself and the man he must pass. What a minute ago appeared to be a single-file formation, with the white man ten steps behind, has suddenly become side-by-side, and yet neither participant ever appeared to step sideways at all. ◐

In this intricate "ballet," to use Jane Jacobs's term (1961), the movements are patterned to minimize tension and allay fears and yet not openly express a breach of trust between the two parties. This "good behavior" is more conspicuous on the relatively well-defended east-west streets of the Village, where many white professionals tend to cluster and where blacks and whites often encounter each other. Such smooth gestural communication is most evident between blacks and whites traveling alone, especially during hours when the sidewalks are deserted. White Villagers' fears seem to run highest then, for that is when the opportunity for harrassment or mugging is greatest.

However, black male strangers confront problems of street navigation in similar ways. This field note illustrates some of the rules city dwellers must internalize:

◐ *At 3:00 Sunday morning I parked my car one street over from my home. To get to my front door, I now had to walk to the corner, turn up the street to another corner, turn again, and walk about fifty yards. It was a misty morning, and the streets were exceptionally quiet. Before leaving the car, I found my door key. Then, sitting in the parked car with the lights out, I looked up and down the street at the high bushes, at the shadows. After determining it was safe, I got out of the car, holding the key, and walked to the first corner. As I moved down the street I heard a man's heavy footsteps behind me. I looked back and saw a dark figure in a trench coat. I slowed down, and he continued past me. I said nothing, but I very consciously allowed him to get in front of me. Now I was left with the choice of walking about five feet behind the stranger or of crossing the street, going out of my way, and walking parallel to him on the other side. I chose to cross the street.*

All these actions fall in line with rules of etiquette designed to deal with such public encounters. First, before I left the safety of my car, I did everything possible to ensure speedy entrance into my home. I turned off the car lights, looked in every direction, and took my house key in hand. Second, I immediately looked back when I heard footsteps so that I could assess the person approaching. Next, I determined that the stranger could be a mugger in search of a victim—one of many possible identities, but naturally the one that concerned me most. I knew that at night it is important to defer to strangers by giving them room, so I established distance between us by dropping back after he passed me. Further, providing for the possibility that he was simply a pedestrian on his way home, I crossed the street to allow him clear and safe passage, a norm that would have been violated had I continued to follow close behind him.

When I reached the corner, after walking parallel to the stranger for a block, I waited until he had crossed the next street and had moved on ahead. Then I crossed to his side of the street; I was now about thirty yards behind him, and we were now walking away from each other at right angles. We moved farther and farther apart. He looked back. Our eyes met. I continued to look over my shoulder until I reached my door, unlocked it, and entered. We both continued to follow certain rules of the street. We did not cross the street simultaneously, which might have caused our paths to cross a second time. We both continued to "watch our backs" until the other stranger was no longer a threat. ◑

In this situation skin color was important. I believe the man on the street distrusted me in part because I was black, and I distrusted him for the same reason. Further, we were both able-bodied and young. Although we were cautious toward each other, in a sense we were well matched. This is not the case when lone women meet strangers.

A woman being approached from behind by a strange man, especially a young black man, would be more likely to cross the street so that he could pass on the opposite side. If he gave any sign of following her, she might head for the middle of the street, perhaps at a slight run toward a "safe spot." She might call for help, or she might detour from her initial travel plan and approach a store or a well-lit porch where she might feel secure.

In numerous situations like those described above, a law-abiding, streetwise black man, in an attempt to put the white woman at ease, might cross the street or simply try to avoid encountering her at all. There are times when such men—any male who seems to be "safe" will do—serve women of any color as protective company on an otherwise lonely and forbidding street.

This quasi "with" is initiated by the woman, usually as she

closely follows the man ahead of her "piggyback" style (see Goffman 1971). Although the woman is fully aware of the nature of the relationship, the man is usually not, though he may pick up on it in the face of danger or demonstrable threat. The existence of this "with," loose and extended as it may be, gives comfort and promises aid in case of trouble, and it thereby serves to ward off real danger. Or at least the participants believe it does.

Eye Work

Many blacks perceive whites as tense or hostile to them in public. They pay attention to the amount of eye contact given. In general, black males get far less time in this regard than do white males. Whites tend not to "hold" the eyes of a black person. It is more common for black and white strangers to meet each other's eyes for only a few seconds, and then to avert their gaze abruptly. Such behavior seems to say, "I am aware of your presence," and no more. Women especially feel that eye contact invites unwanted advances, but some white men feel the same and want to be clear about what they intend. This eye work is a way to maintain distance, mainly for safety and social purposes. Consistent with this, some blacks are very surprised to find a white person who holds their eyes longer than is normal according to the rules of the public sphere. As one middle-aged white female resident commented:

⊙ *Just this morning, I saw a [black] guy when I went over to Mr. Chow's to get some milk at 7:15. You always greet people you see at 7:15, and I looked at him and smiled. And he said "Hello" or "Good morning" or something. I smiled again. It was clear that he saw this as surprising.* ⊙

Many people, particularly those who see themselves as more economically privileged than others in the community, are careful not to let their eyes stray, in order to avoid an uncomfortable situation. As they walk down the street they pretend not to see other pedestrians, or they look right at them without speaking, a behavior many blacks find offensive.

Moreover, whites of the Village often scowl to keep young blacks at a social and physical distance. As they venture out on the streets of the Village and, to a lesser extent, of Northton, they may plant this look on their faces to ward off others who might mean them harm. Scowling by whites may be compared to gritting by blacks as a coping strategy. At times members of either group make such faces with little regard for circumstances, as if they were dressing for incle-ment weather. But on the Village streets it does not always storm, and such overcoats repel the sunshine as well as the rain, frustrating many attempts at spontaneous human communication.

Money

Naturally, given two adjacent neighborhoods representing "haves" and "have-nots," there is tremendous anxiety about money: how much to carry, how to hold it, how to use it safely in public. As in other aspects of Village life, shared anecdotes and group discussions help newcomers recognize the underlying rules of comportment.

Perhaps the most important point of etiquette with regard to money in public places is to be discreet. For example, at the check-out counter one looks into one's wallet or purse and takes out only enough to cover the charge, being careful that the remaining con-tents are not on display. Further, one attempts to use only small bills so as not to suggest that one has large ones.

When walking on the streets at night, it is wise to keep some money in a wallet or purse and hide the rest in other parts of one's clothing—some in a jacket pocket, some in the back pocket of one's jeans, maybe even some in a sock. In this one way would not lose everything in a mugging, yet the mugger would get something to ap-pease him.

A final rule, perhaps the most critical, is that in a potentially violent situation it is better to lose one's money than one's life. Thus the person who plans to travel at dangerous times or in dangerous areas should have some money on hand in case of an assault:

◑ *It was 9:00 P.M., and the Christmas party had ended. I was among the last to leave. John [a forty-five-year-old professional], the host, had to run an errand and asked if I wanted to go with him. I agreed. While I was waiting, Marsha, John's wife, said in a perfectly serious voice, "Now, John, before you go, do you have $10 just in case you get mugged?" "No, I don't have it, do you?"*

Marsha fetched $10 and gave it to John as what was in effect pro-tection money, a kind of consolation prize designed to cool out a pro-spective mugger. As we walked the three blocks or so on the errand, John said, "We've come two blocks, and it's not so bad." His tone was that of a nervous joke, as though he really half expected to encoun-ter muggers. ◑

The reality of the Village is that residents can make their lives

221

safer by "expecting" certain problems and making plans to cope with them. The mental preparation involved—imagining a bad situation and coming up with the best possible solution, acting it out in one's mind—may well be a valuable tool in learning to behave safely on the streets.

Dogs

Dogs play an important role in the street life of the Village. Whether they are kept as protectors or strictly as pets, their presence influences encounters between strangers. Many working-class blacks are easily intimidated by strange dogs, either off or on the leash. Such behavior may be related to social class values, attitudes, or past experiences with dogs. As one young black man said:

◐ *I tell you, when I see a strange dog, I am very careful. When I see somebody with a mean-looking dog, I get very defensive, and I focus on him. I make sure, when the deal goes down, I'm away from it. I'll do what I have to do. But white people have a whole different attitude. Some of them want to go up and pet the dog. Some of these white people will come to the situation totally different from me.* ◐

In the working-class black subculture, "dogs" does not mean "dogs in the house," but usually connotes dogs tied up outside, guarding the backyard, biting trespassers bent on trouble. Middle-class and white working-class people may keep dogs in their homes, allowing them the run of the house, but many black working-class people I interviewed failed to understand such behavior. When they see a white adult on his knees kissing a dog, the sight may turn their stomachs—one more piece of evidence attesting to the peculiarities of their white neighbors.

Blacks seem inclined to see affection for dogs as reflecting race more than class—as telling something about whites in general. It may be that many working-class whites would be just as astounded to witness such "white" behavior toward dogs and might respond like poorer blacks. But as a general rule, when blacks encounter whites with dogs in tow, they tense up and give them a wide berth, watching them closely.

Sometimes a white person taking his dog for a morning stroll will encounter a black jogger, who may act very nervous when confronted by the pair. The jogger slows down and frowns at the dog's owner, who may be puzzled by this reaction toward his "playful young pooch." What began as a "good faith" meeting (a white man and a dog encountering a lone black male on a public street where the intentions of each party might not normally be thought suspect) evolves into a tense confrontation.

In what may seem to be an innocent situation, one can discern profound meaning. The white person and the black person, after repeated encounters of this sort, know something of what to expect; in effect, they become conditioned. The dog owner understands on some level what his animal means to others. The participants may even cooperate in dealing with the dog, passing easily and going about their business. The dog walker will continue on his route, perhaps feeling less afraid than he otherwise would, since the black person backed off and gave him and his dog a wide berth. These themes are expressed by a young black man from the general neighborhood:

◐ *I have this neighbor who lives across from me, he's a brother* [black]. *And the white girls* [living] *above me have a big, giant dog. The dog is huge! I don't know how they keep that big dog in their apartment, 'cause he's so huge. He's friendly, but he's huge. Well, my neighbor is very concerned about this dog. Boy, when that dog gets out in the courtyard, he gets very upset. He told me, now. He told me that he stayed inside one day when they brought the dog out. He wouldn't go outside until they got the dog out of the courtyard. He's very uptight about it. And he hates it when he's walking in the courtyard and the dog runs up on him. But the funny thing about it is that even though they kinda try to discourage the dog from jumping up on him, it happens anyway. Now, I ease up a little bit when I see the dog. It doesn't bother me as much as it does him.*

It bothers me, 'cause he does jump up on you, and I don't like it, to be honest. I don't like no dog running up on me, even if he is tame, running up to me real fast. Well, Joe, my neighbor, gets very, very uptight about that. And it's funny, 'cause they know he gets uptight, and he knows that they know he gets uptight. And the whole thing just gets played out. In a certain way, they just mess with him, without even meaning anything bad by it, I think. It happens. But with me, they know that I'm not as uptight as he is. Yet for me they control the dog a certain way. They're able to grab him before he sees me. They can stop him. But with Joe, they just let the dog get all up on him. I don't know. They just let it play itself out. ◐

Dog-related incidents become part of community lore. The company of a dog allows residents, particularly whites, to feel more secure on the street and gives them more power in anonymous black-white interactions.

To be sure, many white dog owners want to project a friendly presence on the streets, but in public interactions with blacks they find it difficult to do so. The following comments were made by a white Village woman:

◐ *I see how intimidating my dog is. I go out with my dog, and the blacks give me lots of room. I used to walk my son to school, and the children would be flying like leaves in the wind. Oh, the little kids. . . . The kids are hysterically afraid of dogs. For a long time the kids would just scream and run for their mothers, if their mothers were around, and we would have to go through the whole thing about how he was a nice dog. On the other hand, I thought I should not teach them to trust Duke, because where they were coming from, it was not a good thing. Because a lot of people of the community do use dogs to intimidate.* ◐

To be sure, defensive motives for owning dogs reflect a concern about crime and violence in the community. When young blacks see someone, white or black, approaching with a dog, they tend to steer wide of them. Some of the whites are amused by such observations; some are mildly ashamed, like the woman quoted above. Still others take advantage of this cultural difference, employing dogs all the more as agents of defense and protection. Some make a point of having their dogs unleashed, allowing the dog to run away and then calling him back, demonstrating control over the animal. They may order the dog to heel, as though he were a ferocious beast that must be controlled. Through such actions they emphasize their advantage in a potentially volatile public situation and thus assert a measure of control over the streets.

Caring for a dog in the city takes much work, but for many residents of the Village the rewards make it worthwhile. Dogs allow their owners to feel secure on the streets and in their homes. With dogs in tow people look smug, even relaxed, as they encounter strangers. White women with dogs tend not to hurry along when a car slows down beside them. With dogs, some residents will more readily greet strange blacks with a hello.

Dog walkers constitute a "use group" of residents who make Village streets safer for all kinds of people during the early morning hours before work, in the evenings before dinner, and late at night. At these

times people who have come to "know" one another through their
dogs form an effective neighborhood patrol. One can chart their
routes and discover what dog walkers consider to be the neighborhood
boundaries—what streets one does not cross with or without a dog.

George Lewis, for example, is a veteran white Villager who
walks his beloved Irish setter each morning at 8:00. He comes out of
his door with the eager dog on a leash and immediately heads for one
of the north-south Village streets, for fewer front doors face these
streets and residents are less likely to make a scene about where the
setter "does his business." Mr. Lewis travels up to but never across or
along Bellwether Street, separating Northton and the Village. Nor
does he cross Warrington Avenue into the area known as Northton
Annex, even to reach the only vacant lot of any size where a dog
might be allowed to run. The lot is among a group of run-down buildings, and most Villagers, particularly whites, consider the whole
area dangerous. The people who do use the vacant lot are primarily
black dog walkers from Northton or the Village. Mr. Lewis is not the
only Villager who avoids the vacant lot or any blocks north of Bellwether. Indeed, the general dog-walking route seems to involve very
limited travel around two or three of the residential blocks in the
heart of the Village.

By not walking their dogs across Bellwether or Warrington, the
Villagers themselves help create and enforce lines of division between their own neighborhood and Northton. Although one usually
thinks first of stone throwing or other forms of harassment as determining where boundaries are drawn, it is also through daily activities like dog walking that borders are made and remade by people on
both sides of the dividing line.

Within the black community, dogs are used mainly as a means
of protection, whereas the middle-class whites and blacks of the Village generally see them as pets as well. Some lower-class black dog
owners consciously train their dogs to be vicious, thinking that the
meaner the animal, the greater protection he affords. For some, vi-
ciousness is closely associated with the idea of control:

◑ *On Saturday morning at about 11:00, I was walking up Thirty-
fourth Street when I saw a young black man accompanied by a full-
grown Doberman. I noticed him in part because of his shouts at his
dog. "Stop! Stop! You little bastard!" he shouted. He attracted the attention of a few passersby. Then, with fist balled up, he punched the
dog in the side. The dog whined and cowered, but the young man*

continued to hit him, now with a switch. The dog still just whined and cowered.

Two young white women on the sidewalk across the street had stopped to watch. One put her hands to her cheeks in horror but said nothing; they seemed mesmerized by the scene. Others pretended not to notice. After a few minutes of this the man stopped, stood up and pointed to the curb as he moved across the street. "Stay," he said. The dog was now very alert and stayed, his eyes on his master's every movement. When the man reached the other side of the street and had gone some distance down the next block, he slapped his right thigh. At that the sleek black dog bounded across the street like a shot.

I followed the two for some way, and when they reached the next corner the dog dutifully stopped. The man rubbed and patted the animal. Again the man crossed the street, and this time the dog kept his place until the man gave the signal for him to move. The performance gave meaning to the word masterful. For anyone observing this demonstration, the young man was in full control of his dog. And this was not just any old dog but a "vicious" Doberman. Accompanied by his dog, the young man was hardly someone to approach carelessly. ◐

In this way a dog might be thought of not only as a protector, as an extension of oneself, but even as a potential weapon. The message here is, "I'm in control of my 'mean' dog, and if I tell him to, he will bite you." Consistent with this, such an individual may become upset when others are too friendly with his dog, thereby "spoiling him." This forms quite a contrast to the middle-class people of the Village, who encourage others, particularly children, to get to know animals and to be kind to them. This difference again represents a difference in culture that is influenced, if not determined, largely by the social class of the dog owner, not by skin color.

Recently a popular breed has emerged among those who display dogs aggressively. The pit bull is bred to fight other dogs; it is said that it will fight to the death. Among many young black men, this dog is considered meaner than the Doberman. Both are supposed to be ferocious; to tame such a dog reflects positively on the owner.

That control is important to the motives of the dog owner is not missed by a great number of blacks who see whites with dogs. The following account by a young black attests to this:

◐ *Now there's a black fellow who lives in my building. I don't know him at all. I just see him occasionally, we speak. You can see that he's well off, living in the building and all. And he drives like a Riviera. And he has two beautiful boxers. Yeah, they some beautiful dogs! It's funny, when he is outside with them, and they are display-ing their obedience to him, sittin', heelin', runnin' back and forth, and listening to his commands. Two of them, now. The response that he gets from young black kids, he's a little older than me [thirty-five], they respect him to a certain extent. They like him. They see him on the streets, they talk to him, respect him, because he's got these animals and these animals will do what he says. And that's ap-pealing to a lot of folks. You know, and he's gettin' a certain response from people 'cause he's got these dogs. He can go wherever he wants to go, long as he has those dogs.* ◑

In short, to be able to "control" a dog is often a mark of status on the streets, even among total strangers. Among many young blacks, the "meaner" the dog looks, presumably the more status or regard accrues to the master, particularly when the dog is off the leash. When dogs are used as weapons, the ante is raised in the potentially violent game of street life. The following episode, related by a young black man, illustrates this well:

◑ *Once a white guy came with two Dobermans. They don't give a shit about a human. He was walkin' down Bellwether Street. Everybody say, "What's he tryin' to prove?" He stopped at the corner, then walked up the street and came back down and stood on the other side of the corner. "What's up with him? He must be pro-tectin'." So my friend, he go home and get a pistol. He says, "I'm gonna shoot him and both them dogs." That was his way of sayin' that man lookin' for trouble. He'd got beat up by two blacks two nights ago before he came down there. He wanted to see how tough they were when he had his two dogs. They go up to him and say, "What's up?" He said, "What the fuck you mean is up? Two niggers beat me up two nights ago." There was a lady lookin' out the win-dow, she knew there was trouble and called the cops.*

Another guy standin' with a rifle. That guy jumped when he saw that. He didn't know what to do then. [The guy with the rifle] said, "I'll kill you and both them motherfuckin' dogs. So why don't you try lettin' the dogs go, so we can kill both their asses, and you better know how to run." So that white man started to back off. You could tell he was scared. My friends had the guy and he was scared when he saw that. Them dogs ain't nothin' with guns. He let them

*go. He walked away. Then two police cars came up while he walkin'
the street.*

*Somebody told them he come down here and try sic them dogs
on people. So cops stopped him and said, "Hold that fuckin' dog."
That's what the cop said. He told the cops what happened. [The cop]
said, "You recognize any of the guys on the corner?" He said, "No."
"Well, why don't you go down and arrest 'em?" He was a white cop,
nice cop. But he gettin' to the point. Let's see who's wrong and right.
"Where'd it happen?" "Thirty-fourth and Haverford." He wait on
Thirty-eighth and Haverford. "What the fuck you doin' on Thirty-
eighth and Haverford?" He didn't have nothin' to say. So the cop said,
"Why don't you take your dogs and go back where you live at?" He
went back to the Village. Cop came back and told us, "Turn 'round."
That was all he told us, he just drove away. He knew the guy was
wrong. My boy [friend] thanked the officer for bein' understanding.
That was it. That's the way it is down there. Keep the peace. You got
good cops and bad cops.* ◑

Other Safety Rules and Strategies

Dress is an important consideration when walking the Village streets,
day or night. Women wear clothing that negates stereotypical "female
frailty" and symbolizes aggressiveness. Unisex jackets, blue jeans,
and sneakers are all part of the urban female costume. "Sexy" dresses
are worn only when women are in a group, accompanied by a man,
or traveling by car.

Village men also stick to practical, nonshowy clothing. Most
times this means blue jeans or a sweat suit. More expensive clothing
is relegated to daytime work hours or, as for females, travel by car.

The safety of cars and things in them is a major worry. Newcomers learn to park on the east-west streets to avoid nighttime vandalism and theft. They buy "crime locks" and hood locks for their
cars. They learn, sometimes through painful error, to remove attractive items like tape decks and expensive briefcases, or anything that
looks valuable, before they lock up and leave.

Their homes may be similarly barricaded. They sometimes have
chains for their bicycles, bars for their first-floor windows, and dead
bolts for their back doors. Some install elaborate and expensive bur-
glar alarms or keep dogs for the same purpose. They may build high
fences to supplement the quaint waist-high wrought-iron fences from
the early 1900s when the wealthy still claimed hegemony in the area.

Watching from the car as companions go into their houses is a standard precaution for city dwellers. The driver idles the motor out front and keeps an eye on the street until the resident has unlocked the door and is safely inside. This common practice has become ritualized in many instances, perhaps more important as a sign of a caring bond between people than as a deterrent of assault. It helps to make people feel secure, and residents understand it as a polite and intelligent action.

But some people are given to overreaction and to overelaboration of "mug-proofing" behaviors and are likely to see a potential mugger in almost anyone with certain attributes, most noticeably black skin, maleness, and youth. A middle-aged white woman told me this story:

◉ *I had a white taxi driver drive me home once, and he was horrified at the neighborhood I lived in. It was night, and he told me what a horrible neighborhood I lived in, speaking of how dangerous it was here. He said, "This neighborhood is full of blacks. You'll get raped, you'll get murdered, or robbed." I replied, "I've lived here for a long time. I really like this neighborhood." He let me out on the opposite side of Thirty-fourth Street. He said, "OK, you go straight to your door, and I'll cover you." And he pulled out a gun. I said, "Please put it away." But he wouldn't. I was scared to death he was going to shoot me or something as I walked toward the house. It was so offensive to me that this man [did this], whom I trusted less than I trusted any of my neighbors, even those I knew only by sight. I felt sick for days.* ◉

The woman surmised that the taxi driver "must have been from a white ethnic and working-class background." It is commonly assumed among local blacks that such men feel especially threatened by blacks. But some middle- and upper-middle-class whites within the Village are susceptible to similar situational behavior.

Interiors of Public Spaces

Public places such as bars, stores, or banks present a special case; the sense of intimidation and fear is somewhat lessened inside them. One might also expect the estrangement from one's fellows to dissipate and the contrived social distance to narrow, but this does not always happen. Generally, people of different races remain estranged, but they take careful mental notes about one another. It may be that the whites, particularly the newcomers, are more interested in the blacks because this integrated neighborhood represents something foreign to their experience. When whites are out in numbers, or when an otherwise forbidding black male is dressed in clothes that are unmistakably middle-class emblems, the whites are put somewhat at ease. In these circumstances they may "move in on" blacks, taking liberties such as asking the time or directions or even bumping into them without a nervous "excuse me."

Inside a business establishment it is easier to assume that others sharing the space, at least while inside, are committed to a certain level of civility. In the worst situation, one might be able to count on "limited warfare." The establishment, particularly if it has an armed guard, helps to ensure this, and customers may then be concerned to be sociable. If there are arguments or disagreements, they are rarely expected to result in violence. Hence the boldness that may be displayed inside, including smart remarks, arguments, and even punches, is not as likely to take place outside. Many such "fights" are ended when one person raises the stakes to a serious level by saying "Let's step outside!" On the street one cannot take civility and goodwill for granted or count on limited warfare.

Street Wisdom

Those who rely on a simplistic etiquette of the streets are likely to continue to be ill at ease, because they tend not to pay close attention to the characteristics that identify a suspect as harmless. Rather, they envelop themselves in a protective shell that wards off both attackers and potential black allies, allowing the master status of male gender and black skin to rule. Such people often display tunnel vision with regard to all strangers except those who appear superficially most like themselves in skin color and dress.

This is a narrow and often unsatisfying way to live and to operate in public, and many of those who cannot get beyond stiff rules of etiquette decide in the end to move to safer, less "tricky" areas. But most people come to realize that street etiquette is only a guide for assessing behavior in public. It is still necessary to develop some strategy for using the etiquette based on one's understanding of the situation.

Once the basic rules of etiquette are mastered and internalized, people can use their observations and experiences to gain insight. In effect, they engage in "field research." In achieving the wisdom that every public trial is unique, they become aware that individuals, not types, define specific events. Street wisdom and street etiquette are comparable to a scalpel and a hatchet. One is capable of cutting extremely fine lines between vitally different organs; the other can only make broader, more brutal strokes.

A person who has found some system for categorizing the denizens of the streets and other public spaces must then learn how to distinguish among them, which requires a continuing set of assessments of, or even guesses about, fellow users. The streetwise individual thus becomes interested in a host of signs, emblems, and symbols that others exhibit in everyday life. Besides learning the "safety signals" a person might display—conservative clothing, a tie, books, a newspaper—he also absorbs the vocabulary and expressions of the street. If he is white, he may learn for the first time to make distinctions among different kinds of black people. He may learn the meaning of certain styles of hats, sweaters, jackets, shoes, and other emblems of the subculture, thus rendering the local environment "safer" and more manageable.

The accuracy of the reading is less important than the sense of security one derives from feeling that one's interpretation is correct. Through the interpretive process, the person contributes to his working conception of the streets. In becoming a self-conscious and sensitive observer, he becomes the author of his own public actions and begins to act rather than simply to react to situations. For instance, one young white woman had on occasion been confronted and asked for "loans" by black girls who appeared to "guard the street" in front of the local high school. One day she decided to turn the tables. Seeing the request coming, she confidently walked up to one of the girls and said, "I'm out of money. Could you spare me fifty cents?" The young blacks were caught off balance and befuddled. The woman went on, feeling victorious. Occasionally she will gratuitously greet strange men, with similar effect.

A primary motivation for acquiring street wisdom is the desire to have the upper hand. It is generally believed that this will ensure safe passage, allowing one to outwit a potential assailant. In this regard a social game may be discerned. Yet it is a serious game, for failing could mean loss of property, injury, or even death. To prevail means simply to get safely to one's destination, and the ones who are most successful are those who are "streetwise." Street wisdom is really street etiquette wisely enacted.

Among the streetwise, there is a common perspective toward

street criminals, those who are "out there" and intent on violating law-abiding citizens. The street criminal is assumed to "pick his people," knowing who is vulnerable and who is not, causing some people to think that victimization is far from inevitable. This belief gives them confidence on the streets and allows them to feel a measure of control over their own fate. Indeed, avoiding trouble is often, though not always, within the control of the victim. Thus the victim may be blamed, and the streets may be viewed as yielding and negotiable. Consistent with this working conception of street life and crime, the task is to carry oneself in such a way as to ward off danger and be left alone. A chief resource is one's own person—what one displays about oneself. Most important, one must be careful.

Typically, those generally regarded as streetwise are veterans of the public spaces. They know how to get along with strangers, and they understand how to negotiate the streets. They know whom to trust, whom not to trust, what to say through body language or words. They have learned how to behave effectively in public. Probably the most important consideration is the experience they have gained through encounters with "every kind of stranger." Although one may know about situations through the reports of friends or relatives, this pales in comparison with actual experience. It is often sheer proximity to the dangerous streets that allows a person to gain street wisdom and formulate some effective theory of the public spaces. As one navigates there is a certain edge to one's demeanor, for the streetwise person is both wary of others and sensitive to the subtleties that could salvage safety out of danger.

The longer people live in this locale, having to confront problems on the streets and public spaces every day, the greater chance they have to develop a sense of what to do without seriously compromising themselves. Further, the longer they are in the area, the more likely they are to develop contacts who might come to their aid, allowing them to move more boldly.

This self-consciousness makes people likely to be alert and sensitive to the nuances of the environment. More important, they will project their ease and self-assurance to those they meet, giving them the chance to affect the interaction positively. For example, the person who is "streetdumb," relying for guidance on the most superficial signs, may pay too much attention to skin color and become needlessly tense just because the person approaching is black. A streetwise white who meets a black person will probably just go about his or her business. In both cases the black person will pick up the "vibe" being projected—in the first instance fear and hostility, in the second case comfort and a sense of commonality. There are obviously times when the "vibe" itself could tip the balance in creating the subsequent interaction.

Crisis and Adaptation

Sometimes the balance tips severely, and the whole neighborhood reacts with shock and alarm. A wave of fear surges through the community when violent crimes are reported by the media or are spread by word of mouth through the usually peaceful Village. One February a young woman, a new mother, was stabbed and left for dead in her home on one of the well-traveled north-south streets. Her month-old baby was unharmed, but it was weeks before the mother, recuperating in the hospital, remembered she had recently given birth. Word of how the stabbing occurred spread up and down the blocks of the Village. Neighbors said the woman often went out her back door to take out the garbage or call in the dog. But to uninitiated newcomers, the brick streets and large yards seem deceptively peaceful. Crises like these leave in their wake a deeper understanding of the "openness" that characterizes this quaint area of the city.

They also separate those who survive by brittle etiquette from those who—despite increased temporary precautions—can continue to see strangers as individuals. Less than half a block away from the scene of the attack, in a building facing an east-west street, a friend of the young mother was overcome with fear. Her husband was scheduled to go out of town the week after the vicious attack on her friend. She was so frightened that he had to arrange for a neighbor to "baby-sit" with his wife and children at night while he was away.

Security all over the Village was tightened for a time. People who used to go in and out, feeding the birds, shoveling walks, visiting their neighbors and friends, no longer came and went so carelessly. As the news traveled, fear rippled out from the young victim's immediate neighbors to affect behavior in other parts of the Village. One young black man reported that after the attack he was greeted with suspicious stares on his way to Mr. Chow's. "Everyone's looking over their shoulder suddenly," he said. "All black people are suspects."

"It makes you stop and wonder about living here," said one young mother shortly after the stabbing became the main item of conversation. "I've never lived in such a dangerous neighborhood. I run upstairs and leave my back door open sometimes. Like today, I got both kids and took them upstairs, and all of a sudden I said, 'Oh, no! I left the door unlocked!' and I just stopped what I was doing and ran downstairs to lock it." This kind of fear-induced behavior occurs as neighbors work out their group perspective on what is possible, if not probable, in the aftermath of such a crime.

Violence causes residents to tense up and begin taking defensive action again. They may feel uncomfortable around strangers on the streets, particularly after dark. They become especially suspicious of black males. An interview with a young black man from the area sheds some light on how residents react to neighborhood blacks shortly after a violent incident:

◐ *People come out of the door and they're scared. So when they see blacks on the streets they try to get away. Even ones who live right next door. All of a sudden they change attitudes toward each other. They're very suspicious. The guy that killed that lady and her husband down on Thirty-fourth in the Village, he from the Empire [gang]. He tried to rape the lady right in front of the husband—he stabbed the husband and killed him. He'll get the electric chair now; they gave him the death penalty. They caught him comin' out. Wouldn't been so bad, the cops got another call to next door to where he did it at. She was screamin' and the cops heard and came around to the door.*

After that happened, you could feel the vibes from whites. When things like that happen, things get very tense between blacks and whites. And you can feel it in the way they look at you, 'cause they think you might be the one who might do the crime. Everytime they see a black they don't trust 'em. Should stay in their own neighborhood.

That's the Village. They paranoid. ◐

In time the fear recedes. Through successive documentations and neighborhood gossip, Villagers slowly return to some level of complacency, an acceptance of the risks of living in the city. Familiar people on the streets are "mapped" and associated with their old places, much as veteran Villagers have mapped them before. Streets, parks, and playgrounds are again made theirs. When these mental notations remain reliable and undisturbed for a time, a kind of "peace" returns. More and more can be taken for granted. Night excursions become more common. Children may be given a longer tether. Villagers gather and talk about the more pleasant aspects of neighborhood life. But they know, and are often reminded, that the peace is precarious, for events can suddenly shake their confidence again. Mr. Chow's gets robbed, or the Co-op, or someone is mugged in broad daylight.

One mugging was especially disturbing, for the victim was a pillar of stability, familiar on the streets. Mrs. Legget, the eighty-five-year-old white woman, was mugged *again*. As she took her usual afternoon walk, coming down one of the well-traveled north-south streets to her own east-west street, at the intersection near Mr. Chow's, several black girls approached her and demanded her money, which Mrs. Legget gave them. News of this crime reverberated throughout the neighborhood. People were shocked, particularly those from the middle-income white and black communities, but also those from other enclaves of the Village. Who would do such a thing? What sort of person would steal from an eighty-five-year-old lady? She was quite defenseless, with her frail body, failing eyesight, and disarming wit. She has been walking the neighborhood streets for years and is the sort of person "everybody knows"—at least by sight.

Neighbors identify with Mrs. Legget. They are aware of her plight and sympathize with her, even if they do not know her personally. Anyone who does any amount of walking in the neighborhood remembers "that frail old lady with a cane." She is a reference point by which many Villagers gauge their own security. If she can walk the streets, then others, visibly stronger (if less streetwise), can feel capable of maintaining the same rights of passage. Mrs. Legget's freedom of movement stood as a symbol of safety.

Now residents think, "If they'll do it to Mrs. Legget, they'll do it to anybody," and thus the mugging becomes an affront to the whole neighborhood. It transforms an amorphous group into a more consolidated community of "decent people." The neighbors begin to talk and ponder their group position in relation to others, particularly the group from which the muggers are thought to originate, the black youths of Northton, the Village, and other ghetto areas of the city.

People became more circumspect again after the attack on Mrs. Legget. Her daily public presence implied that law-abiding residents had at least partial hegemony over some of the streets during the daylight hours. After the attack, Villagers' plans for taking public transportation became more elaborate. One young woman, a tenant in the apartment building where Mrs. Legget has lived for twenty years, changed her plans to take the city bus home from the Greyhound bus terminal. Instead, she drove her car and paid to park it near the terminal, thus assuring herself of door-to-door transportation for her nighttime return from out of town. "There's a lot of crime going on right now," she told a friend. She was embarrassed, for she usually ridicules the block meetings and homeowners' gripes about theft and vandalism. But Mrs. Legget's mugging shook even the firmest believers in street safety.

Yet like the stabbing of the young mother, this incident eventually passed into memory for most Villagers. Time helps people forget even the most perilous incidents. Neighbors talk and socialize about other things. After a period of using the public spaces uneventfully, suspicion and distrust subside, but they never fade completely. Familiarity is rebuilt and a shared trust in the public spaces is gradually restored.

In this way social knowledge of the immediate area becomes assimilated as stories are shared and retold and a more refined group perspective emerges. This rebuilding of trust occurs by testing the public areas through careful walking and greater-than-usual scrutiny of strangers, particularly young black males. But always and inevitably, things gradually return to "normal." Otherwise life would simply require too much energy.

Conclusion

*I*n the Village-Northton, at least two distinct but overlapping cultures give the appearance of coexisting in relative peace. The first comprises the middle-class whites, along with a small number of middle-class blacks and others. In many respects their values are those associated with the "great tradition" of Western culture; its adherents in the Village see themselves as its vessels and live it out as best they can (see Redfield 1956). Compared with most of their black neighbors, these people appear highly privileged. Some have money, and many are well educated, having grown up in suburban communities and attended some of the finest preparatory schools, colleges, and universities in the country. Others come from urban white working-class families and still feel connections with their old ethnic neighborhoods. At social gatherings in the Village, such ethnic particularities are deemphasized. Most residents are liberal on social issues, but the rise in black-on-white street crime pushes many toward a more conservative stance, in which racial intolerance often emerges (see Wellman 1977; Blumer 1958; Pettigrew 1980a). And the number of conservative homeowners is growing. Generally Villagers are concerned with "good" education for their children, a clean and safe neighborhood, property values, and tolerance toward people who are different from them or deemed less fortunate.

Since whites predominate in this culture, they are generally viewed as its most authentic agents, and "outsiders," particularly lower-income blacks, are inclined to label the culture "white." Essentially, though, it is a middle-class culture; it attempts to incorporate both whites and blacks who share such values, and it tolerates others who might be marginal with respect to their own "native" ethnic groups or life-styles.

A perfunctory look at the Village streets in daytime would lead one to believe that this is indeed a pleasant neighborhood whose residents get along well, and that there is genuine comity among the various kinds of people who live there. And to a large extent this is true. As residents stroll up and down the tree-lined streets, there is

237

often a pleasant show of civility, if not intimacy, between neighbors. On a sunny weekday morning a middle-aged white woman pushes a stroller with a brown baby in it. Approaching a young black woman, she smiles. The woman returns the smile, and both move on. Black youths dressed in expensive jeans and sneakers come around the corner, their loud voices rising as they approach and fading as they disappear. An elderly white man waits for his dog to finish its business by a hedge. Cars pass, including an occasional police car. A middle-aged white woman appears at the corner shepherding a racially mixed group of seven children aged five to seven. She stands between them and the traffic and carefully checks for moving cars, though she has the light. She steps cautiously into the street, while the children are eager to get to the other side. She has her hands full, and passersby watch sympathetically. On this summer morning blacks and whites, males and females, young and old appear to get on well, exchanging pleasantries and even offering help when needed. From this perspective the area does not seem forbidding.

Yet many residents are concerned about the strangers with whom they must share the public space, including wandering homeless people, aggressive beggars, muggers, anonymous black youths, and drug addicts. This concern is expressed in the way people try to adopt a viable street etiquette that they hope will get them safely up and down the streets, maintaining distance between themselves and strangers, particularly black males. Middle-class people, particularly whites, are especially protective of their children, who are closely supervised and usually play outside their own yards only when an adult is present. On the streets, whites are wary of black strangers and give blacks extra scrutiny, particularly when something seems amiss. When approaching their own front doors, residents take an extra measure of care, concerned if a stranger lingers or pays too much attention to them. In conversations on the street, participants divide their attention between partner and street. When they part company they say things like "take care," and they mean it. At night, drivers wait until their passengers signal they are safely inside their houses before moving off. Such behavior belies the notion that this is a fully trusted environment. Indeed, much distrust exists. Residents deal with it by making mental notes on strangers, and they feel more comfortable in subsequent encounters as they place individuals in the local social fabric and can worry about them less.

Increasingly, people see the streets as a jungle, especially at night, when "all cats are gray" and everyone may seem threatening.[1] They are then on special alert, carefully monitoring everyone who passes and giving few people the benefit of the doubt. Strangers must pass inspection. Although there is a general need to view the Village as an island of civility—it has long had the deserved reputation and working conception of itself as one of the most diverse and socially tolerant areas of the city—the underlying sense is that the local streets and public places are uncertain at best and hostile at worst.

This competing view of the area as an urban jungle arises from the existence of the "second" culture: the large black ghetto of Northton, just across the street from the Village. Northton has many stable working-class black families, well-attended churches, fine Victorian architecture, and young people eager to "make something out of themselves." But many characteristics of the jungle can indeed be found there. From the perspective of the Village, among blacks as well as whites, Northton is thought to embody a "little tradition" and has the reputation of being economically depressed and beset by classic urban ills: drugs, crime, illiteracy, poverty, and a high proportion of female-headed families on welfare, as well as one of the highest infant mortality rates in the country (see Redfield 1956). Violent assaults, robberies, muggings, rapes, and murders occur more frequently there.

Things were not always this way. Within recent memory, Northton was a solid working-class black community, with a scattering of middle-class residents (and a few whites). As one middle-aged, long-term black male resident and old head told me:

◑ Oh, in the old days, everybody had a little car, everybody stayed dressed on weekends, everybody went to ball games; they bragged about their kids at Morgan [State University] and Florida A&M, you know. Everybody had kids coming home from college. That don't happen no more. Yeah, man, I remember in my class, in this neighborhood, thirty-five to forty kids went to school [college]. That ain't a lot, but we knew where people were. You know, up at Howard. We saw each other in the summer. Howard, Morgan, Fisk. Some went to Penn State, Westchester. They were all in school. But see, the new batch didn't go to school. And people had them to look up to. We don't have the heroes no more. ◐

1. For an insightful essay that points out the "frontier" character of nighttime relations, see Melbin (1978).

In those days Eastern City had a strong manufacturing employment base. People worked in factories and other industrial concerns in various parts of the city and its immediate environs. Today major manufacturing jobs are vanishing from the metropolitan region, and communities like Northton feel the impact. The problems of Northton, and of the Village and Eastern City, are multifaceted. But the main influence is the changes in the economy and the inability of local black residents and others to make effective adjustments to these changes.

Eastern City's economic base is moving from manufacturing to service to what is called "postindustrial." A ride to the outskirts of the city by train or car reveals plant after plant vacant, where solid residents of Northton once worked. As the factories close or move away, the economic stability of respectable working-class neighborhoods is undermined and the moral and social relations among people are strained. Some may never recover from the dislocation.

This economic pattern is well documented for Eastern City and other major urban areas of the Midwest, East, and Northeast.[2] Large-scale manufacturing concerns seek to locate in areas of cheap land and labor, low tax base, and few environmental restrictions. As they leave Eastern City for Singapore, Ireland, Poland, and "nonmetropolitan" America, they leave behind a vacuum in the city's economy, with the economic and social burdens falling most on those who have fewest resources to deal with them. Revenues are lost to the city because of the diminished tax base (both from industry and from employees), missing wages and their multiplier effects on the local community, and greater welfare costs to support the unemployed and their families. These pressures have been rising since the Reagan administration halted the national policy of "revenue sharing" between the federal government and the cities. And the state government is not forthcoming with needed financial aid. Eastern City is thus caught in a triple crunch. At present the city cannot balance its budget. Attempts to do so force cuts in public services, including support for public schools, police officers, and municipal welfare services. To maintain even minimal levels of service requires that taxes go up.

As taxes rise and threaten to continue rising, and as city services

2. See, for example, the developing literature on this pattern: Kasarda (1989); Stull and Madden (1990); Peterson (1985); Perrucci et al. (1988); and Katz (1989).

decline, other local businesses (not just "primary manufacturing concerns") and middle-class residents consider leaving the city, at least to move to the suburbs. And potential new businesses and residents choose to locate elsewhere. The city has been known to grant tax favors to new enterprises or corporate headquarters to encourage them to locate in the city, but this brings both lost revenues and the need for more city services. These enterprises also provide only a modest number of new jobs, often for nonresidents. So the spiral continues.[3] The resident quoted above continues:

◐ *I don't think the corporations give a shit. I really don't. They have an important part to play. See, they moved out of here. Look at all them plants and stuff; see, those were the jobs these [Northton] people used to have. You take a train out of the city, and for thirty miles you just pass vacant factories, you know, along the tracks, all around town. These were jobs for [local] people.* ◐

The manufacturing economy provided high-paying jobs and could provide training (low skilled) for people with little education and no entering skills. Furthermore, in today's economy even middle-class families require two incomes to live comfortably (see Ehrenreich 1989). Young people graduating from today's underfunded local schools often are not able to read, write, and compute at the level necessary to obtain high-paying jobs. They then become employable only at the lowest levels of the service economy, which pay subsistence wages and offer little training, or must work in "fast food" establishments or similar jobs at wages below what such jobs pay in the suburbs.

Members of the Northton community have not been able to make an effective adjustment to these economic changes. Thus idleness is widespread, numerous young women with children are on welfare, married couples are increasingly rare, and conventional role models are scarce. The "natural" community leadership has suffered in two ways. First, middle-class families who have the resources have left Northton for the suburbs, like their white counterparts in other areas of the city. The weakening of overt housing segregation in parts of the suburbs has allowed blacks to seek better homes and schools elsewhere, leaving Northton without the quality of leadership it enjoyed in the past.

3. For a deft analysis of the sustained attack on the welfare state by the Reagan administration, see Block et al. (1987) and Katz (1989).

Second and even more important, the loss of industries has undermined the traditional leadership of the community, the "old heads." Some of these men and women are now retired on pensions, some are hanging on to the residual manufacturing jobs. But what they used to be able to promise "young boys"—high-paying jobs in exchange for law-abidingness and civility and the work ethic—no longer exists. Faced with persistent racism, youths can hope only for low-paying service jobs, often in the suburbs, or jobs in fast-food restaurants (see Kirschenman and Neckerman 1989). Some old heads have difficulty understanding the young boys' unemployment, so wedded are they to the work ethic, decency, church, and family values. And they are quick to blame them for not wanting to work.

◐ *Our big fatal flaw came around 1972, when the old heads stopped [disengaged]. They didn't go into the street [community work] thing, they went into other things. They didn't come back to protect neighborhoods. There's no more leadership. There was nobody on the corner to talk to the young boys. Everybody on the corner [now] was saying the same criminal, wild, crazy things.*

So for the young, marginally employed men, "community," the work ethic, and family life become less and less part of their world:

They [young men] just imitate what they think it should be. Their own daddies are gone [have left] or never been there [in the home], you know, the one that made the baby, see, he [the father] could be anybody. But see, he [the boy] don't know. The young boy don't have a clue on being a daddy. He hasn't had no practice, ain't seen nothing, and there're no old heads around to show them, because the other batch didn't come along. ◐

The youths mock and patronize the old heads who do remain for not understanding the "way the world really works." The young men may have little desire to engage in the "hard work" their elders performed, even if it were available and had long-term promise. I attribute at least some of this loss of the work ethic indirectly to the social and emotional changes brought on by the civil rights and "cultural nationalist" movements of the 1960s and 1970s, when so many young blacks, determined to forge a positive new identity, proclaimed that they would never subjugate themselves to whites in the "slaves" —physically demanding, dirty work—and "Negro jobs" many of their fathers and grandfathers took for granted. In repudiating the racial caste system, many youths thus trash the work ethic as it relates to work that is thought to solidify one's place at the bottom of the stratification system (see Anderson 1980). Further, when the young boys occasionally see black men working on outdoor construction projects around Eastern City, the blacks are usually doing the hardest and dirtiest work, while the whites are perceived as standing around "shuckin' and jivin'." Such interpretations do not inspire the work ethic. Moreover, the notion of such hard work does not fit with the model of the "good life" they see on television, and black youths tend to be avid watchers, exposed to and influenced by the same "cultural apparatus" (Mills 1962) as youths of the wider society. Consistently, many adjust to the situation of desire for material things coupled with severe economic dislocation by becoming entrepreneurs of drugs and vice—a life that promises thrills, glamour, freedom, and money. The following field note illustrates this tension:

◐ *Outside the barbershop on a corner in Northton, old heads put on hold the dictum, "see but don't see" and steal a closer look at what "must be" a drug dealer. Self-conscious, they try to hide their interest, paying a kind of civil inattention to the show. Others, including a group of young boys nearby, have come over for a look at the "bad ride," but for them the driver is really the main attraction. He is a dealer. That is the way they make sense of the charismatic, close-cropped young black man literally "dripping with gold," dressed in his full urban regalia, including midnight blue Adidas sweat suit and new white sneakers. Rose-tinted glasses thinly shade his eyes. In a show of style, he profiles; lightly stepping into his Lincoln Town Car, he exhibits his cool. He sinks into the richly upholstered front seat, leans on the armrest, and turns up the stereo. His performance is all the more remarkable because of his youth (about twenty-one), which contrasts sharply with his expensive possessions. Local people are intrigued by this figure. Ambivalent, they recoil at his image, but they envy him just the same. The old heads feel especially conflicted; most definitely they condemn his car—which "he did not have to work for." But secretly, some even admire him. He's "getting over," making it, though not in the right way, the way they were taught. They see trouble ahead for him, but he thrives on the risk. He is something of a mystery. The young boys wonder, "How did he do that? How can we be like that?" But they know. Through his displays, he shows them the way. He is only a year or two older than they are, and they can identify with him. His life-style and image beckon, suggesting "maybe you can be like me." ◐*

In the face of related problems of persistent poverty and a lack of

local leadership, the community suffers economic and social breakdown. As the wider regular economy fails them, many young people,
particularly men, seek the underground and adopt its ways.

The drug economy is in many ways a parallel, or a parody, of the
service economy (with an element of glamour thrown in). Rival
drug dealers claim particular street corners to sell their wares. Corners are literally bought and sold, and they belong to the one who
has the power to claim the space for the time being; such claims may
result in territorial disputes that are sometimes settled by violence.
The "owner" has the right to sell drugs there, and he may do so with
a hardly audible, "Psst! Psst! I got the news. I got the news. I got that
girl. I got that bitch. Beam me up, Scotty [*Stark Trek*]. Blow. Pipe.
'Caine." The sellers hawk their wares like newspapers or sports
tickets.

For many young men the drug economy is an employment agency
superimposed on the existing gang network. Young men who "grew
up" in the gang, but now are without clear opportunities, easily become involved; they fit themselves into its structure, manning its
drug houses and selling drugs on street corners (see Merton 1957;
Cloward and Ohlin 1960). With the money from these "jobs," they
support themselves and help their families, at times buying fancy
items to impress others. As one former drug dealer told me:

◐ *Man, you should have seen me. I was the king of the neighborhood. People wanted to run errands for me, wanted to wash my
car, go to the store for me. Girls wanted to have sex. I mean, I had a
9 mm pistol, a .38, and a new Bronco [automobile]. . . . It was nice. I
mean, I took my lady to nice restaurant, bought her things. I helped
my mom out. All her bills are paid. She doin' real good, now. I had
all I wanted.* ◐

Over time these youths also have a hand in creating new markets. Like so many ordinary salesmen, they sell not only to strangers
but to their friends and relatives. At times they literally hook up
others, providing readily available drugs and an atmosphere in which
to "get high." The dealers' sometimes irresistible offer to a potential
customer is, "You get high?" The following narrative by a white police officer shows the tension that results:

◐ *Oh, yeah. We went out on Davis Street [in Northton] yesterday, and we locked up ten or twelve drug dealers. We served search
warrants on three of the drug houses on Davis Street. We had an*

enormous number of police, sixty or seventy officers, 'cause this was a long-term investigation. We videotaped these guys sellin' the drugs. Now, there was two reactions. One of the reactions was, "Boy, this is great." I'm talking about the people along the street. They say, "Thank God! Can you do it some more? Can you keep comin' back and doin' it?" The people [black residents], the friends and family of the people who were arrested for sellin' drugs were mad as hell. Because in effect their friend or family member who's a drug dealer has at least temporarily lost his job! Because that, to those people, is this guy's livelihood. That's where they get their money. "Oh, yeah, let's buy some clothes this week." It's part of the underground economy, and as a result they get to depend on it like most of us would depend on a nine-to-five job where you get a steady paycheck every week. ◑

The changing economic forces have many victims—some obvious, some not so obvious. The most obvious, of course, though the wider culture has often tried not to see them, are the black people of Northton. They bear the immediate burden of the violence and depravity of the drug culture. There is the crack house, for example, a recent addition to ghetto life that mimics the "speakeasy" of another time. Stories circulate of hapless addicts like the man who told the crack dealers to come and take the contents of his house, including the refrigerator, or the "beanpole-thin coke whore" who walked into a convenience store wearing only a trench coat and, opening her coat, said to a male customer, "Can you deal with this?"

There are also the consequences for families of these economic dislocations. A local policeman's account is revealing:

◑ *We went out Friday and served a warrant on Keeney Avenue [in Northton]. And this house easily would not classify for human habitation. The two people that we locked up were living on the third floor. There was a man living on the second floor, one man. And there was a grandmother with about two or three teenagers and three kids under the age of eight, I would say, who were living on the first floor. Ten people living in a totally unlivable house. No heat, no running water. It was dirty. The front porch looked like it was ready to collapse, and the two girls on the third floor, who were both under eighteen, were selling drugs. We had officers go in and make purchases, and when we locked them up, we confiscated about 150 vials of crack. They didn't appear to be strung out. You've got ten people living in a totally unlivable house, including three boys under eight, and you know, what kind of chance do any of these kids have? We see a lot of this kind of thing. The children in Northton, I'm really afraid for them. It's incredible, the odds they're up against.*

When I hear people say we should legalize drugs, because that'll solve the problem, that's absolute idiocy as far as I'm concerned. It's not gonna solve any problems. It may solve one small aspect. It solves the criminality of it. OK, our courts won't be as crowded. Whoopee! More people will contract AIDS. Some of them will be shootin' cocaine. And others will commit crimes in order to even legally buy it. I mean, you've got to spend money to buy cocaine, even if it's legalized and it's a dollar a shot.

You still have to spend good ol' U.S. hard currency to buy it, alright? The tendency among crack addicts, as you say, is to get high and to try to stay high forever. So they are gonna run out of money no matter how cheap we make it, and then they're gonna continue to do those things they do now to get the money to buy the crack. Crime won't be as bad, but it'll still be there. Prostitution will continue. So as a result AIDS is gonna be spread that way. While they're indulging in this act, they're gonna procreate, so you're gonna have more and more, as we see already, crack-addicted babies. The ones addicted at birth are the least of our worries. You look at the history of people who have been mass murderers, and they're almost all people who were abused as children. Don't doubt me when I tell you that out here, right now, within a mile circle of this police station, there are thousands of abused children. Abused in every way you can think of: mentally, physically, emotionally, sexually. They have malnutrition because mom is spending every dime she can get on crack, and there's no food in the house. 'Cause I've been in a whole lot of houses that don't have any food in 'em. And that's the scariest part for me. The future is a whirlwind out there. It's a tornado waitin' to happen, and its gonna tear us apart. ◑

In Northton there are an overwhelming number of poor, female-headed families, a significant proportion of them on welfare. As these families grow older, the children meet the street culture and must come to terms with it. Some dabble in it, experiencing enough to try to pass as hip among their friends; few want to be known as "square" or "lame." For those only loosely anchored to conventional institutions (extended families, churches, or community organizations of one kind or another), the street culture calls loudly and insistently.

Most young boys can no longer earn enough to support a family, in the regular economy or the underground economy or both. Yet they engage in sex for both biological and peer-group reasons and often father children out of wedlock. Over time such behavior becomes incorporated into sex codes that reflect the reality of the situation. The young men often adjust to their financial situation by remaining with their mothers, retaining their "freedom" and all the comforts of home; they may sometimes play the role of man of the house and aid the household through meager financial contributions. But the youth is unwilling to "play house" with the mother of his child, an adaptation his peer group turns into a virtue. The girls are often headed for adolescent pregnancy, but they are doubly unable to provide for their children, with no skills, no provision for child care, and no vision of anything else.

Another set of victims of the changes in the economy are the residents of the Village. First there are the direct effects. The emerging service economy, along with the "compounded inflation" of the past few decades, has made it difficult to live on conventional salaries. A middle-class life in the Village often requires that both spouses be employed, whereas in earlier times one spouse could work and maintain a comparable standard of living. So residents have less time and energy to bring to the life of their community than their parents had, just when fighting to maintain city services or making up for the lack of them is a growing daily issue.

Second are the spillover effects from Northton. The drug crisis has given rise to "zombies" and "pipers," addicts who scavenge the area or who with sad tales aggressively beg for money; some go from door to door in the Village, alarming residents. These people also commit a large amount of the local crime, so residents believe. But unlike ordinary thieves and muggers, crack addicts are desperate people who are not always sensible, and they may take chances ordinary criminals would not risk, thus making the streets and public spaces increasingly dangerous.

Drugs have a profound impact upon the local neighborhoods, and Village residents have become both outraged and fearful. Near where drugs are bought and sold, more crime is committed, including muggings, rapes, and acts of harassment. Telltale pieces of automobile glass littering the streets point to the frequency of car break-ins, as desperate crack addicts search for money to buy a vial of crack. Some residents have had their cars broken into four or five times. Car owners become very angry at the constant stream of nuisance crimes, which they report at local gatherings, where others may share their grief or treat their misfortune as a diversion.

But as these tales reverberate, middle-class people find the area an increasingly difficult place to live, and the suburbs grow more attractive. Such residents may be much inclined to move out of the Village, thinking it unfit for human habitation compared with options in other towns and the suburbs. Hence some do flee, though often not without agonizing or putting up a fight. Those who fight may find themselves becoming increasingly intolerant of anonymous black males. And in public meetings they offer solutions that border on vigilantism or outright racism.

Members of the particularly hard-hit group of progressive liberals of the 1950s and former counterculturalists of the 1960s shudder at such comments, which fundamentally threaten their dream of a diverse and racially tolerant neighborhood. Together they worked to make the Village a place where various kinds of people could live in harmony. Tolerance was their flag. Some of them (who may now be in their seventies) still have high hopes for the area and feel a great social responsibility both to their less fortunate neighbors and to the Village community. Many continue to immerse themselves in time-consuming efforts that promise to make the neighborhood a better place to live. Recently, through the inspiration of Tyrone Pitts, a forty-nine-year-old longtime black resident of Bellwether Street, members of this group have come alive with enthusiasm for ridding the community of drug dealers and crack houses. They join night-time vigils and, with the aid of the police, confront drug houses and their merchants directly. Their activities result in arrests of dealers and harassment of drug buyers, encouraging them to quit those portions of the neighborhood. These people have been so successful that other community groups around Eastern City are adopting their tactics. Together they are known as the Eastern City Antidrug Coalition. And they are strongly supported by local ministers, politicians, black activists, and diverse elements of the community.

But it is easy to see that many of these people are caught between a rock and a hard place. As the "quality of life" in the area appears to decay, their friends, associates, and relatives often wonder why they still live there when it seems such a social and physical wasteland. And the next generation, those who might carry on their work, may have lost faith in their vision or may be preoccupied with making a living. Ironically, if they *are* successful in "making the community a better place to live," then the Village, with its quaint, beautiful, historic homes, will become more attractive to developers, leading to even more gentrification.

At first glance the yuppies who are now coming into the Village appear to be beneficiaries of the economic changes. They move in with more money and can afford to pay the "exorbitant" prices for homes, thus further inflating local housing costs. But equally important for the makeup of the community, the yuppies' interests and values are usually quite different from those of the former counter-culturalists and liberals they join. They tend to exhibit much less "social responsibility" and tolerance toward their poorer neighbors than did their predecessors. For instance the local Village school, established as part of a social movement by progressive liberals, has an excellent citywide reputation, which many of the newcomers disregard. They are often blinded by the assumption that all public schools are inferior, and they readily send their children to private schools, bypassing important opportunities for community involvement. Eventually they may move to the suburbs "for the schools."

For these people the community is like a Venus flytrap. On the surface it seems an agreeable place. Spacious Victorian houses on tree-lined brick streets, cordial, diverse, and sophisticated middle-class neighbors, and the promise of rising property values all are highly attractive to the prospective resident. But after living in the community awhile one experiences car break-ins, burglaries, and public incivility. At dinner parties and other social gatherings the topics of crime and the local [criminal] "element" invariably arise. A neighborhood perspective is hammered out thorough the exchange of "horror stories," though it may be obscured by witty conversation.

For those only weakly committed to city living, particularly middle-class people who have serious difficulty with social diversity and who have clear housing alternatives, the "problem free" suburbs become tempting. After an incident such as a car break-in or a bicycle theft, a "last straw" can make them leave. This temptation becomes especially great when outsiders at work or in overlapping social circles subtly define the area by their inquiries about the quality of life, glibly assume the neighborhood is overrun by ghetto blacks, and treat the area in conversation as a strange place for a "nice" middle-class person to live. Over time, people may simply grow weary of living in the city and succumb to the "shake out" process.

But the yuppies and others may become victims because they have bought property at the high end of the housing marked. As the price of housing ebbs, some middle-class homeowners stay put mainly because they cannot get what they would like for their homes.

Finally, there is the "wider urban community." The general decline in city services and the municipal fiscal crunch, brought about to a large extent by business flight and by drastic budget cuts, including the end of revenue sharing under the Reagan administration, become especially worrisome. Over the past ten years the Reagan budget cuts seem to have had a major impact on community life.[4] Residents read about the way the problems of the homeless, AIDS patients, the proliferation of crack-related orphans, police, schools, and trash removal threaten to overwhelm the city budget. Precisely the moment when the cities needed the most support and the most remedial spending was the point when the budget rug was pulled from under them.

But the Village is different from much of the city in that the forces of development tend to drive property values *up*. These forces include Eastern Tech, Ivy University, the local science research complex, and a proposed new mall at the nearby central train station. These factors appear to augur well for local real estate values, spurring development in the Village and eventually in parts of Northton. In fact, certain segments of the Village community are involved in buying up Village and Northton properties and holding them for future high prices. As this occurs gentrification becomes energized, and the poorer elements of the community are driven out, often into the nearby ghetto. Community residents, particularly the former counterculturalists, view the presence of Eastern Tech in the real estate market with alarm; at best they are skeptical of its designs on the area. But new residents brought in by the developers instead look askance at the presence of any ghetto residents and actively discourage what they see as "ghetto hangouts" in the Village.

In the Village-Northton there are thus multiple victims of the changing economy—and again the departing corporations are deeply implicated. The yuppie who is mugged and the kid who does it; the old head who loses the respect of the kid, who impregnates the teen-

4. For an assessment of the effect of these cuts on other community areas, particularly the end of the federal policy of "revenue sharing," see Logan and Molotch (1987).

age girl, who goes on welfare, which raises taxes, which drives out local companies, which causes unemployment, which causes homelessness, which causes crime, which depresses property values and drives out middle-class residents, which further isolates the poor and the criminal. Each of the groups is frustrated in some way in getting itself together to fulfill the promise of the local area, a promise that is frustrated by increasingly broader structural factors.

These realities try the patience of the most committed urban dweller, particularly Villagers who clearly have other options, sometimes causing them to doubt their earlier commitments to the city, to diversity, and even to social tolerance. Thus many people, particularly recently arrived whites, see residents of the black ghetto as desperate and perhaps dangerous and feel a need to protect themselves. Since social distance is considered protective, law-abiding residents of the Village (including blacks) tend to distance themselves from strange black males by being "short" with them in public encounters. This happens so often that many black males "understand" and may even joke about their public image.

Blacks and whites share many attitudes about the community, especially concerning public safety. To venture out, particularly at night, one must be wary. This is a part of community lore, something everyone, white or black, takes for granted. An even more important part of this lore is that one must beware not of whites but of blacks, especially young males. When a white person is mugged by a black, both blacks and whites "understand" it. When a black person is seriously injured in a mugging, or when whites are the perpetrators, it is more difficult to account for.

Much of this attitude is gained through community perceptions of the ghetto, and it is supported whenever community residents drive through Northton and view the "proof" on the street corners. They see small groups of idle black people who are shabbily dressed, youths carrying loud radios or talking noisily, or what they take to be fights or holdups. Because they have little worthwhile knowledge about the black area, they form a stereotypical picture from what they see. And the people in this picture become the kinds of people they would rather not have close to them. In the mass, these become the people many Villagers try desperately to avoid.

This public order is based on the general association of blacks, particularly males, with a culture of violence and trouble. Whenever there is an account of public incivility involving blacks and whites, blacks are assumed to be primarily at fault. And blacks and whites keep their distance in public, thus remaining strangers who "know" only enough about each other to remain so.

Anonymous blacks in the Village, especially males, often find themselves trying to prove themselves respectable to others they encounter. And because of a lack of understanding by those who rely mainly on local street etiquette and have not yet achieved street wisdom, they seldom can do so to the others' satisfaction. Consequently black males must expend inordinate energy to establish such an identity—in effect, they must campaign for it. A black male approaching the color border in the community must be on "good behavior," or the social situation may be "flooded out" (Goffman 1959). But even then he is usually not fully trusted. As a black person, he is taken first as a representative of the ghetto of Northton. In many ways the black male becomes resigned to the campaign he must wage; it is the norm. But such norms led an air of resentment, distrust, and instability to public encounters between black men and other residents of the Village.

The police who must deal with these situations are also victims in a special way. Many of them share the general prejudice and distrust about black males on the streets. Yet they are charged with maintaining law and order. They often become tense and deal with black youths in threatening or outright abusive ways. But many also put their lives on the line every day when they investigate a crime or quell a disturbance. A white police officer offered the following insight:

◐ *See, this is a mostly black neighborhood. And I have a belief that if you took this problem [drugs and poverty] and didn't change a thing with it and put in the middle of an all-white neighborhood, you would get a much larger reaction to the problem. It would be much more extensive. Because to a large extent white people in the city don't care if black people use crack. As long as they don't come into their neighborhood and rob them, they [whites] don't give a shit. I believe that. Because it's here [in Northton] where there's a lot of poor people and a lot of black people, nobody cares. Or damn few care.* ◐

The Future

I have tried to represent the Village-Northton ethnographically. My account shows some of the ways the changing economy affects Northton and how its negative ramifications victimize residents of the Village as well. As the social breakdown stimulated by crack and by the exodus of companies and local jobs spreads, more and more residents of the area feel the impact in increased crime, uncertainty on the streets, decline in city services, higher taxes, and the exodus of middle-class neighbors.

There are still regular exchanges on the streets of the Village in which people express comity and goodwill toward others of different ethnicity, race, and life-style. The community's ethos and social script call for decency and tolerance toward others, and this definition has become institutionalized. But because they lack knowledge, experience, and familiarity with blacks and black culture, many white newcomers erect a protective wall of prejudice, sometimes expressed through the incessant search for a practical street etiquette, informed by gender and color stereotyping, that will get them up and down the streets safely. As residents come to share a common perspective on their environment, an informal etiquette emerges, including prescriptions and proscriptions about behavior in public, refined through practice, that promises security or at least a minimum of conflict. Through experience, residents adapt and create at least the appearance of an ordered and racially tolerant public space. With time they may gain the capacity to "see through" public situations, to judge "who is who" and to distinguish real danger from false alarms. They may learn to see people rather than race and to rely less on prejudice and stereotyping.

Street wisdom is a way of negotiating day-to-day actions and interactions with minimum risk and maximum mutual respect in a world full of uncertainty and danger. And it can help in building a stronger, more coherent community. But it cannot solve the economic problems faced by Northton, the Village, and the wider community. To correct these problems, seen in many American cities, we must have effective leadership from Washington. One of the most important things the federal government can do is to enact policies that will give young people a serious stake in conventional society, enhancing life chances for them and their children.

In general, education must be given a higher priority. Government and the corporations should be encouraged to help these young people adjust to the new urban reality, first by restructuring urban schools and fortifying them with committed teachers and administrators. With the breakdown of the local community, teachers are frequently called on to perform social welfare work, and many suffer from low morale. At present local schools are overcrowded, and their resources have diminished. If parents fail to paint rooms and do maintenance work, the buildings remain filthy and unattractive.

Child-centered programs must be developed and sustained, with much smaller classes, and fundamentals must be stressed so that students gain the academic and social skills essential to adequately paying employment in the emerging service economy and to success in life. Older youths should receive remedial education on demand, including job training that is long range and of high quality. Ideally this would be on-the-job training with major employers, but it must be some form of gainful employment with an orientation toward growth and an incentive structure of benefits and rewards tied to an individual's development.

In this effort the government must encourage the private sector to take the initiative—to take an interest in the poverty-stricken inner-city neighborhoods and do things they might otherwise see as beyond the call of duty. The welfare of the cities is at stake. Legal employment for idle youths would improve the quality of life for all of us who inhabit the inner city by increasing the tax base, giving these youths a clear stake in the legitimate economy, and encouraging the formation of nuclear families. In addition, high-quality drug treatment and rehabilitation must be available on demand, and young people must be educated or at least warned about the perils of drugs.

If these suggestions are not heeded, we face growing incivility and crime. Drug problems are likely to become far worse, and harder to separate from poverty. This poverty of the city itself will accelerate the breakdown of community and the exodus of middle-class residents, leaving their former neighbors even more isolated. The city will be ringed by the white middle and upper classes, who will venture in only when absolutely necessary. And the urban neighborhoods will become less and less habitable.

Appendix
Characteristics of the Village-Northton Area

Table 1

Population, Demographic Variables, and Housing Characteristics, 1940 to 1980

	1940	1950	1960	1970	1980
Total population[a]					
Eastern City	1,931,300	2,071,600	2,002,500	1,948,600	1,688,200
Northton	17,200	19,400	16,900	12,000	9,100
Village	9,900	13,600	11,500	6,800	6,500
Percentage black					
Eastern City	13	18	26	34	38
Northton	46	78	95	98	98
Village	32	41	65	48	39
Percentage under eighteen years old					
Eastern City	26	26	31	31	26
Northton	33	33	42	41	34
Village	20	23	26	17	11
Percentage sixty-five years old and over					
Eastern City	7	8	10	12	14
Northton	6	6	6	9	12
Village	11	12	12	11	13
Percentage with high-school degree					
Eastern City	19	28	31	40	54
Northton	12	17	16	22	35
Village	28	35	32	53	62
Percentage in college[b]					
Eastern City			2	3	6
Northton	NA	NA	0	1	3
Village			8	26	42

(*continued*)

	1940	1950	1960	1970	1980
Percentage with four years of college and over					
Eastern City	4	5	5	7	11
Northton	1	2	1	2	3
Village	7	8	9	19	31
Working-age population[c]					
Eastern City	1,558,500	1,630,500	1,497,300	1,404,100	1,310,600
Northton	12,900	14,200	11,000	7,600	6,400
Village	8,300	11,000	9,000	5,800	5,900
Percentage in labor force[d]					
Eastern City	56	54	56	57	54
Northton	54	53	57	47	37
Village	58	51	59	50	45
Percentage of labor force unemployed[e]					
Eastern City	17	6	6	5	11
Northton	26	12	14	7	32
Village	17	9	10	8	8
Housing units[f]					
Eastern City	533,300	599,500	649,000	673,500	685,600
Northton	4,600	4,900	4,900	4,100	3,900
Village	3,500	4,300	4,200	2,800	3,200
Percentage owner-occupied					
Eastern City	37	55	59	57	54
Northton	20	30	33	29	31
Village	13	18	18	15	16
Percentage owner-occupied, blacks only[g]					
Eastern City	1	5	10	14	17
Northton	2	21	30	28	31
Village	1	8	12	10	8

	1940	1950	1960	1970	1980
Percentage of units vacant					
Eastern City	5	2	5	5	10
Northton	8	3	11	12	26
Village	12	4	11	10	17
Percentage owner-occupied of all black-occupied units[h]					
Eastern City	10	29	43	47	54
Northton	5	30	36	33	42
Village	6	23	21	20	20

Source: U.S. censuses, 1940–80, by census tract. Northton tracts include most of the neighborhood called "Northton" in this book; Village tracts include all of "the Village" and "the Bottom" and a small part of what might be considered "Northton."

[a] Rounded to nearest hundred.

[b] Figures not available for 1940 and 1950.

[c] Population fourteen years and older, 1940–60; sixteen years and older, 1970 and 1980. Rounded to nearest hundred.

[d] Civilian labor force, 1950–80.

[e] In 1940, those "seeking work," not including those "on public emergency work (WPA, NYA, etc.)."

[f] Rounded to nearest hundred.

[g] Nonwhite owners, 1950 and 1960.

[h] Of all units occupied by blacks, the percentage of owner-occupied units. These figures do not compare directly to overall percentage owner-occupied, which is a percentage of all (including vacant) units. Nonwhite owners, 1950 and 1960.

Table 2

Neighborhood Characteristics, 1980

	Eastern City	Northton	Village
Total population[a]	1,688,200	9,100	6,500
Where living in 1975 (%)			
Living in same house	68%	73%	30%
Living elsewhere in Eastern City	23%	24%	29%
Living elsewhere in Eastern City area[b]	2%	1%	16%
Living outside Eastern City area	6%	2%	24%
Born in Eastern State	73%	67%	56%
Total housing units[a]	619,800	2,900	2,700
Owner-occupied units	378,100	1,200	500
Occupied in 1969 or earlier	64%	80%	59%
Occupied in 1959 or earlier	38%	69%	34%
Renter-occupied units	241,700	1,700	2,100
Occupied in 1969 or earlier	19%	24%	11%
Income[a]			
Median income per household	$13,200	$6,300	$7,200
Mean income per household	16,300	8,700	11,600
Income per wage earner	6,100	2,800	5,500
Labor force[a]	705,300	2,400	2,700
Unemployed	11%	32%	8%
Occupation of employed			
Managerial and professional specialty	20%	11%	39%
Technical, sales, and administrative support	34%	26%	35%
Service occupations	16%	35%	12%
Blue-collar[c]	30%	28%	15%

	Eastern City	Northton	Village
Total families[a,d]	413,000	2,000	700
Married couples living with own children under eighteen years old	29%	15%	20%
Female householders, no husband present, living with own children under eighteen years old	15%	35%	18%
Other families living with own children under eighteen years old	2%	3%	2%

Source: 1980 Census of Population and Housing, Census Tracts, Eastern City, Pa.–N.J.
PHC80-2-283 (Washington, D.C.: U.S. Department of Commerce, 1983).
Note: See table 1 for definition of census tracts.
[a] Rounded to nearest hundred.
[b] Eastern City's SMSA (standard metropolitan statistical area) includes the seven counties surrounding the city—four in Pennsylvania and three in New Jersey.
[c] Precision production, craft, and repair occupations, and operators, fabricators, and laborers.
[d] Households in which the primary householder and one or more other persons are related by birth, marriage, or adoption. These include families without children under eighteen years old.

References

Abrahams, Roger D. 1970. *Deep down in the jungle*. 2d ed. Chicago: Aldine.

Allen, Walter R. 1978. The search for applicable theories of black family life. *Journal of Marriage and the Family* 40:177–29.

Anderson, Bernard E., and Isabel V. Sawhill, eds. 1980. *Youth employment and public policy*. Englewood Cliffs, N.J.: Prentice-Hall.

Anderson, Elijah. 1978. *A place on the corner*. Chicago: University of Chicago Press.

———. 1980. Some observations on black youth employment. In *Youth employment and public policy*, ed. Bernard E. Anderson and Isabel V. Sawhill, 64–87. Englewood Cliffs, N.J.: Prentice-Hall.

———. 1986. Of old heads and young boys: Notes on the urban black experience. Unpublished paper commissioned by the National Research Council, Committee on the Status of Black Americans.

Arensberg, Conrad M. 1937. *The Irish countryman*. New York: Macmillan.

Auletta, Ken. 1982. *The underclass*. New York: Random House.

Banton, Michael. 1964. *The policeman and the community*. New York: Basic Books.

Becker, Howard S. 1963. *Outsiders: Studies in the sociology of deviance*. New York: Macmillan.

———. 1970. *Sociological work*. Chicago: Aldine.

Becker, Howard S., et al. 1961. *Boys in white: Student culture in medical school*. Chicago: University of Chicago Press.

Berry, Brian J. L., and Russell Hardin, eds. 1982. *Rational man and irrational society? An introduction and sourcebook*. Beverly Hills, Calif.: Sage.

Berry, Brian J. L., and John D. Kasarda. 1977. *Contemporary urban ecology*. New York: Macmillan.

Billingsley, Andrew. 1968. *Black families in white America*. Englewood Cliffs, N.J.: Prentice-Hall.

Bittner, Egon. 1967. The police on Skid Row. *American Sociological Review* 32(October): 699–715.

Black, Donald J., and Albert Reiss, Jr. 1967. Police control of juveniles. *American Sociological Review* 35(February): 63–77.

Blackwell, James. 1984. *The black community: Diversity and unity*. New York: Harper and Row.

Block, Fred, et al. 1987. *The mean season: The attack on the welfare state*. New York: Pantheon.

Block, Richard. 1977. *Violent crime*. Lexington, Mass.: Lexington Books.

Bluestein, Barry, and Bennett Harrison. 1984. *The deindustrialization of America*. New York: Basic Books.

Blumer, Herbert. 1958. Race prejudice as a sense of group position. *Pacific Sociological Review* 1 (Spring): 3–6.

———. 1969. *Symbolic interactionism*. Englewood Cliffs, N.J.: Prentice-Hall.

Bourdieu, Pierre. 1986. The forms of capital. In *Handbook of theory and research for the sociology of education*, ed. J. G. Richardson. New York: Greenwood Press.

Bordua, David, ed. 1967. *The police*. New York: John Wiley.

Burgess, Ernest W., ed. 1926. *The urban community*. Chicago: University of Chicago Press.

———. 1967. The growth of the city. In *The city*, ed. Robert E. Park and Ernest W. Burgess. Chicago: University of Chicago Press.

Clark, Kenneth B. 1965. *Dark ghetto*. New York: Harper and Row.

Cloward, Richard A., and Lloyd Ohlin. 1960. *Delinquency and opportunity: A theory of delinquent gangs*. Glencoe, Ill.: Free Press.

Coleman, James. 1988. Social capital in the creation of human capital. *American Journal of Sociology* 94:S95–S120.

Cox, Oliver C. 1948. *Caste, class, and race: A study in social dynamics*. New York: Modern Reader Paperbacks.

Cressey, Paul F. 1938. Population succession in Chicago. *American Journal of Sociology* 44:59–69.

Danziger, Sheldon, and Daniel Weinberg, eds. 1986. *Fighting poverty*. Cambridge: Harvard University Press.

Dash, Leon. 1989. *When children want children*. New York: William Morrow.

Davis, Allen F., and Mark H. Haller. 1974. *The peoples of Philadelphia: A history of ethnic groups and lower-class life, 1790–1940*. Philadelphia: Temple University Press.

Doeringer, Peter, and Michael Piore. 1971. *Internal labor markets and manpower analysis*. New York: McGraw-Hill.

Dollard, John. 1932. *Criteria for the life history*. New Haven: Yale University Press.

Doyle, Bertrand W. 1937. *The etiquette of race relations*. New York: Schocken Books.

Drake, St. Clair, and Horace Cayton. 1962. *Black metropolis*. New York: Harper and Row.

DuBois, W. E. B. 1899. *The Philadelphia Negro*. Philadelphia: University of Pennsylvania Press.

———. 1965. *The souls of black folks*. In *Three Negro classics*. New York: Avon Books. Originally published 1903.

Edelman, Marian Wright. 1987. *Families in peril: An agenda for social change*. Cambridge: Harvard University Press.

Ehrenreich, Barbara. 1989. *Fear of falling: The inner life of the middle class.* New York: Pantheon.

Elwood, David T. 1986. The spatial mismatch hypothesis: Are there teenage jobs missing in the ghetto? ed. Richard B. Freeman and Harry J. Holzer. In *The black youth employment crisis,* Chicago: University of Chicago Press.

———. 1988. *Poor support: Poverty in the American family.* New York: Basic Books.

Erickson, Kai. 1966. *Wayward Puritans.* New York: John Wiley.

Evans-Pritchard, E. E. 1940. *The Nuer: A description of the modes of livelihood and political institutions of a Nilotic people.* New York: Oxford University Press.

Farley, Reynolds. 1984. *Blacks and whites: narrowing the gap?* Cambridge: Harvard University Press.

Fine, Gary Alan, and Sherryl Kleinman. 1979. Rethinking subculture: An interactionist analysis. *American Journal of Sociology* 85:1–20.

Fischer, Claude S. 1977. *Networks and place: Social relations in the urban setting.* New York: Free Press.

———. 1982. *To dwell among friends: Personal networks in town and city.* Chicago: University of Chicago Press.

Fogelson, Robert. 1977. *Big city police.* Cambridge: Harvard University Press.

Frazier, E. Franklin. 1939. *The Negro family in the United States.* Chicago: University of Chicago Press.

———. 1957. *Black bourgeoisie.* New York: Free Press.

Freeman, Richard B. 1976. *Black elite: The new market for highly educated black Americans.* New York: McGraw-Hill.

———. 1986. Create jobs that pay as well as crime. *New York Times,* Sunday, 20 July.

Freeman, Richard B., and Harry J. Holzer, eds. 1986. *The black youth employment crisis.* Chicago: University of Chicago Press.

Furstenberg, Frank. 1976. *Unplanned parenthood.* New York: Free Press.

Gale, Dennis E. 1979. Middle-class resettlement in older urban neighborhoods: The evidence and the implications. *Journal of the American Planning Association* 45(July):293–304.

Gans, Herbert. 1962. *The urban villagers.* New York: Free Press.

Geertz, Clifford. 1983. *Local knowledge: Further essays on interpretive anthropology.* New York: Basic Books.

———. 1988. *Works and lives: The anthropologist as author.* Stanford, Calif.: Stanford University Press.

Gibson, William. 1980a. The alleged weakness in the black family structure. In *Family life and morality: Studies in black and white,* by William Gibson, 55–73. Lanham, Md.: University Press of America.

──────. 1980b. The question of legitimacy. In *Family life and morality: Studies in black and white*, by William Gibson, 41–54. Lanham, Md.: University Press of America.

Gitlin, Todd. 1987. *The sixties: Years of hope, days of rage*. New York: Bantam.

Glasgow, Douglas G. 1980. *The black underclass: Poverty, unemployment and entrapment of ghetto youth*. New York: Random House.

Goffman, Erving. 1959. *The presentation of self in everyday life*. Garden City, N.Y.: Doubleday.

──────. 1961. Role distance. In *Encounters*, by Erving Goffman. New York: Bobbs-Merrill.

──────. 1963. *Behavior in public places*. New York: Free Press.

──────. 1971. *Relations in public*. New York: Harper and Row.

──────. 1974. *Stigma*. Englewood Cliffs, N.J.: Prentice-Hall.

Green, Arnold W. 1941. The cult of personality and sexual relations. *Psychiatry* 4:343–48.

Hammond, Boone E., and Joyce A. Ladner. 1969. Socialization into sexual behavior in a Negro slum ghetto. In *The individual, sex, and society*, ed. Carlfred B. Broderick and Jessie Bernard, 41–51. Baltimore: Johns Hopkins University Press.

Hannerz, Ulf. 1969. *Soulside*. New York: Columbia University Press.

Hawkins, Darnell F., ed. 1986. *Homicide among black Americans*. Lanham, Md.: University Press of America.

Heiss, Jerold. 1975. *The case of the black family*. New York: Columbia University Press.

Hershberg, Theodore. 1974. Free blacks in antebellum Philadelphia. In *Peoples of Philadelphia*, ed. A. F. Davis and M. H. Haller. Philadelphia: Temple University Press.

Hirsch, Susan E. 1978. *Roots of the American working class: The industrialization of crafts in Newark, 1800–1860*. Philadelphia: University of Pennsylvania Press.

Horowitz, Ruth. 1983. *Honor and the American dream*. New Brunswick, N.J.: Rutgers University Press.

Hughes, Everett C. 1945. Dilemmas and contradictions of status. *American Journal of Sociology* 50:353–59.

Hunter, Albert. 1974. *Symbolic communities: The persistence and change of Chicago's local communities*. Chicago: University of Chicago Press.

Jacobs, Jane. 1961. *The death and life of great American cities*. New York: Random House.

Jaynes, Gerald D., and Robin M. Williams, Jr., eds. 1989. *A common destiny: Blacks and American society*. Washington, D.C.: National Academy Press.

Jencks, Christopher. 1988. Deadly neighborhoods. *New Republic*, June, 22–32.

Kasarda, John. 1988. Jobs, migration, and emerging urban mismatches. In *Urban change and poverty*, ed Michael G. McGeary and Laurence E. Lynn. Washington, D.C.: National Academy Press.

Kasarda, John D. 1989. Urban industrial transition and the underclass. *Annals of the American Academy of Political and Social Science* 501 (January): 26–47.

Katz, Jack. 1988. *Seductions of crime: Moral and sensual attractions in doing evil*. New York: Basic Books.

Katz, Michael B. 1989. *The undeserving poor: From the war on poverty to the war on welfare*. New York: Pantheon.

Katznelson, Ira. 1981. *City trenches*. New York: Pantheon.

Kilson, Martin. 1981. Social classes and intergenerational poverty. *Public Interest* 64 (Summer): 55–78.

Kirschenman, Joleen, and Kathryn M. Neckerman. 1989. "We'd love to hire them but . . .": The meaning of race for employers. Paper presented at the Social Science Research Council Conference on the Truly Disadvantaged, 19 October, at Northwestern University, Evanston, Illinois.

Kochman, Thomas. 1972. *Rappin' and stylin' out*. Urbana: University of Illinois Press.

Kornblum, William. 1974. *Blue collar community*. Chicago: University of Chicago Press.

Labov, William. 1986. Language structure and social structure. In *Approaches to social theory*, ed. Siegwart Lindenberg, James S. Coleman, and Stephan Nowak. New York: Russell Sage.

Ladner, Joyce. 1973. *Tomorrow's tomorrow*. New York: Doubleday.

Landry, Bart. 1987. *The new black middle class*. Berkeley: University of California Press.

Lane, Roger. 1967. *Policing the city*. Cambridge: Harvard University Press.

Lewis, Diane K. 1975. The black family: Socialization and sex roles. *Phylon* 36:221–37.

Lewis, Hylan. 1955. *Blackways of Kent*. Chapel Hill: University of North Carolina Press.

Lewis, Oscar. 1966. *La vida: A Puerto Rican family in the culture of poverty—San Juan and New York*. New York: Random House.

Lieberson, Stanley. 1980. *A piece of the pie: Blacks and white immigrants since 1880*. Berkeley: University of California Press.

Liebow, Elliot. 1967. *Tally's corner: A study of Negro street corner men*. Boston: Little, Brown.

Lofland, Lyn. 1973. *A world of strangers*. New York: Basic Books.

Logan, John R., and Harvey L. Molotch. 1987. *Urban fortunes: The political economy of place*. Berkeley: University of California Press.

McGeary, Michael G., and Laurence E. Lynn, eds. 1988. *Urban change and poverty*. Washington, D.C.: National Academy Press.

McIntyre, Jennie. 1967. Public attitudes toward crime and law enforcement. *Annals of the American Academy of Political and Social Sciences* 374:34–46.

McLanahan, Sara, Irwin Garfinkle, and Dorothy Watson. 1988. Family structure, poverty, and the underclass. In *Urban change and poverty*, ed. Michael G. McGeary and Laurence E. Lynn. Washington, D.C.: National Academy Press.

Mangum, Garth L., and Stephen F. Seniger. 1978. Ghetto life styles and youth employment. In *Coming of age in the ghetto: A dilemma of youth unemployment*, by G. L. Mangum and S. F. Seniger. Baltimore: Johns Hopkins University Press.

Manning, Peter K. 1977. *Police work: The social organization of policing.* Cambridge: MIT Press.

Matza, David. 1964. *Delinquency and drift.* New York: John Wiley.

Mead, George Herbert. 1934. *Mind, self, and society.* Chicago: University of Chicago Press.

Melbin, Murray. 1978. Night as frontier. *American Sociological Review* 43 (February): 3–22.

Merton, Robert. 1957. Social structure and anomie. In *Social theory and social structure.* Glencoe, Ill.: Free Press.

Milgram, Morris. 1976. *Good neighborhood.* New York: Norton.

Mills, C. Wright. 1962. Man in the middle: The designer. In *Power, politics, and people: The collected essays of C. Wright Mills*, ed. Irving L. Horowitz. New York: Oxford University Press.

Molotch, Harvey. 1972. *Managed integration: Dilemmas of doing good in the city.* Berkeley: University of California Press.

————. 1976. The city as a growth machine: Toward a political economy of place. *American Journal of Sociology* 82:309–32.

Morris, Aldon. 1984. *The origins of the civil rights movement: Black communities organizing for change.* New York: Free Press.

Moynihan, Daniel Patrick. 1972. The schism in black America. *Public Interest* 27 (Spring): 3–24.

Myrdal, Gunnar, et al. 1944. *An American dilemma: The Negro problem in America.* New York: Harper and Row.

Nathan, Richard. 1987. Will the underclass always be with us? *Society* 24 (March-April): 57–62.

Niederhoffer, Arthur. 1969. *Behind the shield.* New York: Doubleday.

Park, Robert E. 1936. Human ecology. *American Journal of Sociology* 42:1–15.

Park, Robert E., and Ernest W. Burgess. 1967. *The city.* Chicago: University of Chicago Press.

Perkins, Eugene. 1975. *Home is a pretty dirty street.* Chicago: Third World Press.

Perrucci, Carolyn C., Robert Perrucci, Dena B. Targ, and Harry R. Targ. 1988. *Plant closings: Intentional context and social cost.* Hawthorne, N.Y.: Aldine De Gruyter.

Peterson, Paul, ed. 1985. *The new urban reality.* Washington, D.C.: Brookings Institution.

Pettigrew, Thomas. 1973. Attitudes on race and housing: A social-psychological view. In *Segregation in residential areas,* ed. A. Hawley and V. Rock. Washington, D.C.: National Academy of Sciences.

———. 1980a. Prejudice. In *Harvard encyclopedia of American ethnic groups,* ed. Stephan Thernstrom, 820–29. Cambridge: Harvard University Press.

———. 1980b. *The sociology of race relations.* New York: Free Press.

Pipes, Harriette, and Rosalyn Terborg-Penn. 1985. Historical trends in perspectives of Afro-American families. *Trends in History* 3(3–4): 97–111.

Pope, Hallowell. 1969. Negro-white differences in decisions regarding illegitimate children. *Journal of Marriage and the Family* 31: 756–64.

Radzinowicz, Leon, and Marvin Wolfgang, eds. 1971. *The criminal in the arms of the law.* New York: Basic Books.

Rainwater, Lee. 1960. *And the poor get children.* Chicago: Quadrangle Books.

———. 1966. Crucible of identity: The lower-class Negro family. *Daedalus* 45: 172–216.

———. 1969. Sex in the culture of poverty. In *The individual, sex, and society,* ed. Carlfred B. Broderick and Jessie Bernard, 129–40. Baltimore: Johns Hopkins University Press.

———. 1970. *Behind ghetto walls.* Chicago: Aldine De Gruyter.

Redfield, Robert. 1960. *The little community* and *Peasant society and culture.* Chicago: University of Chicago Press.

Reiss, Albert J. 1971. *The police and the public.* New Haven: Yale University Press.

Reiss, Albert, J. and Michael Tonry, eds. 1986. *Communities and crime.* Chicago: University of Chicago Press.

Rossi, Peter H. 1989. *Down and out in America.* Chicago: University Chicago Press.

Rubinstein, Jonathan. 1973. *City police.* New York: Farrar, Straus and Giroux.

Schulz, David A. 1969. *Coming up black: Patterns of ghetto socialization.* Englewood Cliffs, N.J.: Prentice-Hall.

Schuman, H., and B. Gruenberg. 1970. The impact of city racial attitudes. *American Journal of Sociology* 76: 213–61.

Shaw, Clifford, and Henry McKay. 1942. *Juvenile delinquency and urban areas.* Chicago: University of Chicago Press.

Short, James F., Jr., 1971. *The social fabric of the metropolis.* Chicago: University of Chicago Press.

———. 1990. *Delinquency and society.* Englewood Cliffs, N.J.: Prentice-Hall.

Short, James F., Jr., and Fred L. Strodtbeck. 1965. *Group processes and gang delinquency.* Chicago: University of Chicago Press.

Simmel, Georg. 1971. *Georg Simmel on individuality and social forms.* Ed. Donald N. Levine. Chicago: University of Chicago Press.

Sitkoff, Harvard. 1981. *The struggle for black equality.* New York: Hill and Wang.

Smith, Neil, and Peter Williams, eds. 1986. *Gentrification of the city.* Boston: Allen and Unwin.

Stack, Carol B. 1974. *All our kin: Strategies for survival in a black community.* New York: Harper and Row.

Staples, Robert, ed. 1971. *The black family.* Belmont, Calif.: Wadsworth.

Stull, William, and Janice Fanning Madden.1990. *Postindustrial Philadelphia: Structural changes in the metropolitan economy.* Philadelphia: University of Pennsylvania Press.

Sumka, Howard J. 1979. Neighborhood revitalization and displacement: A review of the evidence. *Journal of the American Planning Association* 45 (October): 480–87.

Sutherland, Edwin. 1937. *The professional thief.* Chicago: University of Chicago Press.

Suttles, Gerald D. 1968. *The social order of the slum.* Chicago: University of Chicago Press.

———. 1972. *The social construction of communities.* Chicago: University of Chicago Press.

Szelenyi, Ivan. 1983. *Urban inequalities under state socialism.* New York: Oxford University Press.

Taeuber, Karl, and Alma Taeuber. 1965. *Negroes in cities.* Chicago: Aldine.

Taub, Richard P., D. Garth Taylor, and Jan D. Dunham. 1984. *Paths of neighborhood change: Race and crime in urban America.* Chicago: University of Chicago Press.

Tenhouten, Warren. 1970. The black family: Myth and reality. *Psychiatry* 2:145–73.

Thompson, Daniel C. 1963. *The Negro leadership class.* Englewood Cliffs, N.J.: Prentice-Hall.

Thrasher, Frederic M. 1927. *The gang: A study of 1,313 gangs in Chicago.* Chicago: University of Chicago Press.

Treiman, Donald. 1966. Status discrepancy and prejudice. *American Journal of Sociology* 71:651–64.

Turnbull, Colin. 1961. *The forest people.* New York: Simon and Schuster.

Turner, Ralph. 1967. *Robert Park on social control and collective behavior.* Chicago: University of Chicago Press.

————. 1978. The role and the person. *American Journal of Sociology* 84:1–23.

Valentine, Charles A. 1968. *Culture and poverty: Critique and counterproposals.* Chicago: University of Chicago Press.

Wacquant, Loic J. D., and William J. Wilson. 1989. The cost of racial and class exclusion in the inner city. *Annals of the American Academy of Political and Social Science* 501 (January): 8–25.

Wagner, Helmut. 1970. *Alfred Schutz on phenomenology and social relations.* Chicago: University of Chicago Press.

Warr, M. 1980. The accuracy of public beliefs about crime. *Social Forces* 59:456–70.

Wellman, David. 1977. *Portraits of white racism.* New York: Cambridge University Press.

Weppner, Robert S. 1977. *Street ethnography.* Beverly Hills, Calif.: Sage.

Whyte, William Foote. 1943. A slum sex code. *American Journal of Sociology* 49:24–31.

————. 1981. *Street corner society.* 3d ed. Chicago: University of Chicago Press.

Williams, Terry M. 1989. *Cocaine kids.* Reading, Mass.: Addison-Wesley.

Williams, Terry M., and William Kornblum. 1985. *Growing up poor.* Lexington, Mass.: D. C. Heath.

Willie, Charles V., ed. 1970. *The family life of black people.* Columbus, Ohio: Charles E. Merrill.

Willie, Charles V., and Janet Weinandy. 1970. The structure and composition of "problem" and "stable" families in a low-income population. In *The family life of black people,* ed. Charles V. Willie. Columbus, Ohio: Charles E. Merrill.

Wilson, James Q. 1968. The police and the delinquent in two cities. In *Controlling delinquents,* ed. Stanton Wheeler. New York: John Wiley.

————. 1971. *Varieties of police behavior: The management of law and order in eight communities.* New York: Atheneum.

Wilson, William J. 1980. *The declining significance of race.* 2d ed. Chicago: University of Chicago Press.

————. 1985. Cycles of deprivation and the underclass debate. *Social Service Review* 59 (December): 541–59.

————. 1987. *The truly disadvantaged.* Chicago: University of Chicago Press.

Wilson, William J., and Robert Aponte. 1985. Urban poverty. In *Annual review of sociology,* vol. 11, ed. Ralph H. Turner and James F. Short, Jr. Palo Alto, Calif.: Annual Reviews.

Wirth, Louis. 1928. *The ghetto.* Chicago: University of Chicago Press.

Wolf, Eleanor. 1963. The tipping point in racially changing neighborhoods. *Journal of the American Institute of Planners* 29:217–22.

Wolfgang, M., and F. Ferracutti. 1964. *The subculture of violence*. London: Tavistock.

Zorbaugh, Harvey W. 1929. *The Gold Coast and the slum*. Chicago: Univer- of Chicago Press.

Index